Anonymous

Fourth report of the Commissioners

For the Exhibition of 1851 to the Right Hon. Sir George Cornewall Lewis, one of Her Majesty's principal secretaries of state

Anonymous

Fourth report of the Commissioners
For the Exhibition of 1851 to the Right Hon. Sir George Cornewall Lewis, one of Her Majesty's principal secretaries of state

ISBN/EAN: 9783337717919

Printed in Europe, USA, Canada, Australia, Japan

Cover: Foto ©ninafisch / pixelio.de

More available books at **www.hansebooks.com**

FOURTH REPORT

OF

THE COMMISSIONERS

FOR THE

EXHIBITION OF 1851,

TO THE

RIGHT HON. SIR GEORGE CORNEWALL LEWIS, Bart., &c. &c.

ONE OF HER MAJESTY'S PRINCIPAL SECRETARIES OF STATE.

Presented to both Houses of Parliament by Command of Her Majesty.

LONDON:
PRINTED BY GEORGE E. EYRE AND WILLIAM SPOTTISWOODE,
PRINTERS TO THE QUEEN'S MOST EXCELLENT MAJESTY.
FOR HER MAJESTY'S STATIONERY OFFICE.

1861.

TABLE OF CONTENTS.

	PAGE
REPORT	5

APPENDIX:—

A. EVIDENCE given before the NATIONAL GALLERY SITE COMMISSION in 1857 in favour of the adoption of the KENSINGTON GORE SITE for the NEW NATIONAL GALLERY - 41

B. CORRESPONDENCE between HER MAJESTY'S COMMISSIONERS and the LORDS COMMISSIONERS of HER MAJESTY'S TREASURY in reference to the KENSINGTON GORE ESTATE - 88

C. ACT of PARLIAMENT (21 & 22 Vict. c. 36.) for releasing the COMMISSIONERS' LANDS on REPAYMENT of MONIES granted in aid of their FUNDS - 100

D. DEED of GIFT by JOHN SHEEPSHANKS, Esq., of his COLLECTION of PICTURES and DRAWINGS, in Trust, to form the Nucleus of a NATIONAL GALLERY of ART in connexion with HER MAJESTY'S DEPARTMENT of SCIENCE and ART; and MINUTE of the PRESIDENT of the BOARD of TRADE thereon - 102

E. CORRESPONDENCE between HER MAJESTY'S COMMISSIONERS and HER MAJESTY'S GOVERNMENT on the Subject of the ANIMAL PRODUCE MUSEUM - 105

F. REPORT of the SELECT COMMITTEE of the HOUSE of COMMONS appointed in 1860 to inquire and report concerning the SOUTH KENSINGTON MUSEUM - 109

G. AGREEMENTS between HER MAJESTY'S COMMISSIONERS and the HORTICULTURAL SOCIETY for the LEASE to the SOCIETY of a Portion of the COMMISSIONERS' ESTATE at KENSINGTON GORE, together with the NEW CHARTER granted to the SOCIETY - 118

H. EVIDENCE given by the SECRETARY to HER MAJESTY'S COMMISSIONERS before the SELECT COMMITTEE of the HOUSE of COMMONS on the BRITISH MUSEUM (1860) - 147

I. CORRESPONDENCE between HER MAJESTY'S COMMISSIONERS and the SOCIETY of ARTS respecting the proposed EXHIBITION of 1861 - 160

K. CORRESPONDENCE on the Subject of the INTERNATIONAL EXHIBITION of 1862 166

L. CHARTER of INCORPORATION of the COMMISSIONERS for the EXHIBITION of 1862 - 190

M. DEED of GUARANTEE given to SECURE an ADVANCE to be made by the BANK OF ENGLAND to the COMMISSIONERS for the EXHIBITION OF 1862 - 198

N. ACCOUNT of the RECEIPTS and EXPENDITURE of HER MAJESTY'S COMMISSIONERS from January 1st, 1856 to December 31st, 1860 - 202

Map of Estate - To face Title.

FOURTH REPORT

OF THE

COMMISSIONERS FOR THE EXHIBITION OF 1851,

TO THE

RIGHT HON. SIR GEORGE CORNEWALL LEWIS, BART., &c. &c.

One of Her Majesty's Principal Secretaries of State.

SIR,

In conformity with the provisions of the Supplemental Charter which Her Majesty was graciously pleased to confer upon us on the 2nd December 1851, we have the honour to transmit to you, for the purpose of its being laid before Her Majesty for Her approbation, the Fourth Report of our proceedings as Commissioners for the Exhibition of 1851.

It appears unnecessary to repeat on the present occasion the statements made by us in our former Reports explanatory of the objects for which we received our incorporation as a permanent Commission, or to do more than briefly recapitulate the general results of our labours up to the date of our Third Report on the 16th April 1856, as set forth in that Report.

It was shown by us on that occasion that the various steps requisite for perfecting the Kensington Gore Estate, and rendering it fit for the national objects to which it was intended to apply it, were then nearly completed; that in the three years that had elapsed since our scheme for the promotion of Art and Science in their practical bearings upon productive industry was put forward, the most marked and satisfactory results had been attained, and that Parliament had recognized the importance of the objects in view by liberal pecuniary contributions, and had enabled the Government to give practical effect to the public demand for increased means of instruction in Science and Art by the establishment and development of the

Third Report.

large and important Department of Science and Art devoted to that especial purpose, and the benefits of which were made to extend over the whole country, instead of being confined to the metropolis.

After pointing out that satisfactory relations had been established between the Government and ourselves, and arrangements made for securing harmony of action in all that related to the appropriation of the site purchased at the joint expense of the public and the Royal Commission, we alluded to the recommendations of the Committee of the House of Commons on the National Gallery appointed in the year 1853, in favour of the removal of the National Gallery to the Kensington Gore Estate, and we specified numerous collections and museums connected with Science and Art that had been either established or largely extended since the date of our Second Report. The results of the Paris Universal Exhibition of 1855 were referred to by us as serving to confirm the conclusions at which the experience of the Exhibition of 1851 had already compelled us to arrive, as to the importance of systematically imparting instruction in Science and Art to the industrial classes of the community, to enable them to maintain their position in the markets of the world; and we showed in conclusion, how a practical beginning had been made, with the support of Parliament, towards the realization of the comprehensive scheme in contemplation of which the Kensington Gore Estate was purchased, by means of the erection of the structure now known as the South Kensington Museum, which, whilst being sufficiently extensive to provide for the more immediate wants of the public, would not interfere with the ultimate adoption of measures calculated to make permanent provision for those wants on a scale worthy of the nation.

It will now be our duty to report to you, for submission to Her Majesty, the various steps that have been taken by us in the discharge of the duties graciously entrusted to us by Her Majesty, in the period of five years that has elapsed since the presentation of our Third Report.

It will probably be more convenient that, instead of attempting to follow a strict chronological order in reporting our proceedings, we should rather describe them in connexion with the several subjects to which they respectively relate; and we will accordingly commence by pointing out the altered position occupied by us towards the Government in respect of the ownership of the Kensington Gore Estate at the present period, as compared with that existing at the time of our last Report, together with a statement of the circumstances which have led to the change in question.

In conformity with the recommendation of the National Gallery Committee of 1853, to which reference was made in our Third Report, Her Majesty's Government addressed a communication to us in the early part of 1856, in which they requested to be informed whether we were prepared to convey to them a site on our estate sufficient for the erection of a National Gallery, with suitable approaches and a sufficient surrounding space; and, if so, what were the precise boundaries of the space which we would be prepared to give up for this object. To this communication we returned a reply to the effect that we were prepared to give up so much of the estate as might be required for the site of the new National Gallery, with suitable approaches and a sufficient surrounding space, to the intent that it might be vested in the Commissioners of Public Works in trust for the proposed object, such portion of the estate to be taken from the main block lying within the great boundary roads. We added, with reference to the request to be informed of the precise boundaries of the space which we would be willing to give up for the purpose, that, in the absence of more precise information as to the nature and extent of the building intended to be erected, we could only declare our readiness to place at the disposal of the Government so much of the main block as might be needed for the full and complete execution of any plan for the erection of the National Gallery that might be subsequently decided upon.

Circumstances leading to dissolution of partnership with Government. National Gallery question.

Her Majesty's Government accordingly introduced a Bill into the House of Commons in June 1856, entitled, "A Bill to provide a Site for a new National Gallery," with a view of giving effect to the recommendations of the National Gallery Committee of that House, by securing the requisite site on the Kensington Gore Estate. On the second reading of the Bill, however, on the 27th June 1856, an amendment was moved by Lord Elcho, and carried against the

Government by a majority of 153 to 145, to the effect that "An humble address be presented to Her Majesty, praying Her Majesty to be graciously pleased to issue a Royal Commission to determine the site of the new National Gallery, and to report on the desirableness of combining with it the Fine Art and Archæological Collections of the British Museum, in accordance with the recommendation of the Select Committee on the National Gallery in 1853."

It should here be observed, however, that the recommendation of that Committee in favour of the issue of a Royal Commission related solely to the second of the two subjects referred to in Lord Elcho's amendment, and that the Committee, in fact, decided, by a majority of 8 to 3, against referring the question of the site of the Gallery to a Royal Commission.

National Gallery Site Commission.

Her Majesty was pleased, in conformity with the address of the House of Commons, to issue Her Royal Commission in the sense indicated in the Address, on the 17th December 1856, the Commissioners appointed being six in number, viz., Lord Broughton, the Dean of St. Paul's, Mr. C. R. Cockerell, Professor Faraday, Mr. Richard Ford, and Mr. George Richmond.

The more important part of the evidence given before the Commission in favour of the adoption of the Kensington Gore site will be found in Appendix A.

The Commissioners finally reported in June 1857 in favour of retaining the National Gallery on its present site in Trafalgar Square, after coming to an unanimous resolution that, "after the consideration of the various sites suggested to the Commissioners, they are of opinion that their choice is confined to the site of the present National Gallery, if sufficiently enlarged, and the estate at Kensington Gore."

It appears, however, that of the original number of six Commissioners, three only, viz., Lord Broughton, the Dean of St. Paul's, and Mr. Cockerell, concurred in this Report, one of the remainder (Mr. Richmond) having opposed it, and voted in favour of the site of the Kensington Gore Estate, another (Professor Faraday) having declined to vote, and the third (Mr. Ford) having resigned shortly after his appointment.

Since the presentation of this Report, no further steps have been taken in reference to the question of the site of the new National Gallery beyond a notice being given by the Chancellor of the Exchequer at the commencement of the Session of 1858 for the appointment of a Select Committee "to inquire into the proposed sites for a National Picture Gallery, and into the plans for the enlargement of the British Museum." This notice of motion fell to the ground owing to the change of Government which took place immediately afterwards.

The temporary arrangements made for the custody and exhibition in the meantime of a portion of the pictures belonging to the National Gallery, for which no room can be found in the present Gallery, will be referred to at a later part of this Report.

Matters having arrived at this position, and there being no immediate prospect of Her Majesty's Government being enabled to take any effectual steps for putting an end to the state of uncertainty that had so long existed, we found ourselves compelled early in 1858 seriously to consider our own position. While on the one hand the Government and the general public had derived the advantages to which we will be our duty presently to refer, from the purchase of the Kensington Gore Estate,—a purchase originated by ourselves, and towards which we had so largely contributed; on the other hand we had ourselves obtained no return whatever for our outlay, beyond the few reserved rents for houses on the estate in the occupation of tenants, for the grazing of the land, &c. And whilst waiting for the decision of the Government on the subject of the National Gallery and the other institutions under Government control, we had been precluded from all independent action or from carrying into execution any plans of our own for a period of more than five years.

Although we remained as earnest as ever in our desire to co-operate with Her Majesty's Government in promoting the plans for the development of which the joint purchase of the estate was made in 1852, it appeared to us to be neither desirable nor advantageous that the existing state of uncertainty and inaction should be further prolonged; and we therefore decided to address to the Government the communication which will be found in Appendix B.

EXHIBITION OF 1851.

Offer to dissolve partnership with Government.

In that communication, after referring to the peculiar nature of the tenure of the estate, rendered necessary by its divided ownership, and pointing out that the position occupied by us in relation to the Government had tended seriously to interfere with the prosecution of our plans for the advancement of Science and Art, we stated that if the Government had arrived at the conviction that it was no longer advantageous to carry out the original plan by means of a joint partnership with the Commission, we had on our part come to the conclusion that it would be right for us to offer to relieve the Government from any existing embarrassment by taking upon ourselves the entire execution of our own plans for the promotion of Science and Art in the manner that might appear to us best adapted for the purpose, and in conformity with the principles and objects set forth in our Second Report. We then proceeded to express our readiness, in the event of Her Majesty's Government concurring in this opinion, to repay to them the whole of the sums advanced by Parliament towards the purchase of our estate, amounting to 177,500*l*., together with a moiety of the net rents received from the estate, amounting to 3,879*l*. 4*s*. 2*d*., the whole of the estate being made in return the absolute property of the Commissioners.

Offer accepted by Government.

To this proposal a reply was returned by the Lords of the Treasury (see also Appendix B.) to the effect that their Lordships were fully sensible of the inconvenience, delay, and even pecuniary loss which had arisen from the relations which the existing arrangement between the Government and ourselves had rendered inevitable; and that they concurred with us in the opinion that the double ownership and authority of Her Majesty's Government and ourselves offered serious impediments to the active prosecution of any one uniform plan for the appropriation of the estate to the important purposes connected with the promotion of Science and Art to which we were desirous of devoting it. Their Lordships added that, under these circumstances, they considered that the objects which Parliament had in view in making grants of public money, as well as the interests of Science and Art, would be most effectually promoted by adopting our proposal; and they stated, in conclusion, that they would defer to a future occasion the consideration of the

FOURTH REPORT OF COMMISSIONERS.   11

measures which might be necessary with reference to the position occupied by the Department of Science and Art on our estate.

At the same time we thought it desirable to put upon record a detailed memorandum recapitulating the circumstances which originally led to the connexion which had hitherto united the Government and ourselves as joint owners of the estate, and explaining the reasons for the proposed dissolution of that connexion. (See Appendix B.)

In conformity with the understanding thus arrived at, a Bill was introduced into Parliament by the Government in the Session of 1858 for the purpose of carrying into effect the proposed dissolution of partnership. This Bill, which passed into law on the 12th July 1858, under the title of "An Act for releasing the lands of the Commissioners for the Exhibition of 1851, upon the repayment of monies granted in aid of their funds" (21 & 22 Vict. c. 36.) is given in Appendix C. *Act of Parliament.*

. By Clause I. of this Act, it was provided that on the repayment by us of the sum of 181,379*l*. 4*s*. 2*d*. (being the amount of the two above mentioned sums of 177,500*l*. and 3,879*l*. 4*s*. 2*d*.) our estate should be absolutely released and discharged from the agreement existing between the Treasury and ourselves respecting the appropriation of the property as defined in the Treasury Minute of the 15th February 1853 (see Appendix D. to our Third Report); and from all trust, obligation, control, claim, and demand to which it might be subject in respect of the sums granted by Parliament; with a proviso that if such payment were not made within six months from the passing of the Act there should be added to the sum in question a further sum equal to one half of the net rental accruing to the time when such payment should be made.

Clause II. of the Act empowered the Lords of the Treasury to require that the outlying portion of the estate occupied by the Department of Science and Art should be retained in the occupation and for the use of Her Majesty's Government for purposes connected with Science or the Arts so long as they might think fit; and to direct that the payment of such portion of the sum of 181,379*l*. 4*s*. 2*d*. as they might think fit, not exceeding what might appear to them to be the value of the piece of land in question, might be postponed so long as it was so retained. The clause further provided that on the payment by us of the residue, after deduction of the amount of which the payment might be so postponed, their Lordships should issue a warrant releasing the residue of the estate from the before-mentioned agreement and all trust, obligation, control, claim, and demand as aforesaid.

Retention of part of land for Department of Science and Art.
In pursuance of the power vested in them by Clause II. of the Act, the Lords of the Treasury required that the piece of land in question should be retained for the purposes mentioned, and were pleased to fix its value (on the basis of the actual cost incurred in acquiring it, with the addition of the expenditure for roads and approaches properly applicable to it) at the sum of 60,000*l.*, leaving a balance payable by us to Her Majesty's Government of 121,379*l.* 4*s.* 2*d.*

We had not made our proposal for the repayment of the advances made by Parliament towards the purchase of the estate without previously satisfying ourselves that there was a reasonable prospect that the necessary funds could be procured by means of a mortgage of the estate, and further that the interest on such mortgage could be provided for by means of letting upon building leases the outlying portions of the estate.

Loan of 120,000l. on mortgage of part of the estate.
When it had been decided as above-mentioned that the sum immediately payable by us to the Government should be fixed at the sum of 121,379*l.* 4*s.* 2*d.*, we entered into negociations with the view of raising 120,000*l.* on a mortgage of the estate, or a portion of it, and finally succeeded in borrowing that sum at 4 per cent. interest from the Commissioners of Greenwich Hospital, upon the security of the various outlying portions of the estate (with the exception of the piece occupied by the Department of Science and Art) together with the upper portion of the main square of the estate.

Issue of Treasury warrant releasing the estate.
The necessary payment into the Exchequer having been made by us within the period of six months specified in the Act, the Lords of the Treasury issued to us the Warrant therein provided for, releasing the whole of the estate, (except the portion retained for the use of the Department of Science and Art,) from the Government lien upon it, in the terms before recited.

For the purpose of meeting the annual interest upon the loan from the Greenwich Hospital Commissioners, we took the necessary steps for letting, upon building leases, the various outlying portions of the estate, which being separated from the main square by the great roads surrounding it, and being of a disjointed and fragmentary character, could not be made use of in connexion with our general scheme for the appropriation of that main square. The outlying pieces in question, four in number, and containing respectively $3\frac{1}{4}$, $1\frac{1}{2}$, $5\frac{1}{4}$, and $1\frac{1}{4}$ acres, will be found indicated in the plan prefixed to this Report. While the ground rents derived by us from these portions of the property amount to a sum sufficient to defray the interest on the mortgage, we have reason to believe that the sale of the fee simple of them, if hereafter determined upon, would raise a sum sufficient to pay off the mortgagees' claims upon the estate in respect of the loan of 120,000*l*.

Letting of outlying pieces on building leases.

We may take this opportunity of stating that the various steps described by us in our Third Report as being in the course of execution for perfecting and completing the estate, have all been carried to a satisfactory conclusion. The plan prefixed to this Report will be found to be accompanied by such detailed particulars as to render it unnecessary for us to enter upon the subject at greater length here, or to do more than invite attention to the plan in question.

In our last Report we submitted a brief statement of the circumstances attending the recent establishment by Her Majesty's Government, with the sanction of Parliament, of the Department of Science and Art; and we mentioned that, in consequence of the approach of the time when it would be necessary for the Department to give up its temporary occupation of Marlborough House, Her Majesty's Government had in contemplation the adoption of arrangements for the removal of the Department to the Kensington Gore Estate.

That removal took place in the course of the year 1856, the sum of 10,000*l*. being voted by Parliament to defray the expenses of the removal and the cost of the various buildings, &c., required for the service of the Department.

Removal of Depar of Science and Art to the estate.

EXHIBITION OF 1851.

South Kensington Museum. The erection of the iron museum building, for which the sum of 15,000*l.* was voted by Parliament in the Session of 1855, was meanwhile proceeded with under our directions, and formal possession of it handed over to the Department on its completion, on the 30th March 1857.

Opening by Her Majesty. On the 20th June of the same year the Museum was formally visited by Her Majesty previous to its opening to the general public, and, under the name of the South Kensington Museum, has, since that time, continued to enjoy a very large amount of public favour.

The Reports presented to Parliament annually by the Department of Science and Art (which was transferred in 1857 from the Board of Trade to the Education Department of the Privy Council), will be found to contain full particulars of the proceedings of the Department, and to afford gratifying evidence of the success that has attended its establishment on the Kensington Gore Estate, whilst its constantly increasing importance and extending sphere of usefulness, and local and provincial connexion, fully confirm and corroborate the views originally expressed by us, as to the necessity of the establishment of such a Department, and the beneficial influence which it was calculated to exert upon productive industry.

Success of Museum. The number of visitors to the Museum in the period of three-and-a half years, between its opening and the close of 1860, was no less than 1,810,640, viz., 268,291 in the second half of 1857; 456,288 in 1858; 475,365 in 1859; and 610,696 in 1860; and although the fact of its being opened at night on certain evenings of the week (and which has been appreciated as an invaluable boon by the working classes of the metropolis), has, of course, tended to increase the total number of visitors, the necessity of keeping the Museum free from crowds on certain days for the purposes of study, by imposing a small charge for admission on those days, has, on the other hand, had the effect of greatly limiting that number.

Collections exhibited in South Kensington Museum. We mentioned in our last Report that the collections which the Museum appeared to us to be calculated to contain were the Educational Museum, the nucleus of which was then possessed by the Government; the Museum of Patented Inventions, belonging to the Commissioners of Patents; the Animal Produce Museum, the property of ourselves; and the Museum of Ornamental Art, belonging to the Department of Science and Art, and at that time temporarily exhibited in Marlborough House.

The whole of these collections have since been deposited in the South Kensington Museum, where they have all been greatly extended and developed; but, in addition, several other important collections have been placed in the Museum, some of them being the property of the public, and others belonging to private bodies. In the former category may be specified the Art Library, the Sheepshanks Gallery of Pictures, the Museum of Construction and Building Materials, the Food Museum, and the Collection of Photographic Reproductions, all the property of the Department of Science and Art; and also the British portion of the Collection of Pictures, belonging to the Trustees of the National Gallery, including the Turner and Vernon Galleries, which have been provisionally deposited, with the sanction of Parliament, in fire-proof buildings, erected at a cost little exceeding 8,000*l*., in the rear of and communicating with the iron museum building, in consequence of Marlborough House, where they were previously exhibited, being required to be given up for the use of His Royal Highness the Prince of Wales. In the second category are included a valuable Collection of Sculpture, mainly formed and contributed by the Sculptors' Institute; and an important Collection of Specimens of Architecture, chiefly the property of the Committee of the Architectural Museum, and formerly deposited in Cannon Row.

It will appear from the above statement that as many as eleven or twelve distinct Collections illustrative of Science or Art, which have been called into existence to satisfy the public wants, but for none of which accommodation could be found elsewhere, have already been located on this portion of the Kensington Gore Estate, thus strongly confirming the opinions expressed by us on the subject of the advantage to be derived by the public from the acquisition of the property, whilst the unexpectedly large and constantly increasing number of visitors to the Collections in question proves conclusively that the distance of the site from the centre of the metropolis, which was so often urged as an insuperable objection to it, has not in any way operated to its prejudice.

EXHIBITION OF 1851.

Sheepshanks Gallery.

We give in Appendix D. the deed of gift, dated the 2nd February 1857, whereby Mr. Sheepshanks presented to the nation his valuable Collection of original Pictures and Drawings, the work of British artists, now known as the Sheepshanks Gallery, together with the Minute of the President of the Board of Trade accepting the gift. The gift is stated to be made with the view to the establishment of a Collection of Pictures and other Works of Art, fully representing British Art, and it was an express condition of the gift that the gallery to be erected for the purpose, and which Mr. Sheepshanks desires to be called "The National Gallery of British Art," should be built on our Kensington Gore Estate, or else in the public Parks or Gardens at Kensington. The Collection includes 233 paintings in oil, and 103 drawings and sketches. The sum of 3,500*l.* was voted by Parliament in 1857 for the erection of a building adapted for the reception of Mr. Sheepshanks' gift, and the Gallery was opened by Her Majesty in the month of June in that year, simultaneously with the opening of the South Kensington Museum, in the immediate rear of which it is placed.

Animal Produce Museum presented by Commission to Government.

With reference to the "Animal Produce Museum" above referred to, it will be remembered that in our last Report we mentioned the steps that had been taken by us in conjunction with the Society of Arts, for the formation of such a Museum, to complete, in respect of the Animal Kingdom, the link already existing in the case of the Mineral and Vegetable Kingdoms of the great Class of Raw Materials, in the shape of the Museum of Practical Geology in Jermyn Street, and the Museum of Economic Botany at Kew; and we then stated that the Collection in question had become our sole property, on our reimbursing to the Society the whole of the outlay incurred by them in connexion with the Museum (pp. 32 and 33). We subsequently incurred a considerable expenditure in developing the Collection and providing the necessary fittings, &c., and finally presented it to Her Majesty's Government, for the use of the Department of Science and Art, on the sole condition of measures being adopted for its permanent preservation and exhibition, and for its future further development, as opportunities might offer. The correspondence that passed on the subject between the

Government and ourselves is given in Appendix E. The interest at all times taken by the public in the Animal Produce Museum, as shown by the crowded state of the gallery in which it is exhibited, has been very remarkable. No portion of the Collections, with the exception, perhaps, of the Picture Galleries, appears to excite a greater degree of attention on the part of the visitors to the South Kensington Museum. Its value as a means of promoting that industrial instruction, on the importance of which we have dwelt so fully on former occasions, cannot but be very great.

We may take this opportunity of mentioning that we erected at our own cost, at an expense of 2,000*l*., the refreshment and retiring rooms which are situated at the entrance to the Museum, and that we made a free gift of them on their completion to the Department of Science and Art. We also expended out of our own funds a sum of 3,000*l*. in providing fittings for the Museum buildings, irrespective of the outlay incurred by us on the fittings for the Animal Produce Museum, and a grant made by us for fittings for the Architectural Museum. *Erection of refreshment rooms, &c., at cost of 5,000l., and presented by Commission to Government.*

Whilst the establishment and development of the Department of Science and Art has been attended by these gratifying results in respect of that portion of its duties more immediately connected with the metropolis, and dependent upon metropolitan support, the local and provincial success attending its exertions will be seen by the fact that in addition to 10 metropolitan schools, the number of provincial Art Schools and branches had increased from 34 in 1853 (the first year of the establishment of the new Department) to 86 in 1860; whilst the total number of persons receiving instruction in 1860 in the schools of the Department and in the public schools connected with them, was as many as 89,481. The Travelling Collection of Works of Art belonging to the Department had been sent to 31 places in the four years ending with 1860, and been visited by nearly 400,000 persons. The Art Library not only affords great facilities for day and evening study to the Students of the Department, and persons occupied in productive industry in the Metropolis, but its contents are circulated throughout the country, upon the demand of *Statistics of progress of Department of Science and Art.*

local schools; 2,000 books and drawings were so circulated in 1860 in the provincial seats of industry.

Science Schools and Classes have also been established at Aberdeen, Accrington, Banbury, Birmingham, Bristol, Dedham, Edinburgh, Glasgow, Gloucester, Halifax, Haslingden, Hollingwood, Huddersfield, Manchester, Middlesboro'-on-Tees, Slaithwaite, Slough, and Wigan, in Institutions connected with the East Lancashire and Cheshire Union of Mechanics' Institutions, and Classes in connexion with the Miners' Association of Cornwall and Devon, and seven Schools and Classes in the Metropolis.

House of Commons' Committee on South Kensington Museum.

A Select Committee was appointed by the House of Commons in the Session of 1860, "to inquire and report concerning the South Kensington Museum," and their Report is given in Appendix F. The Committee came to the conclusion "that the South Kensington Museum, in respect of its action, as well throughout the United Kingdom as in the metropolis, is exercising a beneficial influence, and that it is fully deserving of continued Parliamentary support." They further reported "that additional space for the accommodation and exhibition of the Art Collections should be provided at once," by means of completing and glazing over the quadrangle of brick buildings commenced by the Sheepshanks, Vernon, and Turner galleries, at a cost of 17,000l.; and also that it was necessary to remove the wooden schools and dilapidated houses on the ground occupied by the Department, and at once to provide in their place safe buildings for official residences and the Art Training Schools, at an additional cost of 27,000l.

In accordance with the recommendation of the Committee, the sum of 17,000l. was voted last year to provide the suggested accommodation in the rear of the iron museum building, which latter building the Committee reported that they saw no occasion for disturbing at present, as it could be usefully employed and might well be allowed to stand for some years to come.

We understand that a further vote for 15,000l., being part of the above-mentioned sum of 27,000l., is proposed in the Estimates for the present year to be taken towards providing permanent buildings in lieu of the present wooden schools and old houses alluded to in the Committee's Report.

Although many of the previous particulars respecting the South Kensington Museum and the operations of the Department of Science and Art may be found in the Annual Reports presented to Parliament by the Department, we cannot refrain from adverting to the happy realization of the views originally put forward by us which they indicate, and expressing our satisfaction at seeing them carried out to so remarkable an extent.

Our official connexion with the Department has of course ceased since the date of the dissolution of our partnership with the Government.

We will now proceed to refer to the steps that have been taken by us towards the execution of our scheme for laying out the main square of the estate, since we became the sole owners of it, commencing with a statement of the circumstances connected with the grant of a lease by us to the Horticultural Society of the central portion of that main square, and with the formation on that spot of the ornamental gardens now in course of execution by the Society. *Lease to Horticultural Society.*

In the month of January 1859 we received a communication from the Society, requesting to be informed whether we would be willing to receive a proposition for renting the middle of our main square; and if so, upon what terms.

The Horticultural Society being a body formed "for the improvement of Horticulture, both ornamental and useful," and being one of the societies enumerated by us in our Second Report as engaged in the promotion of the interests of Science and the Arts, to aid in the promotion of which we were ourselves incorporated, it appeared to us that this application was well worthy of our serious consideration, and we came to the conclusion that a compliance with it might be made subservient to laying the foundation of our general plan for the future appropriation of the main square of the estate, at the same time that we were satisfied that the intended operations of the Society would extend the influence of the Science and Art of Horticulture upon productive industry, and thus directly tend to promote the objects of our incorporation.

After lengthened negociations with the Society, we entered into an arrangement with them for leasing to them for a period of 31 years from the 1st June 1861, a space of about 22 acres in the centre of our main square, as indicated in the Plan prefixed to this Report, upon condition that it should be laid out as an ornamental garden, with the necessary accompaniment of terraces, steps, fountains, &c., and with the addition of a conservatory or winter garden at the north end, at a total estimated cost of 50,000*l.*; we ourselves undertaking to erect at our own expense and also at an estimated cost of 50,000*l.*, arcades of an architectural character to enclose the area leased to the Society, and to execute the earthworks requiring to be executed preparatory to the laying out of the gardens. The arcades in question, whilst being complete in themselves, were designed by us at once to serve to unite into a harmonious whole any buildings that might be hereafter erected between them and the main roads of our estate, in furtherance of our general objects, and also to secure the gardens against any future interference or encroachment, as those objects were gradually developed.

We also agreed that the rent to be paid to us by the Society should be ascertained with reference to the receipts of the Society in each year, and that before any rent was paid to us, the Society should be allowed to deduct from the gross receipts from the gardens, in addition to the sum required to meet all current expenses, the amount that might be payable by them for interest on the money borrowed by them for the works on the land. The rent to be paid to us was to be a sum equal to the interest payable by us on the money borrowed for the execution of the portion of the works agreed to be undertaken by ourselves, or so much of this interest as the surplus receipts after the above specified deductions might amount to. And if the surplus exceeded this interest, a further sum equal to a moiety of the residue.

A committee of six persons, three to be nominated by ourselves and three by the Society, was agreed to be appointed for the purpose of regulating the amount to be deducted from the gross receipts for the current expenses of the gardens, and a general veto with regard to the management of the grounds has been reserved to us. The Society are entitled to apply for a renewal of the lease for a further period of 31 years two years before the expiration of the original term, in which case we shall either be bound to grant a renewal upon the same terms as the original lease, or, if we decline to renew it, to compensate the Society by the payment of a sum in no case less than 15,000*l.*, and which may be greater if the Society have not then paid off the whole of the debenture debt originally incurred by them for the execution of the works on the land, as in that case we have agreed to take upon ourselves the payment of a certain portion of that debt.

Various other stipulations have been entered into with reference to our mutual rights over the arcades, the conditions under which the lease shall be forfeited in the event of the continued non-payment of rent by the Society, the application of a portion of the Society's annual profits to the liquidation of their debenture debt, and other matters, which will be found fully set forth in the three several agreements that we have entered into with the Society, which are contained in Appendix G. That Appendix also contains a copy of the new Charter that has just been granted to the Society by Her Majesty, re-incorporating them, with extended powers, under the name of "The Royal Horticultural Society."

The works agreed to be executed by the Society and ourselves are now being pushed forward with all practicable speed, and although the long continued frost of last winter has seriously retarded our operations, we still look forward to its being possible for the Society to open the gardens for their first great show on the day originally fixed upon, viz., the 5th June next.

We may here mention that we have granted permission for the erection in the new Horticultural Gardens of the intended memorial of the Great Exhibition of 1851, towards the cost of which the sum of about 6,000*l.* has been provided by public subscription, and the execution of which has been entrusted by the subscribers to Mr. Joseph Durham.

Exhibition Memorial.

For the purpose of carrying out the arrangements made between us and the Horticultural Society, involving a total expenditure of at least 100,000*l.*, it became necessary for both parties to take steps for raising their respective quotas. The interest felt by the public

Steps taken by Commission and Society to raise sums required for

new Gardens.

in the proposed new Gardens is shown by the fact that the whole of the sum of 50,000*l.* required to be raised by the Society was obtained in a short time by the issue of life-memberships and by donations to the extent of 10,000*l.* (since increased to 15,200*l.*), the remaining 40,000*l.* being raised on the security of debentures, carrying 5 per cent. interest and giving a right of admission to the Gardens. The Society have since determined to raise a further sum of 10,000*l.* on Debentures, making the amount borrowed by them 50,000*l.* Our quota of 50,000*l.* was raised by means of a loan from the Commissioners of Greenwich Hospital, from whom, as already mentioned, we had previously borrowed the sum of 120,000*l.*, for the purpose of paying off the Government lien upon our estate. The loan was made upon the security of the lower portion of the main square of the estate, which was not included in the original mortgage, combined with the security of the land embraced in that mortgage, and at a rate of interest equal to about $4\frac{1}{4}$ per cent., which we propose to pay out of the rental receivable by us from the Horticultural Society under our agreement with them.

British Museum Committee of House of Commons.

A Select Committee of the House of Commons having been appointed in 1860, " to inquire how far and in what way it may be desirable to find increased space for the extension and arrangement of the various Collections of the British Museum, and the best means of rendering them available for the promotion of Science and Art," an application was made to us by the Committee for the purpose of ascertaining the price that would be asked by us for such portion of our land as might be required for the purposes of the British Museum.

Resolution of Trustees of British Museum.

It should here be mentioned that at a special general meeting of the Trustees of the British Museum, held on the 21st January 1860, a majority of nine to eight of the Trustees had adopted a resolution (based upon the evidence collected by a sub-committee of their body,) to the effect that it was "expedient that the Natural History Collections be removed from the British Museum, inasmuch as such an arrangement would be attended with considerably less expense than would be incurred by providing a sufficient addional space in immediate contiguity with the present building of the British Museum."

The site to which it was proposed by the Trustees to remove the Natural History Collections was our estate; and it was to the resolution on the subject arrived at by them that the appointment of the Select Committee of the House of Commons was in some degree owing.

It appeared to us that, as the British Museum was an important national institution, we should only be carrying out our original intentions by dealing in a liberal spirit with any proposal that might be made to us for removing a part of its collections to our site, should Parliament be desirous of making such removal; and we accordingly came to the conclusion that the price to be asked for our land, in the event of Her Majesty's Government applying for any portion of it for the national purposes in question, should be 10,000*l.* per acre (being not more than one-half of what we had reason to believe to be its present actual value), and at the rate of 5,000*l.* per acre for that small portion of it where the necessity of arching over the ground under our agreement with the Horticultural Society, would leave no ground-floor space available; and we authorized our Secretary to attend before the Committee and give evidence to that effect on the 12th July last. The evidence accordingly given by Mr. Bowring will be found in Appendix II.

The Committee reported, in opposition to the decision of the Trustees of the British Museum above quoted, that they had "arrived at the conclusion that sufficient reason has not been assigned for the removal of any part of the valuable collections now in the Museum, except that of Ethnography, and the portraits and drawings." *Report of House of Commons' Committee*

The following amendment, proposed by Mr. Lowe, the Vice-President of the Committee of Council on Education, had previously been negatived by the Committee: "Considering the little connexion between the Natural History Collection with the other collections of the Museum, the applicability of the principle of division of labour to Museums, the unsatisfactory nature of the fanciful principle of a 'collection of collections,' the high price of land at Bloomsbury, the fact that a very small part of the Natural

History Collection was included in the collection purchased from Sir H. Sloane, the very imperfect state of the Zoological Collections, and other arguments which have been set forth in the earlier part of this Report, your Committee cannot recommend the retention of the Natural History Collections at Bloomsbury as a permanent arrangement."

The price of land at Bloomsbury above alluded to appears from the evidence given before the Committee to be from 40,000*l.* to 50,000*l.* per acre, as compared with the price of 10,000*l.* per acre asked by us for a site on our estate.

The Committee prefaced the above-quoted resolution against the removal of any of the British Museum Collections by statements showing that while the expense of obtaining the necessary additional land adjoining the present site and erecting the necessary buildings thereon, would not exceed 300,000*l.*, the cost of removal to the Kensington Gore Estate would be 620,000*l.*, in addition to further expenses for a Departmental Library, packing and removing the collections, and extensive fittings and cases. It might be supposed that these statements were scarcely reconcileable with the fact just mentioned that the cost of land at Bloomsbury was four or five times as great as that at which the land on our estate could be obtained for a great national purpose; but it appears on examination that the two different amounts of 300,000*l.* and 620,000*l.* relate to entirely different calculations as to what the extent of the space allotted to the Natural History Collections should be, and that they consequently do not admit of any comparison being drawn between them; the 300,000*l.* representing the cost of the purchase of two acres of land at Bloomsbury and of the erection of two acres of buildings thereon, whilst the 620,000*l.* represents the cost of five and a half acres of land and buildings on the Kensington Gore Estate.

We are not aware whether Her Majesty's Government have come to any decision in consequence of the Report of the British Museum Committee.

We have now to report the different steps that have been taken by us in connexion with the proposed International Exhibition of

FOURTH REPORT OF COMMISSIONERS.

862, for the conduct of which Her Majesty has lately been pleased to issue Her Royal Charter of Incorporation to the Commissioners named therein.

The question of a repetition of the Great Exhibition of 1851 was taken into consideration by the Council of the Society of Arts at the beginning of 1858, and resolutions favourable to such repetition taking place in the year 1861 were then adopted by them and circulated amongst the commercial public. At the close of the same year the Society brought the matter officially under our notice, transmitting a copy of the Resolutions referred to, and enquiring whether we would be willing to entertain the question of ourselves undertaking the management of the proposed Exhibition.

Proposed International Exhibition of 1861.

To this communication we returned a reply to the effect that we considered that we could only be justified in complying with this application upon its being made to appear to us not only that the scheme in question met with the general sympathy and support of the public to an extent sufficient to warrant a reasonable confidence of success, but also that the necessary funds would be at once forthcoming for the purpose of defraying the expenses of the Exhibition. We added that we had ourselves no funds applicable to the purposes of the Exhibition, and that we had no information before us on which to found an opinion as to the amount of public support that might be anticipated for the undertaking; and we stated in conclusion that on being made acquainted with the result of any inquiries on this subject which might be instituted by the Society, we would proceed to consider (should that result prove to be satisfactory) how far it might be in our power to contribute to the success of the Exhibition, and also to determine the position to be taken by us with respect to its management.

The Society of Arts replied to this letter on the 11th March 1859, stating that they would do all in their power to furnish us with the information desired by us, especially by means of obtaining subscriptions to a proposed guarantee fund of 250,000*l.*, considering such a subscription as a sufficient test of the probability of success. The letter also set forth various general considerations to show why, in the opinion of the Society, the proposed Exhibition was likely to elicit still more definite and valuable results than the Exhibition of 1851.

Intended Exhibition abandoned.

The war in Italy broke out at about this time, and threatened to be of long continuance, and as the disturbed state of the Continent gave little hope that the Exhibition, so far as its international character was concerned, could be held with success, the Council of the Society of Arts passed a resolution at the beginning of June 1859 to the effect that it was of opinion that, under these circumstances, the Exhibition should be postponed to a more favourable opportunity. In this resolution we expressed our entire concurrence, and the original proposal of holding a second Great Exhibition in 1861, or exactly ten years after the first one (in accordance with the views on the subject long held by the Society of Arts) was accordingly abandoned. Appendix I. will be found to contain the correspondence that passed between the Society of Arts and ourselves in reference to the proposed Exhibition of 1861, as distinguished from that now actually intended to be held in 1862.

International Exhibition of 1862.

The Italian war having been unexpectedly brought to an early conclusion, the question of holding a second great International Exhibition in 1862 (it being now too late to make the necessary arrangements for holding it in 1861) was again revived by the Society of Arts, who forwarded to us on the 8th March 1860 a copy of a proposed guarantee agreement for securing the means of holding the Exhibition, and asked to be informed whether we were willing to grant a site on our Kensington Gore Estate for the purposes of that and future Exhibitions, and for other purposes tending to the encouragement of Arts, Manufactures, and Commerce,

Draft guarantee agreement.

and, if so, on what terms. The following were the principal conditions of the draft guarantee agreement in question:—No subscriber was to be liable unless the deed was signed to the extent of at least 250,000*l.*, and in the event of loss attending the Exhibition each subscriber was to contribute in rateable proportion to his subscription to liquidate such loss. Earl Granville, the Marquis of Chandos, Mr. Thomas Baring, Mr. Dilke, and Mr. Thomas Fairbairn were to be invited to be the five Trustees of the Exhibition. Application was to be made to us for a site on estate for the Exhibition, and the trustees were to erect whatever [buil]dings, whether permanent or temporary, they might think [nece]ssary for the purpose, but on the express condition that at least [one-]third of the sum so expended by them should be employed in [erec]tions of a permanent character, suitable for decennial or other [exh]ibitions, and when not so used, suitable for other purposes tending [to t]he encouragement of Arts, Manufactures, and Commerce, such [per]manent buildings to be vested in the Society of Arts. In the [eve]nt of there being a surplus, it was to be applied to the [enco]uragement of Arts, Manufactures, and Commerce in such [ma]nner as the subscribers might determine at a meeting to be called [for] the purpose. In the event of there being a loss which the [Soc]iety of Arts declined to liquidate, the permanent buildings above [me]ntioned were to be sold, and if, after such sale, there still remained [a] deficit, the ultimate loss was to be borne by the subscribers [rat]eably, as already stated.

As we were not at that time in possession of sufficient information [as] to the ability of the Society of Arts to carry out their proposal to [ho]ld an Exhibition in 1862, we felt ourselves unable to return an [im]mediate answer to the application of the Society; but on the 8th [Ju]ne 1860 the Society addressed a further communication to us [re]newing their application, and acquainting us, as an evidence of the [in]terest felt by the public in the proposed Exhibition, that as many [as] 455 persons had already intimated their intention to subscribe to [th]e proposed guarantee fund sums amounting in the aggregate to [£]98,350*l.*, and also stating their opinion that the amount subscribed [w]ould be largely and rapidly increased when they could announce [th]at arrangements for the grant of a site on our estate had been [de]finitively entered into with us. They also informed us that the [am]ount which it was intended to invest in the permanent buildings [al]ready spoken of was to be at least 50,000*l.*, and called attention [to] the liberality with which the Society had surrendered their claim [to] a share of the surplus profits of the Exhibition of 1851.

In reply to their application we informed the Society of Arts that [w]e should be happy to grant rent free until the 31st December [1]862, for the purposes of the Exhibition of 1862, the use of the [w]hole of the land on the main square of our estate lying on the

Terms assented to by Commission. Loan of 16 acres of land.

south side of the arcades and entrances to the gardens of the Horticultural Society, estimated at 16 acres (see the plan prefixed to this Report) on the understanding that all the buildings to be erected for the Exhibition, whether permanent or temporary in their character, should be subject to our approval, and that all the temporary buildings should be removed within six months after the close of the Exhibition, if required by us; the Trustees of the Exhibition being at liberty on the other hand to remove the buildings termed permanent if the Exhibition should be attended with pecuniary loss. We further expressed our readiness to grant to the Society, in recognition of their long-continued services in advancing the interests of the Arts and Manufactures, and especially in preparing the way for the Great Exhibition of 1851, a lease for 99 years at a moderate ground rent of those permanent buildings, if retained on our ground, on condition of not less than the sum of 50,000*l.*, named in the Society's letter of the 8th June, being expended on them by the Trustees, and of their not covering more than one acre of ground; and also on condition of their being used solely for holding Exhibitions and for purposes connected with the promotion of Arts and Manufactures (the omission of the word *Commerce* being intentional on our part, as will be seen by reference to Appendix K. No. 5).

Lease to Society of Arts of permanent buildings.

With respect to the Society's application that we should appropriate a portion of our estate for the purpose of future exhibitions analogous to the proposed Exhibition of 1862, we informed them that with the view of meeting their wishes as far as was consistent with our public duty, and at the same time bearing in mind our obligations to our mortgagees, we would undertake, in the event of the payment to us of the sum of 10,000*l.* out of the profits (if any) of the Exhibition of 1862, to reserve for the purposes of another international exhibition in 1872, to be conducted by such body as might be approved by us, the remainder of the land now proposed to be lent by us for the Exhibition of 1862 that was not covered by the permanent buildings already referred to, such reservation not interfering in any way with the free use by us of that land in the intervening period.

Reservation of land for Exhibition in 1872.

The Society of Arts acquainted us in reply that the terms proposed by us were entirely satisfactory to them in their general scope and

Acceptance of terms.

FOURTH REPORT OF COMMISSIONERS.

er; but we deemed it necessary to state to them, with refer-
an assumption on their part that it was our intention that the
y whom the contemplated Exhibition of 1872 should be con-
, should be nominated by the Society, subject to our approval,
ey were in error in this respect, seeing that we felt it to be
istent with the duty which we owe to the public to fetter our
of free action with regard to future Exhibitions, by entering
ny engagement, either expressed or implied, as to the body by
such Exhibitions should be conducted; and that we must
ourselves entirely free to act on this, as on all other points
cted with such undertakings, in the manner that should appear
at the time to be most conducive to the success of the object
d in view.

ese conditions having been arranged with us, the Society *Negociations between Society of Arts and proposed Trustees.*
d into correspondence with the five gentlemen named in the
guarantee deed as the proposed Trustees for the management
Exhibition, with a view to obtaining their definite acceptance
trust thus offered to them.

compliance with the wishes expressed by the proposed Trustees *Application of Society of Arts to Commission to manage Exhibition, under certain restrictions.*
e course of that correspondence, the Society of Arts again wrote
on the 24th October last to inquire whether we would be pre-
, *whilst preserving the conditions of the guarantee agreement,* the
al provisions of which have been already enumerated by us
26), either to undertake ourselves the management of the
ibition or to afford to the undertaking that more limited amount
sistance which two of the proposed Trustees (Lord Granville
Mr. Baring) made, in a letter a copy of which was forwarded to
the Society, the condition of their accepting the proffered
eship (see Appendix K., Enclosure to No. 6). The letter in
ion stated that they were of opinion that our body, with certain
fications of its working arrangements, would furnish the best
of directing the Exhibition, but intimated their readiness, in
event of our not being willing to undertake the labour and
nsibility of managing it, to accept the office of Trustees of the
ibition (their proposed three colleagues having already accepted
office without reserve), upon condition of our expressing an
ion favourable to the holding of another Exhibition, and the

proposed mode of management, and of our consenting to advise the Trustees as to certain important principles, and of some of the members of our Finance Committee being willing to give them their advice occasionally on other matters.

The question submitted for our consideration was therefore whether, on the one hand, we would be willing ourselves to manage the Exhibition, not with entire liberty of action, and in such manner as we might deem best adapted to ensure its success, but subject to the provisions of a guarantee agreement in the preparation of which we had not been in any way concerned, and the provisions of which might prove to be calculated seriously to impede us in the discharge of our duties; or whether, on the other hand, leaving the Exhibition to be managed by Trustees, as originally proposed, we would be prepared to assist the undertaking to the more limited extent above indicated.

It appeared to us, upon full consideration, that it would be inconsistent with our responsibility towards the Crown, and with the position occupied by us under our Charter of Incorporation, to accede to a proposal for undertaking ourselves the management of the Exhibition of 1862, accompanied, as in the present instance, by such a serious restriction as that of the maintenance of all the conditions of the guarantee agreement insisted upon as a *sine quâ non* by the Society of Arts; and the more so, seeing that in the previous application of the same nature made to us by the Society to undertake the management of the Exhibition of 1861, then contemplated, no restriction of any kind was sought to be imposed upon us.

But even if the above-mentioned difficulty had not existed, the terms of the draft guarantee agreement itself appeared to offer a most serious obstacle to our assuming the management of the proposed Exhibition. One of the most prominent conditions of that agreement was, that the conduct of the Exhibition should be entrusted to a body of Trustees, five in number, and specifically named in the agreement when the public were invited to become subscribers to it. Although provision was made for filling up any vacancy that might occur in the number, no reservation was made to provide for the possible contingency of an entire change in the character of the managing body; still less did the agreement contemplate that the Exhibition should be managed by us in particular. It therefore appeared to us that the whole agreement would fall to the ground, releasing the guarantors from all liability, had so fundamental an alteration been introduced as that involved in the transfer of the management to ourselves from the small body of Trustees specifically provided for in the agreement.

Under these circumstances we felt that we had no alternative but to express to the Society our regret that we were unable to entertain the question of managing the Exhibition.

<small>Commission could not accept proposal to manage Exhibition if restricted as proposed.</small>

We added, however, with respect to the more limited question raised by the alternative alluded to by Lord Granville and Mr. Baring, that we should be happy to meet the wishes of the Society to that extent, and to render any support and assistance to the undertaking that might be consistent with our position as a chartered body and with the powers conferred upon us by our Charter of Incorporation. We therefore expressed our general approval of the object which the Society of Arts had in view in organizing the scheme of the proposed Exhibition; and showed, by reference to the liberal terms upon which we had already stated that we were prepared to place at their disposal the ground necessary for the purposes of the Exhibition, how ready we were to co-operate with the Society in the matter, and that we had confidence in the mode of management by means of Trustees, proposed by the Society and sanctioned by the parties to the guarantee agreement. We also stated that we should be happy to communicate with the Trustees from time to time upon any points, whether of principle or of detail, connected with the undertaking upon which they might think proper to seek our advice; and concluded by mentioning that, with the view of facilitating those communications as far as possible, it would afford us much pleasure, when the Trust was definitely constituted by the acceptance of the whole of the five gentlemen who had been requested to act as Trustees, to elect as Members of our Commission, under the powers conferred on us by our Charter of Incorporation, those two of the five Trustees who were not already members of the Commission, viz., Lord Chandos and Mr. Fairbairn.

<small>Facilities offered by Commission.</small>

EXHIBITION OF 1851.

Acceptance by proposed Trustees.

Upon this reply being communicated by the Society to the proposed Trustees, those gentlemen announced, on the 22nd November last, their willingness to accept the Trust, on the understanding that the Society took measures forthwith for giving legal effect to the Guarantee, and for obtaining a Charter of Incorporation satisfactory to them.

Alteration in original terms as to permanent buildings.

During the interval required for the preparation of the necessary legal powers, the Trustees proceeded to take such provisional steps as their position permitted, including a consideration of the arrangements in connexion with the erection of the buildings required for the Exhibition, and came to the conclusion that it would be impossible for them, without serious injury to the general interests of the undertaking, to carry out literally the condition laid down by us in our previous correspondence with the Society of Arts, that the permanent buildings erected by the Trustees, and intended to be leased to the Society of Arts, should not cost less than 50,000l. and not cover more than one acre of ground (see page 28). The Trustees informed the Society of Arts that while it did not appear, from the general tenor of the correspondence between the Society and ourselves, that any question of principle was intended on either side to be involved in the specification of the sum of 50,000l., they had reason to believe that the general objects had in view in stipulating for the expenditure of a certain sum on a certain area might be realized in a manner satisfactory both to the Society and to ourselves, although the amount to be spent on the permanent buildings to be leased to the Society at the close of the Exhibition were reduced. They proposed that the buildings in question should consist of the central portion (occupying a little less than an acre) of certain picture galleries facing Cromwell Road, that it was intended to erect, and asked for such a modification of the above-mentioned condition as would admit of a reduction of the amount required to be spent on the permanent buildings from 50,000l. to a sum of not less than 20,000l.

We informed the Society, in reply to their request that we would assent to the modification desired by the Trustees, that we were prepared to give our assent accordingly, upon condition of there being expended upon those permanent buildings at the close of the Exhibition, if the necessary funds existed, such portion of the difference between the original sum of 50,000*l*. agreed to be spent thereon and the reduced amount that might be so expended under the concession now made by us as might, in our judgment and that of the Trustees, be deemed requisite for the completion, in a suitable architectural manner, of the buildings to be leased to the Society.

The reason for our making this stipulation was, that we felt that if we allowed any permanent buildings to be retained on the site, it was important that they should be sufficiently handsome in an architectural point of view, which could not be the case if no larger amount were expended upon them than the limited sum proposed by the Trustees. By the arrangement agreed to by us the retention of the buildings would not disfigure the estate or offer any impediment to the ornamental execution of any future building scheme on the property, which might otherwise be seriously interfered with if so small a sum as that desired by the Trustees were expended on so large an area as that intended to be covered by these buildings.

It is obvious that the above alteration in the terms originally agreed to between the Society of Arts and ourselves, combined with the alteration which it involved in the stipulations contained in the draft guarantee agreement, was one greatly to the benefit of the subscribers to the guarantee, and greatly tending to lessen the chance of their being eventually called upon to contribute any portion of the sums respectively guaranteed by them. By the original stipulations the Trustees were required to expend *at least* one-third of the total sum expended by them on buildings for the Exhibition in the erection of permanent buildings to be leased to the Society of Arts, at the same time that there was no limit whatever upon the amount which the Trustees might choose so to spend. By the altered arrangement, however, the total sum that the Trustees are empowered to expend on the buildings in question under any circumstances is a *maximum* of 50,000*l*., and even a considerable portion of that sum (that to be expended on the architectural completion of the permanent buildings) is not to be spent in the first

c

instance, but only in the event of the Exhibition being successful. The liability of the Guarantors was thus, in fact, reduced from an unlimited *minimum* to a limited *maximum*.

<small>Further loan of land to the Trustees for purposes of Exhibition.</small>
Whilst this matter was under discussion a further important question arose as to the sufficiency of the space agreed to be lent by us for the purposes of the Exhibition, and which, as already mentioned, amounted to about 16 acres ; and the Trustees found it necessary to address a communication to us on the subject, representing that additional space was imperatively required, and applying for the loan of an unoccupied portion of our land lying between the Western Arcades of the Horticultural Gardens and Prince Albert's Road (the same land, in fact, as that which we were prepared to devote, if desired, to the purposes of the British Museum), whereby an additional exhibiting space of about four acres would be obtained; and also applying for the loan of the South Arcades of the Gardens, for the supply of refreshments, both inside and upon them, to the visitors to the Exhibition.

After communicating with the Horticultural Society, who, under their lease from us, are to enjoy a right of promenade in the Arcades in question, and who met the wishes of the Trustees in a liberal spirit, we acquainted the latter that we were prepared to grant them the use of the additional land applied for, and also of the South Arcades (thus sacrificing for the time the large rental expected to be derived by us from letting stalls in those Arcades, as previously intended by us) upon condition of the Trustees providing a permanent wall and roof to the South Arcades, and a permanent wall to the West Arcades, in place of the temporary ones about to be constructed by us. We felt it necessary to make this stipulation, in order to prevent the possibility of the stability of either of those Arcades being endangered by the manner in which it was proposed to employ them in connexion with the Exhibition.

The correspondence on the subject of the International Exhibition of 1862 that has taken place between ourselves and the Society of Arts and the Trustees of the Exhibition, and the general purport of which has been above stated by us, is given in Appendix K.

<small>Grant of Charter to Trustees.</small>
Her Majesty was pleased to grant a Charter of Incorporation to the Trustees, as desired by them, on the 14th February last. By that

FOURTH REPORT OF COMMISSIONERS. 35

Charter they have received the title of "The Commissioners for the Exhibition of 1862;" and as it contains various stipulations based upon the agreements made by us with the Society of Arts and the Trustees, and otherwise has a direct connexion with our own proceedings, we deem it right to append a copy of it to this Report. (Appendix L.)

The guarantee deed having been duly executed to the necessary extent of 250,000l., the certificate of the Commissioners to that effect was published in the "London Gazette" of the 15th March; and all the requisite preliminaries having been completed by the issue of that certificate, the Commissioners have entered upon the active discharge of their important and arduous duties, which we earnestly trust they may be enabled to carry to an entirely successful issue. Execution of guarantee deed.

A copy of the Guarantee Deed, to which signatures for nearly 400,000l. have been affixed up to the present date, is given in Appendix M.

In continuation of the return of our financial position, submitted in Appendix C. to our Third Report, we beg to append a statement of our receipts and expenditure in the period between the 1st January 1856 and the 31st December 1860, duly audited by the Governor and Deputy Governor of the Bank of England. (See Appendix N.) Financial position of Commission.

The annual statements of our receipts and expenditure which we announced our intention in our last Report of presenting, have been regularly prepared by us, and forwarded to the Home Office accordingly, for presentation to Her Majesty.

It now only remains for us, in conclusion, to submit a brief recapitulation of the various particulars set forth in the course of this Report. Conclusion.

The circumstances which led to the complete change in the position towards Her Majesty's Government previously occupied by us, and the dissolution of our partnership in the Kensington Gore Estate, which took place two years ago, leaving us the sole owners of the property, have been detailed. It has been seen, however,

c 2

that the Government, in the exercise of the discretion vested in them by the Act of Parliament passed for the purpose of dissolving the partnership, have retained the large outlying portion of the estate on which the South Kensington Museum is erected, for the use of the Department of Science and Art; and have thus made provision for the progressive development of that portion of the scheme for the promotion of Art and Science in their practical bearings upon productive industry put forward by us in our Second Report, which may be considered as more immediately dependent upon the aid of Parliament, and subject to Government control.

The most satisfactory results have already been obtained from the action of the Department in question, while the most marked success has attended its exertions not only in the metropolis but in the provinces; and the Report of the House of Commons Committee of last year on the South Kensington Museum states emphatically that that Museum " is fully deserving of continued Parliamentary support." The remarkable number of visitors to the Museum in the period of three and a half years during which it has been established on the estate, amounting to nearly two millions, has given conclusive evidence, not only of the interesting and instructive character of the numerous collections exhibited in it, but of the fact that its situation on the western side of the metropolis does not interfere with its accessibility and popularity, whilst there is no site in London, with the exception of the Kensington Gore Estate, where the necessary space could have been obtained, not only for the ultimate requirements of the Department, but for its present wants.

The various outlying portions of our estate, irrespective of the piece occupied by the Government as above stated, have been let by us on building leases, in order to provide the funds required to enable us to pay the interest on the large sum borrowed by us on mortgage for the purpose of paying off the Government lien upon the property; and we have shown the satisfactory progress that has already been made by us in the appropriation of the remainder of the estate, comprising the main square of between 50 and 60 acres. It has been seen that we have devoted the central portion of it, to the extent of more than 22 acres, to the establishment on it of a great

FOURTH REPORT OF COMMISSIONERS.

ciety whose especial object is the promotion of the Science of
rticulture, thus carrying out one of the objects originally contem-
ted by us, whilst this manner of appropriating this portion of the
operty has permanently established an ornamental centre to serve
the interior court to any buildings which may be hereafter
cted between the Horticultural Arcades and the fine open roads
structed by us round the main square.

The arrangements that have been made by us with the Society of
ts and the Commissioners for the Exhibition of 1862 for the loan
 a portion of the estate for the purposes of that Exhibition have
o been explained in this Report, where we have shown that a
rther portion of the main square, amounting to 16 acres, and
bsequently increased to 20 acres, has been lent by us as a site for
e Exhibition buildings, and that we have agreed to grant to the
ciety of Arts a lease of the permanent buildings proposed to be
cted, to the extent of an acre, to be used by them for holding
hibitions and for purposes connected with the promotion of Arts
d Manufactures. We have also agreed to reserve 16 acres of
 same land for an Exhibition to be held in 1872, under certain
ditions.

Out of the total extent of land originally purchased by us in
52, amounting to 85 or 86 acres, the various appropriations that
ve already been made for the purposes of the Department of
ience and Art, the construction of roads, the Horticultural
rdens, the Exhibitions of 1862 and 1872, and the erection of
ivate houses, have absorbed, more or less permanently, not less
an 70 acres, so that only 14 or 15 acres, or about one-sixth of the
nd forming the Kensington Gore Estate, remain at present unap-
opriated to the development of the purposes contemplated by our
arter; and even four acres of that amount have been temporarily
nt for the Exhibition of 1862. Whilst we cannot but look upon
is as a most satisfactory result, and as one affording every prospect
 the ultimate and entire accomplishment of the important objects
r the promotion of which the estate was originally purchased by
 under the powers conferred upon us by Her Majesty, it will be
r duty, in the new and independent position now occupied by us,
 persevere in our exertions to attain that end, and to endeavour to

merit a continuance of that confidence and favour which Her Majesty has been graciously pleased to extend to us throughout the whole period of our incorporation.

Given under our Corporate Seal at the Palace of Westminster, this Third day of May 1861.

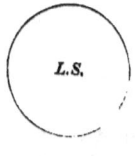

L.S.

EDGAR A. BOWRING,
Secretary.

ALBERT.
GRANVILLE.
BUCCLEUCH.
CHANDOS.
DERBY.
ROSSE.
PALMERSTON.
PORTMAN.
OVERSTONE.
TAUNTON.
J. RUSSELL.
G. C. LEWIS.
W. F. COWPER.
B. DISRAELI.
T. MILNER GIBSON.
W. E. GLADSTONE.

ROBERT LOWE.
A. Y. SPEARMAN.
W. CUBITT.
C. L. EASTLAKE.
CHARLES LYELL.
R. MURCHISON.
THOMAS BARING.
THOMAS BAZLEY.
G. P. BIDDER.
RICHARD COBDEN.
C. WENTWORTH DILKE.
THOMAS FAIRBAIRN.
T. F. GIBSON.
JOHN GOTT.
LEONARD HORNER.
HENRY THRING.

APPENDIX.

APPENDIX A.

Evidence given before the NATIONAL GALLERY SITE COMMISSION in 1857, in favour of the adoption of the KENSINGTON GORE Site for the NEW NATIONAL GALLERY.

I.—EVIDENCE of the Right Hon. Sir GEORGE CORNEWALL LEWIS, Bart., M.P., Chancellor of the Exchequer.

LEWIS.

2775. *Chairman.*] I think that on the 5th of June last year you presented a Bill to Parliament, which was prepared by yourself and Mr. Wilson—a Bill having this title, " To provide a Site for a new National Gallery," which Bill was then read a first time, and the second reading of it was appointed for the 9th of the same month of June. Was that so?—It was.

2776. I believe that the second reading did not take place on that day, and that the Bill was put off two or three times, and that on the 27th of the same month, Lord Elcho made a motion for an address to the Crown, and that motion being carried by a small majority—eight, I think—the Government proposed that the Bill should be read a second time on the following Monday; but on that day the order of the day for that second reading was discharged, and the Bill was withdrawn?—Yes, that was what passed.

2777. Will you be so good as to look and see if that is the Bill (*handing a Bill to the witness*)?—Yes, that is the Bill.

2778. Have you had occasion lately to look at the report of the speech which you made upon that occasion?—Yes, I have lately refreshed my memory by reading over the report of the speech in Hansard's Debates.

2779. I find that in that speech you are reported to have made use of these expressions, "With regard to the Site of the new National Gallery, all we propose at present is, that the nation should consent to take from the Exhibition Commissioners a half or some part of the ground which they possess at Kensington Gore." Did you say that?—Yes, that was the effect of what I stated.

2780. I wish to know whether, in accordance with those expressions of yours, the Bill, in fact, decided the question of the site?—The question which we considered to be decided by that Bill was, that all doubt would be put an end to with respect to the title to the land which we proposed to accept as a site for the intended National Gallery of Pictures. The

APPENDIX A.

LEWIS. Commissioners are doubtless aware that that land is held at present on a peculiar tenure. The Commissioners for the Exhibition purchased a portion of the site, for which they paid 165,000*l*. Another portion of that site was paid for by Parliament, to the amount of 177,500*l*., so that the entire cost of the land at Kensington Gore amounts to 342,500*l*. I am not aware that the boundaries between the land purchased by the Commissioners and the land purchased by the Government have ever been set out; but it has been agreed that the Government should have a certain control over the land belonging to the Commissioners; and that no appropriation of it should be made without the consent of the Treasury. So that the Government is the owner of a portion—we will say, in general terms, one-half—and has a control over the appropriation of the other half. But then it might be said, if Parliament was to vote a sum of money, and a building was to be erected upon any portion of the site, it might be uncertain whether the land entirely belonged to the Government; and I believe the whole of it was, in fact, conveyed to the Commissioners; so that the estate is legally vested in the Exhibition Commissioners, although more than half of it was paid for by the Government. The Exhibition Commissioners are desirous of making any such arrangement as may facilitate the views of the Government; but in order to remove any legal doubts which might be raised as to the title, it was thought desirable that this Bill should be passed, the effect of which would be to vest in the Government so much of the land as might be used for the purpose of a National Gallery. It consists of only one clause, which, if the Commissioners will allow me, I will read to them. "It shall be lawful for the Commissioners of Her Majesty's Treasury to select, and cause to be marked out or defined, such part of the said land purchased by the said Commissioners for the Exhibition of 1851" (the whole of it was so purchased, in fact, so that that description would apply to the whole of the site) "and being within the area aforesaid, as to the said Commissioners of the Treasury may appear suitable for the purpose of a site of a new National Gallery, with proper surrounding or adjoining space and approaches; and it shall be lawful for the said Commissioners for the Exhibition of 1851, by deed under their common seal, to be enrolled among the Records of the Court of Exchequer, to convey the land so selected and marked out or defined to the Commissioners of Her Majesty's Works and Public Buildings, to be held by such last-mentioned Commissioners in trust for the purpose aforesaid." The effect of that clause would have been, the Exhibition Commissioners being prepared to convey the land, that the land would have been vested in perpetuity in the Commissioners of Works. Therefore, any money voted by Parliament would have been employed in erecting a building upon land to which the Crown or the Government had a perpetual title. Such was the effect of this Bill. The Government certainly did consider that the question was

APPENDIX A. 43

decided that this site should be used for the erection of a National Lewis.
Gallery for Pictures. They did not carry their views beyond that one
destination of it, namely, that a National Picture Gallery should be
erected on this site—that part of the case they considered to be settled—
and it was with that view that they made the application to Parliament.
But they did not intend to apply for any vote of money to erect the
building in last Session. All they intended to do was to pass that Bill,
and in the present Session they would have applied to Parliament for a
vote of money to commence the building. That was the view of the
Government.

2784. It was to be solely for a Picture Gallery ?—Solely for a Picture
Gallery.

2785. You did not contemplate combining the archæological or the
artistic treasures of the British Museum with the pictures in the projected National Gallery—that was not part of your object?—No; but
we intended, in conformity with the recommendation of Colonel Mure's
Committee, to advise the Crown to issue a Commission to inquire into
that subject. The present Commission was issued (as the Commissioners
are aware) in consequence of the vote which was carried by the House
of Commons for an address to the Crown. But if the Government had
been left to exercise its own discretion, it would have limited the inquiry
of the intended Commission to the question of the removal of the collections of art, or any other portion of the British Museum. That we
thought ought to have been made a separate inquiry. Colonel Mure's
Committee, although the terms of the Address are somewhat ambiguous,
limited its recommendation of an inquiry simply to the question of the
British Museum; it did not recommend that there should be any inquiry
upon the subject of the site.

2786. May I ask you whether the Government had come to any detailed
determination with respect to the National Gallery, supposing your Bill
had been carried, besides the selection of a site ?—According to the view
of the Government, the question of a site for the National Gallery involves
two important considerations. The first is the expense of acquiring a
sufficient site; and the second, the adequacy of that site for the wants of
the intended gallery. Now, the entire extent of the site at Kensington
Gore is 86 acres. The Gore House Estate consisted of 21 acres; there
is a part which is called the Villars Estate, consisting of 48 acres, and
Lord Harrington's estate of 17 acres, making altogether 86 acres. Now
86 acres is a large space to command in the neighbourhood of London,
and that was one of the considerations which very much influenced the
Government in giving the preference to this site. Next, there was the
consideration that it was paid for—the whole of the purchase-money of
the Government had been actually paid; the remaining portion of the
purchase-money had been paid by the Commissioners, and their land

presented as a gift to the Government. Therefore, the site belonged to the nation, and no further outlay was necessary; it was not necessary to go to Parliament for any further grant for purchasing land. Now the Commissioners are of course aware that when any question of building arises in or near London, one of the great sources of expense is the site. It is not merely the building, but it is the difficulty of obtaining land in the proper place, and to the proper extent. We thought that the circumstances of this site were such, with respect both to its position and its area, as to render it very eligible; moreover, we could not overlook the fact that it was our own, and that no further money was needed for the acquisition of it. Those were two important elements in the decision. Then we had to consider that Colonel Mure's Committee had expressed a decided opinion against the site at Trafalgar-square. They not only said that the existing National Gallery was insufficient, but they also expressed a decided opinion against Trafalgar-square as the site for any National Gallery— they condemned it altogether. They went into a great deal of evidence upon the subject of the destruction of pictures by smoke, and other atmospheric influences. Now I really cannot myself pretend to form any opinion upon that question; there was certainly strong evidence adduced to show that pictures did suffer in that position. How far that evidence may be conclusive I can for myself form no judgment. I will only say that persons of great authority did express that opinion. But what I confess weighs with me much more than the supposed deleterious influences upon the surface of the pictures is the want of space. The room of the present National Gallery is wholly inadequate, and there is great difficulty in obtaining additional room. In the first place, it would be necessary to pull down the workhouse behind the National Gallery. Then there is the barrack, and I believe that the Horse Guards and the War Department make great objection to the removal of that barrack, which is considered an important military position in the metropolis. I believe there is some dictum of the Duke of Wellington's upon the subject; and, in fact, the Horse Guards are not at all willing that the barrack should be removed. Under those circumstances, the space which can be acquired seems not to be sufficient. Now that is an important element in the question, because the National Gallery, which originally consisted of a small number of pictures, has received considerable augmentations, and my belief is, that if there were more space provided, it would receive still greater augmentations. Since the foundations of the National Gallery were laid, the Vernon pictures have been added, and there is no room to hang them in the National Gallery; they are all now in Marlborough House. Then there are the Turner pictures, many of which are not yet hung, and of which only a portion are hung in Marlborough House. All this arrangement is owing to the want of space. Marlborough House in a short time will be wanted for the Prince

APPENDIX A.

of Wales, and these pictures must necessarily be removed. Then there is the Sheepshanks Collection, which, perhaps, the Commissioners have seen; it is considered, and justly considered, a most interesting and valuable collection of pictures. Those have been given to the nation upon the express condition that they should be provided with a building at Kensington Gore; therefore, with regard to that portion of the collection, some building must be erected at Kensington Gore—we could not consistently with the terms of the deed of gift put them on any other site. Then there is also a collection of pictures not yet formed, but which will have to be formed before long, owing to an address of the House of Lords, and a vote of Parliament last Session, and a minute of the Treasury, which has since been issued—namely, for the formation of a Gallery of Historical Portraits. Now that collection might no doubt be separated from the general National Gallery, but still it seems that there would be no place so appropriate for it, as one in combination with that gallery. Putting all those circumstances together, we arrive at the conclusion, that a site of considerable size would be convenient for the National Gallery. Then there is another thing to be considered, which is, that although, no doubt, Parliament has been liberal in making grants for the National Gallery, by far the larger portion of it is owing to donations; and I think there is very little reason to doubt, that if we had the means of providing for pictures, in a good light and handsome rooms, and in a place accessible to the public, where they could be seen to advantage, owners of pictures, who are unwilling that, after their death, their collections should be left to the chances of hereditary succession, and should be, perhaps, brought to the hammer and dispersed, would, in many instances, from public spirit, be disposed, to leave them to the nation. We know that, in former times, Sir Francis Bourgeois intended to leave the collection which is now in the Dulwich Gallery to the nation, but, I believe the Chancellor of the Exchequer of that day would not provide a sufficient building for the purpose, and accordingly it was left to Dulwich College. There we have an instance of a valuable collection, which is put in a place not very accessible to the public, and which would be much better disposed of in connexion with a National Gallery. Perhaps the same thing might happen with other collections. Now there is a remark which I observe Lord Monteagle has made this Session upon the subject in the House of Lords, which is deserving of attention. On the 16th of February, when speaking upon the Sheepshanks Collection of Pictures, he said, "We had a very fine collection" (that means the National Gallery), "but he believed the public were not quite in possession of the facts as to how it had been got together, for, both in that and the other House of Parliament, he had heard the collection discussed as if it were mainly or altogether the creation of the State, and principally purchased out of the national resources, whereas, in point of fact,

LEWIS.

we were indebted for it much more to the generosity and public spirit of private individuals, than to any liberality which Parliament had shown in the matter." Then he showed how the collection had been formed. He said, "From 1824 to 1856, 112 pictures were purchased for the National Gallery by the State, and 433 were the gifts of private individuals. The special gifts of pictures to the nation included 16 by Sir G. Beaumont, 6 by William the Fourth, 35 by the Rev. W. H. Carr, 15 by Lord Farnborough, 8 by his late valued friend, Lord Colborne, 3 by Mr. Samuel Rogers, and 156 by Mr. Vernon." If to those we add the gifts of Turner and Mr. Sheepshanks, I think it is manifest that our National Gallery has been formed more by donation than by purchase; and it is a fair inference from that fact that we may look for its future increase, rather to the liberality of individuals than to the grants of Parliament. Now, there is nothing which is so likely to induce individuals to make such gifts to the nation as the provision of a sufficient and properly situated National Gallery, admitting, from time to time, of increase, as the collection may be enlarged. Therefore I confess it seems to me that, provided it is admitted that the formation of a National Gallery of Pictures is a national object, which I think seems now pretty generally conceded, it would be an excellent investment for the nation to build a good National Gallery on a site which is sufficiently large to admit of additions to the gallery from time to time. Those were the principal grounds upon which the Government came to the conclusion to build upon this site. They also looked carefully to all the different alternatives which were proposed, namely, to the different sites which had been suggested as preferable to Kensington Gore site, and, if it is the wish of the Commissioners, I will state in detail the reasons which determined them to reject each one of those sites in succession. There is one other point which I have overlooked, which, perhaps, I may be permitted to add. There are, at Hampton Court, pictures which might, with advantage, be added to the National Gallery. Whatever objections may be made to Kensington Gore, upon the score of distance, must apply much more forcibly to Hampton Court. It may, perhaps, be doubted whether, for example, the cartoons of Raphael, and some of the more important and interesting pictures at Hampton Court, might not, with the permission of the Queen, be removed to a National Gallery, and become valuable portions of it. All that, of course, implies the command of a greater space than there is at present; because at present not only is the National Gallery incapable of receiving any additions, but it cannot even accommodate those pictures which properly form a portion of it.

2787. I understand you to say, that it was not part of the Government plan to have a building, or to provide space for a building, which was inevitably to combine sculpture with painting?—Decidedly not. We considered that question as altogether undetermined. In fact, so far as

APPENDIX A.

we had come to any determination upon the subject, it was not to disturb the British Museum, but to leave all the sculptures in their present position. All that we had decided to do was to build (if I may borrow the term) from the Munich Gallery) a Pinacothek at Kensington Gore. We intended to make it as little expensive in the first instance as possible, but to build it upon such a plan as would admit of enlargement from time to time, as future circumstances might suggest.

2788. That is to say,—as would admit of enlarging the building as well as adding to the collection, in the original structure?—Just so; to admit of successive enlargements to the building, for the purpose of accommodating any additions which might be made to the collection, either by purchase or gift.

2789. [*Dean of St. Paul's.*] It would be a great general plan, of which portions might be successively carried out?—Exactly so.

2790. [*Professor Faraday.*] Did the plan include any distinct proposal to exclude other kinds of buildings from the neighbourhood of the gallery at Kensington Gore? was the rest of the ground to be kept quite clear?— Yes; we certainly contemplated that it should be left quite open to the decision of Parliament—that if they might think it desirable to make provision for buildings for any other purpose, any portion of the site might be employed for such other purpose. We did not expect that the National Gallery would occupy 86 acres of land, and we certainly thought that if any purposes connected with Science, for instance Scientific Collections, or rooms for learned societies, or any object of that sort, could be conveniently attained upon that site, it would be very proper for the consideration of Parliament. At the same time that did not enter at all into our plan; we contemplated it, but we did not provide for it. We intended to do nothing that would in any way interfere with the accomplishment of such a design; but we did not make it at all a part of our proposal. Our proposal was perfectly simple; we said, We propose to take from the Commissioners a valid title to so much land as we want to build upon, so that there shall be no question that the building which we are about to erect, being defrayed by public money, shall be in perpetuity the property of the Government. Having secured that land, we intended to build upon it a Picture Gallery, limiting the construction, in the first instance, to so much as would accommodate the pictures which we had got, and would admit of enlargement for the reception of any pictures which we might hereafter acquire.

2791. For my own part, I have a strong feeling that the accommodation of the public must be a thing to be considered. The access of what I may call the multitude is an item in my mind—one amongst many important considerations. Can you favour us with any thoughts upon this subject?—Of course it cannot be denied that Trafalgar-square is a much more central position than Kensington Gore—that everybody

APPENDIX A.

Lewis. must see at first sight—but we started upon the assumption, that a Committee of the House of Commons had almost unanimously decided that Trafalgar-square was not a fitting place for a National Gallery. Then the question arose, to what place shall it be removed? It was necessary to find some site other than Trafalgar-square. If one of the grounds upon which Trafalgar-square was considered an unfitting site for a National Gallery, was the injury to the surface of the pictures, it seemed idle to remove it to Burlington House, which was at no great distance from Trafalgar-square, or to St. James's Palace, as other persons proposed, which was merely at the other end of Pall Mall. It seemed desirable to go to such a distance from the town as would at any rate, if it did not altogether exclude these impurities of the air, diminish them materially. On the other hand, we thought it not desirable to go to such a distance as would render it a journey to visit the Picture Gallery. It seemed to us that Kensington Gore was a fair medium between those two extremes. It is sufficiently distant from the centre of the town to be free from the chief part of the impurities which load the air in the very smoky parts of the metropolis, and, at the same time, it is not so remote as Hampton Court, or the present Crystal Palace, and, therefore, not situated at a distance which requires a person to devote a considerable portion of the day to visit it. The fact of the enormous crowds which flowed to the Crystal Palace, in Hyde Park, proves experimentally that the distance is not so great as to deter the population of this town from visiting an exhibition in that district. Now, the proposed site at Kensington Gore is just opposite the place where the Crystal Palace stood, in Hyde Park, and that seemed to us to show conclusively, that although it was not so central as Trafalgar-square, nevertheless, it was not so distant but that vast numbers of persons, without any material inconvenience, could visit it. Those were the grounds upon which we thought it was not so distant as to be materially inconvenient. No doubt we are owners of the site of Burlington House. It is paid for. We might pull down Burlington House, and build upon that site a National Gallery; but of course the Commissioners are aware that the site of Burlington House is not nearly so large as that of Kensington Gore—it is nothing approaching it.

2792. *Dean of St. Paul's.*] What is the extent?—It is about three acres—whereas you will observe that this is 86 acres.

2793. *Chairman.*] Of course you are aware that every one of the recommendations which you say induced the Government to prefer Kensington Gore to Trafalgar-square, was stated in the Report of the Committee of 1848 (composed of Lord John Russell, Sir Robert Peel, Mr. Hume, Lord Morpeth, Mr. Goulburn, Mr. Baring Wall, Mr. Charteris, the Earl of Lincoln, Sir Benjamin Hall, the Marquis of Granby, Mr. Parker, Mr. Wakley, Mr. D'Israeli, Mr. Vernon Smith, and Mr. Bankes) to belong to Trafalgar-square, viz., "the commanding nature of the site, its accessibility and nearness to the chief thoroughfares," "the aids to economy," and " the space for further enlargement,"—and they concurred unanimously in the opinion that, taking all those considerations into account, Trafalgar-square was the preferable site?—The Report of that Committee was under the consideration of Colonel Mure's Committee, and they came to a totally different result. I presume they had the benefit of all the arguments, and all the evidence adduced by the former Committee. But I confess, with great deference to the able persons who formed that Committee, that it seems to me to be impossible to maintain that, however accessible Trafalgar-square may be, the site is sufficiently spacious, or sufficiently admits of successive enlargements. It seems to me that the great objection to the site of Trafalgar-square is its narrowness.

2794. But if the space now occupied by the barracks at the back of the National Gallery, and if the baths and wash-houses of St. Martin's parish and the workhouse were added thereto, would not there then be quite sufficient space for all the objects which you contemplate?—This, of course, assumes that the additional space can be obtained. I suppose that we might negociate with the parish authorities for the purchase of the workhouse, provided they could be provided with a site elsewhere. They probably would ask a very high price for it. With regard to the barracks, I am not prepared to say that the War Department would consent to abandon that site. I know that great objections have been made hitherto. Whether any other ground can be obtained in that part of the town, I cannot say, but I know, that hitherto they have considered it essential that this site should be retained as a barrack, not merely on account of the space, but on account of the peculiar position of the barrack at the intersection of several great lines of communication.

2795. That was the opinion, I think, of the then Commander-in-Chief, Lord Hardinge, as communicated by the then Quartermaster-General?—Yes; I believe Lord Hardinge had a very strong opinion upon the subject; therefore I could not say that it would be possible to obtain the site of that barrack. With regard to the wash-houses, I presume that they might be made a matter of negociation. Of course this Commission must be aware that when a Government, who themselves have no special knowledge upon the subject, undertake to decide a question of this sort, they must, to a great extent, be determined by authority, and in this instance, there was the authority of the most recent tribunal which had investigated the subject, namely, Colonel Mure's Committee. They, with a knowledge of all the previous inquiries, and all the evidence which had previously been taken, came almost unanimously to a decision that Trafalgar-square was not a place fitted

D

for the National Gallery. They expressed a decided and clear opinion upon that point.

2796. *Dean of St. Paul's.*] I think they did not express an opinion as to any particular site?—They expressed a preference for Kensington Gore; by a majority they came to a decision in favour of Kensington Gore.

2797. *Chairman.*] A very small majority?—Yes: it was not a very decided recommendation, nor was it an unanimous one; but, nevertheless so far as there was an inclination expressed by that Committee, it was in favour of the Kensington Gore site. But they expressed a clear, and I think, an all but unanimous opinion in favour of the removal from Trafalgar-square.

2798. *Dean of St. Paul's.*] I think you said that the Government had had under consideration certain other sites, which you would not be unwilling to communicate to the Commission. Of course the Commission are exceedingly anxious to know what sites are available, in order that they may fully exhaust the subject?—We considered all the sites which had been proposed. I will either mention them myself, or will answer any questions.

2799. Will you have the goodness to mention them? There may be some which have not occurred to us?—One of the sites which was most strongly recommended was some site in Kensington Gardens.

2800. *Chairman.*] There were two sites in Kensington Gardens, one at Bayswater and the other near the Palace?—One of those sites was discussed, I think, in the Report of Colonel Mure's Committee.

2801. *Mr. Richmond.*] The one near the sunk wall which divides Kensington Gardens from the old Deer Park was, I think, the one agreed, on all hands, to be the best?—There were two sites mentioned in Kensington Gardens; one was somewhere on the site of the present Palace, or very near it, between the present Palace and the water; and another was a site on the side of Kensington Gardens, nearly fronting the Kensington Gore Estate, almost close to it, in fact. The view which we took was, that looking to the very strong objections which were made by the public, even to the temporary occupation of any part of the Park (for we considered Kensington Gardens as practically part of Hyde Park) for the Crystal Palace in 1851, we did not feel ourselves at liberty even to entertain the project of appropriating any part of the Parks for purposes of building. We believed that the public, generally, set so high a value upon maintaining the integrity of the Parks, that we considered it quite out of the question, until we had altogether exhausted every other possible site in the neighbourhood of the metropolis, to propose to take any portion either of Hyde Park, or St. James's Park, or Kensington Gardens.

APPENDIX A.

1802. Or Regent's Park—did that come under your consideration?—
I do not think anybody proposed Regent's Park. There might be
objection, perhaps, to Regent's Park. I am speaking now merely
St. James's Park, the Green Park, Hyde Park, and Kensington
dens. We believed that the strongest objection was entertained,
ss a case of absolute necessity could be made out, against appro-
ting any portion of them to the purposes of a building. With regard
he site which immediately overlooked, one may say, the estate of
ington Gore, it seemed almost a wanton act to take a portion of
e Park, when you might have, as it seemed to us, an equally eligible
on the other side of the road. The distance from London was
ical. The Kensington Gore site was equally accessible, rather more
sible, in fact, and there was much greater command of additional
on the Kensington Gore side than on the side of the Park; there-
we thought that that plan was, of all others, the plan which had
to recommend it. Then there was the plan of pulling down
ington Palace, and appropriating that site to a National Gallery.
ieve that has even now many friends. That plan, we thought, was
e to most powerful objections. In the first place, Kensington Palace,
approached from the back, is considerably more distant than Ken-
on Gore; and as the principal objection to Kensington Gore was
distance, the objection to Kensington Palace seemed far stronger
to Kensington Gore, on the principal ground on which the question
debated. Then Kensington Palace is the property of the Crown.
e Crown consents to part with it, it can, according to the present
only part with it for a sum equivalent to its value; because,
ugh the Crown property is made over to the nation for the life of
eigning Sovereign, still it is considered as the property of the Crown,
he nation has only a life interest in it, and when the land is made
in perpetuity to the nation, an equivalent sum must be voted to
rown, and invested in land. Therefore in taking the site of Ken-
on Palace, we should have had to buy it in the same way as we
l have had to buy it from a private individual, even if the Crown
onsented to part with it. Then I would observe, that although at
moment, perhaps, the apartments in Kensington Palace may not be
or other means may be found of accommodating the persons who
odged in Kensington Palace, it is to be borne in mind that the
n has a young family growing up—that in some few years there
be Princes and Princesses who will require apartments, who must
dged by means of public grants, and that Kensington Palace is a
nient place in which the Royal Family may be furnished with
ments. Therefore to destroy Kensington Palace, is to destroy a
ce, which would probably be wanted for the use of the Royal
ily within no long time. When you have a great deal of vacant

Lewis. land it seems a wanton act, and one of reckless expense, to demolish a building such as Kensington Palace, which, although it may not be a very splendid specimen of architecture, is nevertheless not an unsightly building. It is a large pile, and has existed for some years—it is connected with historical recollections, and I cannot see that there is any sufficient justification for choosing that particular spot of ground to build upon, when there is so much land in the neighbourhood which is not built upon. I confess it seems to me that the reason for selecting Kensington Palace as the site of the new National Gallery altogether fails, and that no one, looking to his responsibility to the country, could, with any propriety, make such a proposition. Therefore those two sites, we thought, were condemned conclusively by the arguments against them.

2803. *Chairman.*] When you say "those two sites," do you include that recommended by the Commission in 1851, at Bayswater, as one of them (*showing a plan to the witness*)?—No, this is the one I mean (*pointing to another plan*).

2804. *Dean of St. Paul's.*] That was recommended by Lord Seymour's Commission?—I do not think we considered it.

2805. *Mr. Richmond.*] That was on the north side of the Park; yours was on the south side?—Yes.

2806. *Chairman.*] Did you consider the recommendation of appropriating that portion of Kensington Gardens (*pointing to the plan*) an encroachment which would be so objectionable as not to be adopted under any circumstances? I speak of the site recommended in 1851 by the Commission composed of Lord Seymour, Lord Colborne, Sir Charles Eastlake, Mr. Ewart, and Sir Richard Westmacott?—I should state, certainly, that that was not one of the sites which, so far as I know, was under the consideration of the Government. I have no distinct idea of ever having heard it suggested before. With regard to distance, I should think it is open to pretty much the same objection as Kensington Gore. The distance is nearly the same from any central point of London as Kensington Gore. It is liable to the same objection of being a detraction from Kensington Gardens, which I think the public would view with very great jealousy, particularly the persons living on the northern side of Hyde Park, and it would also be open to the further objection of not being conveniently susceptible of increase, from time to time, as new additions might be made to the collection. In order to increase it, it would be necessary to cut off a larger portion from Kensington Gardens, an avenue, for instance, and a walk; it would be necessary, probably, to destroy the avenue, to stop up the walk, to cut down trees, and altogether to diminish the space.

2807. The Commissioners of 1851 did not seem to think that that objection would apply to their plan. It is clear that it is a very small

APPENDIX A. 53

space which they propose to take off. If any further additions were required to the building, they could only be made by carrying the space backwards, and this plan shows that that space could only be obtained by cutting down an avenue, and by stopping up one of the principal walks in Kensington Gardens, namely, that walk which leads from the bridge, at the end of the Serpentine River, to the basin in front of Kensington Palace.

2808. *Dean of St. Paul's.*] Were there any other sites which were under the consideration of the Government?—Yes, there were other sites. One of the sites, which I think Lord Elcho recommended, was St. James's Palace. It was proposed to pull down St. James's Palace, and build on that site a National Gallery, in combination with rooms for drawing-rooms and levees. It was said that the company returning from levees and drawing-rooms might walk through the National Gallery. Now, in the first place, the same objection which applies to demolishing Kensington Palace also applies to demolishing St. James's Palace. I do not mean to say that St. James's Palace has any great architectural recommendations; but it answers the purpose of a palace, it contains apartments which the Queen can assign to members of the Royal Family, or to members of Her household. There are reception rooms for drawing-rooms and levees; and it serves purposes which must be served in some other place, and at a further expense of public money, if the present building is pulled down. Then, as to the improvement of site, it seems to me that whether the National Gallery is at one end of Pall Mall or at the other is very immaterial, and that no great advantage will arise from removing it so short a distance. As to the idea of the company from the drawing-rooms and levees passing through the National Gallery, I can hardly conceive anything less recommended by convenience; because I presume it would be necessary to exclude the public on those days from the National Gallery. It could not be intended that ladies in diamonds and trains should walk through the rooms when the public were admitted; therefore it would be necessary to exclude the public on those days, which would be an inconvenience. Then persons coming from a drawing-room or a levee, I imagine, would very seldom wish to stop to see pictures; they probably would simply walk through the rooms and go to their carriages and return home. Therefore, I cannot see that there is the smallest convenience or fitness in attempting to combine a National Picture Gallery with the rooms for levees and drawing-rooms. For those reasons we came to the very decided conclusion, altogether to reject the idea of pulling down St. James's Palace. One of the plans, which was at the same time proposed, was to pull down Marlborough House.

2809. *Chairman.*] Lord Elcho proposed that?—The Queen is empowered by Act of Parliament (13 & 14 Vict. cap. 78) to settle Marlborough House on the Prince of Wales, in such manner that he may have

LEWIS.

APPENDIX A.

and enjoy the same immediately after he shall have attained the age of eighteen years and thenceforward during the term of the joint lives of Her Majesty and His Royal Highness. It is at present used only temporarily, with the consent of Her Majesty, for objects connected with Art, during the minority of His Royal Highness. The Government has no power to dispose of the building, and unless it is impossible to find ground elsewhere, I cannot see anything which would justify a Government, which is responsible for its acts, in proposing to deal in so very summary and arbitrary a manner with buildings which, at present, have a totally different and necessary appropriation. Then I believe that there was some plan for a National Gallery at Whitehall.

2810. It was only mentioned in the debate?—I do not distinctly remember what part of Whitehall it was. I think Lord Elcho mentioned some part of Whitehall. Land in Whitehall is extremely expensive, and is wanted very much for other purposes, and it does not strike me that any advantage would be derived from building a National Gallery in Whitehall. The space between the street and the river is confined, and altogether, I should think that it is about as little fitted for a National Gallery as any part of London which could be found. Whatever site is selected, some objection can be made to it. One must consider the alternatives, and take that site which, on the whole, has the largest number of recommendations, and to which the fewest powerful objections apply. Having carefully considered all the different alternatives, and exhausted, as we thought, the subject, we came to the conclusion, after a perfectly unprejudiced investigation, that upon the whole the site of Kensington Gore was the best for the intended purpose.

2811. Did you consider the question of the removal of the pictures to the British Museum?—I cannot say that it was one of the subjects of consideration. I cannot say that at that time any suggestion was made of removing the pictures to the British Museum. The only proposal which we considered was that of removing from the British Museum certain portions of the collection. One proposal was to remove all the Marbles, and to combine them with the Picture Gallery; to have, in short, a Glyptothek and a Pinacothek in one. That plan we rejected. We saw no reason for disturbing the arrangement of the British Museum. We limited ourselves to the provision of a Picture Gallery. Then it was also proposed to take away the Natural History Collections from the Museum. In order to avoid the necessity of removing the Marbles, on account of the want of space, and of combining them with the Picture Gallery, it was said that sufficient space might be obtained for the marbles, with the further additions which may be made to them, by removing the Natural History Collections in the British Museum, and by transferring them to some other site, possibly to Kensington Gore. That was a plan which we considered. I do not mean to say that it might not be desirable,

APPENDIX A. 55

under certain circumstances, to remove the Natural History Collections LEWIS.
from the British Museum. At the same time, it must be remembered,
that one of the great attractions of the British Museum is the collections
of Natural History. A large number of the persons visiting the British
Museum go to see the collections of Natural History. They also visit
the antiquities, but they are much attracted by the collections of Natural
History; and my belief is, that if the British Museum consisted simply
of books and of antiques, the number of visitors would be materially
diminished. How far that is an argument against their removal, it is
for the Commissioners to consider, but such, I believe, would be the
result. Those were the two plans which we considered, and we came to
the conclusion not to combine the antiquities and the sculptures with the
picture gallery; and with regard to the Natural History Collections, not
to take any step for the present. But we did intend, in the event of
Parliament having agreed to our plan, and if they had consented to build
a picture gallery at Kensington Gore, to issue a Commission, similar to
the present Commission, to inquire into the best mode of dealing with
the want of space which undoubtedly exists at the British Museum. It
would then have been open to that Commission to have made any recommendation which they thought fit.

2812. You did not come to so decided an opinion, I think, with respect
to the removal of the Natural History from the British Museum as you
did with regard to the breaking up of the Antiquarian Department?—
No, we only came to a decision not to make any recommendation at that
moment. But we fully recognize the fact that the British Museum is at
present scarcely adequate to the demands upon it, and that every year
renders it more inadequate, and that it is quite clear that something
must be done before long, if it is to furnish a sufficient accommodation
for all the different objects which are sent to it. We believe that the
library is amply sufficient: that there is now adequate accommodation
for all the books which it is likely to receive for many years to come.

2813. *Dean of St. Paul's.*] Have you mentioned all the sites which
were under the consideration of the Government?—Yes.

2814. *Chairman.*] Have you considered the site which has been lately
a good deal recommended, in the middle of the Regent's Park?—No; I
do not think that any such site was suggested.

2815. Mr. *Richmond.*] There was one other site proposed, namely,
that near the sunk wall, which was spoken of very much. It of course
comes within the prohibitions which you have alluded to, it being in the
very centre of the Park?—I never heard that suggestion before. However, it would be open to the same fatal objection, as I consider it, of
being a detraction from the Park, and requiring, moreover, large
approaches to be made, and room for carriages. For instance, at present
cabs and omnibusses are not admitted into the Park. If you make a

APPENDIX A.

Lewis. National Gallery in the centre of the Park, you can hardly refuse to allow public conveyances to approach it; you can hardly say that hackney cabs should not be allowed to drive up to the National Gallery. Then you would have at once to alter the rule with regard to the admission of hackney cabs into the Park. This is a rule which has never yet been relaxed. It is not merely a rule which the Crown or the Government might wish to maintain, but I believe the public would object extremely to the admission of hackney cabs into the Park: it is considered a matter of public convenience that they should not be admitted, and still less omnibusses. The moment that you build a National Gallery in the centre of the Park, or in Kensington Gardens, you would at once have to deal with that question.

2816. And you do not think that you would have to deal with it if the National Gallery were planted at Kensington Gore?—Clearly not.

2817. It was given in evidence by, I think, several competent persons (I refer particularly to Sir William Cubitt), that if the National Gallery were placed on the site of Kensington Gore, it would necessitate the formation of a road through the Park, that the northern part of the town would complain so much of going round by Park-lane, or else going round by the town of Kensington, that in the end there must be a road from the northern part of the town to the National Gallery?—I should altogether dispute that inference. I do not think there would be such an influx of persons into the National Gallery as to make it necessary to bisect the Park by a road. The persons who now have to go from what is called Tyburnia to Belgravia have to go round the Park at one end or the other, and I do not think that the existence of a National Gallery in Kensington Gore would render a different state of things necessary. The Kensington Gore site is extremely accessible, because there is the Brompton-road on the one side and the Kensington-road on the other, and the Commissioners have made roads from north to south; therefore nothing can be at present more accessible than it is, and all those difficulties of the approaches are entirely got over.

2818. The project was to have a sunk way and a tunnel under Rotten-row?—I was not aware of any such plan, but I confess it does not seem to me that there would be any necessity for such an arrangement.

2819. Professor *Faraday*.] Has the site of Devonshire House ever been brought under your consideration?—When the proposal was made last year, I do not think it was known that Devonshire House was in the market, or offered for sale. I have since heard, along with other people, that there is an idea that Devonshire House might be purchased by the Government. Of course it would be a very expensive purchase. I do not know what the extent of the site may be. I presume that it would not be very different from Burlington House.

2820. Mr. *Cockerell*.] It is rather larger; there are about three acres

APPENDIX A. 57

at Burlington House, and about three and a half at Devonshire House? LEWIS.
— The Commissioners are not embarrassed with the difficulties which a
Government have to encounter when they propose large money votes to
the House of Commons. I hope that they will bear in mind that looking
at this as the practical question, if we have to go to Parliament to ask
them to vote not only the expense of a large building but also the expense
of the purchase of a site to the extent of 150,000l. or 200,000l., the
difficulty of obtaining the consent of the House of Commons is greatly
increased, and the probability of a satisfactory practical solution of the
question is much augmented. What the Government sincerely desired
was to obtain at as reasonable a cost as the circumstances of the case
admitted, a commodious and a spacious building for the reception of the
pictures now forming the National Gallery, together with all such other
pictures as might, at no distant period, probably be added to it, and we
believed that the proposal which we made, through, of course, it.was not
free from valid objections, as scarcely any proposal which you can make
is free, was nevertheless less objectionable than any other which could be
substituted for it. We thought that it was a very advantageous bargain
for the country, to take a site which had cost 150,000l. from the
Exhibition Commissioners, and which cost the Government nothing, and
that the large area which that purchase, together with the purchase from
our own grants produced, would afford advantages which could not be
derived from any other site.

2821. Accessibility seems to be the great object of the public, both in
favour of artists, and in favour of those attending the courts of law, and
the inhabitants of the east and north ends of London. Recreation for
those who are waiting in Westminster Hall and on Parliament, having
an hour or a couple of hours to spare, who may go to Charing Cross, or to
a central position with very great advantage, and pass their time with
great profit. That has been felt very much in the public mind it appears,
and very reasonably. It is contended that such a distance as Kensington
Gore would hardly be found to be accessible for useful purposes, either to
the artist or to provincials and strangers?—That, of course, is a matter
of judgment. I believe that the attendance at the National Gallery has
gone on steadily diminishing for some years; that it is less now than it
was some years ago, which seems to show that the situation has no such
very great attractions to strangers and others. With regard to those
who attend courts of law, and the Houses of Parliament, I am afraid,
judging from my own experience, that they are not very often visitors at
the National Gallery; that their time is too much occupied to admit of
their finding much leisure for seeing pictures, at least during the busy
period of the year. With regard to the inhabitants of the north of
London, it certainly must make very little difference whether they go to

Kensington Gore or to Trafalgar-square, for one radius of a circle is not longer than another radius. No doubt, to persons living in the east of London, it is somewhat farther to go to Kensington Gore than it is to go to Trafalgar square, but I believe, as far as I can judge from the habits of the persons who visited the Crystal Palace, that what people do who visit the Picture Galleries, particularly strangers, is, that they devote a certain portion of a day to the purpose, when they are not otherwise occupied; and whether the journey takes them ten minutes more or less, backwards and forwards, does not much matter to them. If a person did not walk —if he went in a conveyance—the distance, we will say, from Charing Cross to Kensington Gore would not occupy above twenty minutes, or, at the most, half an hour,—half an hour would be a very large allowance. The distance from Devonshire House to Kensington Gore could not take a person above a quarter of an hour, and even to walk, it could not take him above half an hour. Therefore, it does not strike me that the argument of distance is a very powerful one.

2822. Mr. *Richmond.*] The fact is, I think, that during the exhibition of the Crystal Palace, which certainly was an extraordinary one, and was open five or six months, six millions of persons visited it?—Yes; everybody knows that the crowds were so great that it was difficult to make head against the stream. I do not mean to say that the attraction of the Crystal Palace was not far greater than the attraction of a Picture Gallery could be. I am aware that the cases are not strictly parallel. Still it is the fact that a very large number of persons did go daily to the Crystal Palace, that the distance was not so great as to form any material obstacle. Now I remember perfectly well the argument about Hyde Park. When Hyde Park was first proposed, it was said that there were great objections to it; and I know that the Government of the day entertained doubts whether they would allow it to be so used. I also know that those who were favourable to the plan (and they were at that time, I believe, in a very small minority, although it succeeded so well afterwards,) said that it was essential to the success of the Crystal Palace to have the site in Hyde Park, that if it was taken to a greater distance, —if it was taken a mile or two miles further,—it would entirely fail, and that the whole success of the project depended upon the Government allowing that site to be used. I believe that that anticipation was correct, and if the Crystal Palace, instead of being in Hyde Park, had been in Richmond Park or Bushy Park, my belief is, that instead of millions going, there would have been thousands only; and that it would just have made the difference between complete success and almost complete failure. Therefore, although I do not at all say that the cases are strictly parallel, still I do say that the crowds which flocked to the Crystal Palace prove that the distance was not a material obstacle to visiting it. In

APPENDIX A'.   59

that way I think, it is a strong argument in favour of the site at Kensington more.   — LEWIS.

2823. In Mr. Bowring's evidence before Colonel Mure's Committee, there are some statements of figures—that, in 1852, 305,203 persons visited the Zoological Gardens, that at Kew Gardens there were 231,010, at Hampton Court 173,391, and at the British Museum 507,973 ?—I am told that the annual accounts kept of the visitors to those establishments show, that while the number of persons visiting the National Gallery has gone on annually diminishing, the number of visitors to the places at a little distance from London has regularly gone on increasing, so that distance is not so great an impediment as might be supposed. The facility of communication at present, the cheapness of public conveyances, and other things, enable persons to go to these places.

2824. *Chairman.*] One of the reasons of the result which you have just mentioned, is that they wish to get out of town, to get fresh air independently of the object which they go to visit ?—Yes.

2825. Professor *Faraday.*] The use of this great gallery, being as much for the preservation of the pictures as for that kind of instruction of the public which they get by going casually to it, has any idea ever suggested itself to the Government with regard to having a place for the preservation of the highest works of art and other places of a more ordinary character for the instruction of the people ; whether, in fact, a diffusion of the centres of instruction with one of preservation would not be the desirable course to take ?—Undoubtedly that has been one of the main objects which the Government have had in view. They have thought that the present National Gallery, from its confined space, and the small number of pictures which it accommodates, affords very imperfect instruction as well as gratification to the public, and that the national uses and advantages of a Picture Gallery might be greatly increased if there was more power of enlarging the collection. That is one of the principal objects which we have had in view. It is a question, for instance, whether it might not be desirable to have copies of some of the greatest works of art. If you have a copy, for instance, of the Transfiguration, or if you have copies of some of the largest church pictures in different parts of Europe, of course you must have a great deal of space to contain them. Everybody knows that one of the great difficulties, with regard to pictures, is the space which is necessary for properly hanging them and exhibiting them. That is one of the obstacles to the acquisition of pictures by private individuals. There are very few persons who can hang up a large picture. I think it is quite worthy of consideration, whether, if Parliament were disposed to be liberal, and to enlarge the National Gallery beyond what would accommodate pictures purchased by the nation and given to the nation, some addition of that sort would not be highly expedient. My belief is that it would be expedient—at the same

Lewis. time I cannot say that the Government intended to propose any plan of that sort; but they certainly contemplated it as a matter which would be desirable. I need not say that its adoption would very much depend upon the view which Parliament might take of the propriety of supporting such an institution. Many persons in the House of Commons have an objection to that which they consider as something which is intended merely for the benefit of the educated classes, and which they think is not appreciated by the bulk of the population. I believe myself that this is a narrow view of the utility of a National Gallery. On the contrary, I consider it as a valuable part of a system, if one may so say, of public instruction. I think, too, that persons who take that view do not understand the real sentiments of the working classes. I believe that now there is, amongst a large portion of the working classes, a desire to see public institutions of that sort enriched; and that they would not grudge the appropriation of a portion of the taxation of the country to improving them. At the same time the Commissioners are doubtless aware that there are persons in the House of Commons who do not at all share those views, and who would very much object to large grants being made for a National Picture Gallery. Therefore the Government must proceed cautiously and gradually in such matters; but, as far as my own opinion goes, I have no hesitation in saying that I should consider that a very valuable part of a National Picture Gallery.

2826. *Dean of St. Paul's.*] Would not accessibility be peculiarly important to that class of persons of whom you have just been speaking?—Accessibility seems to me to be a relative term.

2827. Easy and cheap access?—By accessibility you may mean that which is in the most central spot of London. Now that which is in the most central spot of London is necessarily in a very crowded spot—is necessarily in a spot in which there is great difficulty in obtaining land, and in which, from the enormous cost of ground where it is sold literally by the inch, you must be cramped as to space. I certainly consider myself that Kensington Gore is perfectly accessible, in this sense, that there are approaches to it from all directions, and that you can reach it in a limited time from any part of the metropolis. It is not so central as Trafalgar-square, but it is perfectly accessible.

2828. *Mr. Cockerell.*] The necessities of space for a National Gallery bear a very small proportion to the space appropriated at Kensington Gore. I look upon it that four acres would furnish abundant space for a Pinacothek for 100 years to come?—Yes, I quite admit that that is the truth. The space is far greater than is at all needed for the purposes of a National Gallery; but four acres of land are not easily obtained in any of the central parts of London.

2829. Three acres or three and a half acres would furnish a prodigious resource for many years from this time?—No doubt.

APPENDIX A.

LEWIS.

2830. *Chairman.*] I think you say that the Government did not consider the advantages which might attach to the site of Devonshire House?—I should think myself that the difference between Devonshire House and Burlington House may be considered as practically very limited. Burlington House has already been acquired, and we could, if we thought fit, dislodge the learned societies which now occupy it, and propose a grant for building upon that area.

2831. *Dean of St. Paul's.*] Excepting that the front of Devonshire House is perfectly open, and looks upon the Park, and behind there are Lansdowne Gardens and Berkeley-square?—Yes; but as far as area and position are concerned, there is no great difference.

II.—EVIDENCE of Mr. BOWRING.

BOWRING.

2832. *Chairman.*] You still are Secretary, I believe, to the Commission of 1851?—I am.

2833. You were examined at considerable length before Colonel Mure's Committee in 1853, were you not?—I was.

2834. Have you lately looked at the evidence which you gave on that occasion?—Yes; I have just been reading it over again.

2835. Has any change to any extent taken place with reference to the Gore Estate since you gave that evidence?—Yes; there have been some important changes. The great roads, varying from 80 to 100 feet in width, which were then only contemplated, have all been made. Some considerable purchases of property in Gore-lane, projecting very awkwardly into the estate have been effected, and, altogether, the estate has assumed a much more compact and complete condition than formerly.

2836. Has any change taken place in the extent. I see it is stated to be 86 acres?—It remains very nearly the same in extent. Not exactly the same. This wedge, composing Gore-lane, has been purchased (*showing the same*). But, on the other hand, there has been an exchange recently of a small outlying piece here (*pointing to the plan*) for a smaller piece lying within the main square (*showing the same*), which it was important to secure. Therefore, I think, we may assume that the increased acreage which we have obtained by the Gore-lane purchases is counterbalanced by the decreased acreage caused by the exchange, so that the extent of the estate remains virtually as nearly as possible the same as before.

2837. *Mr. Cockerell.*] The frontage of Gore-lane has not been purchased?—No, with the exception of the reversion to the houses on the western side.

2838. *Dean of St. Paul's.*] Does Gore-lane still exist?—It is closed as a public thoroughfare. We have power, under our Act of Parliament, to obtain the whole of the coloured part of Gore-lane; but we do not at present touch this block, which is now occupied by first-class houses.

2839. What is the name of that row of houses?—I think they call it Kensington Gore or Lower Kensington Gore. There are two distinct terraces, containing six houses each, one consisting of first-class houses, and the other of rather smaller ones.

2840. *Mr. Richmond.*] Do you know the length of lease of those two rows of houses?—They are long leases, and we have no power over them at present, nor have we over Lord Auckland's property, known as Eden Lodge.

2841. *Chairman.*] We have had some evidence from the Chancellor of the Exchequer, as to the objects of the Commissioners in purchasing that estate, and also as to the circumstances under which they offered part of the site of it for a National Gallery. Therefore it will be hardly necessary to trouble you with any question in that respect. But if you have anything to tell us, which you consider that we are not likely to be aware of, we shall be glad to hear it?—I believe that there has been a good deal of misapprehension as to the part taken by the Royal Commissioners for the Exhibition of 1851, with regard to this site. It has been assumed, and frequently stated, that they have attempted to thrust it upon the public. I may, perhaps, be allowed to state briefly the real circumstances of the case. On referring to the Report of the House of Commons' Committee of 1850, on the National Gallery, it will be seen that there was a very strong intimation there given in favour of the removal of the National Gallery. The Committee did not positively recommend its removal from the existing site, being, as they stated, ignorant of the character of the new site which might be chosen; but they expressed a decided opinion against any enlargement of the present building on the present site, and the whole tenor of the recommendation was in favour of the removal. In the following year, a Commission was appointed by the Treasury, at the head of which was the present Duke of Somerset, the other members being Lord Colborne, Sir Charles Eastlake, Sir Richard Westmacott, and Mr. Ewart, to inquire into the question of a site for the National Gallery. They made a Report, in which they proposed three alternative sites. The exact position of the first, or the one preferred by them, was not specifically mentioned in the Report, because it was an estate which would have to be acquired by purchase, and if it were known that the Government wished to buy it, the price would of course be raised against them. But those Commissioners intimated that it was in the immediate neighbourhood of the Parks, and facing Hyde Park. They then proceeded to say that if the Government were unwilling to incur the outlay involved in such a pur-

APPENDIX A. 63

cha[se], there were two other sites adapted for the site of a National Bowring.
Ga[lle]ry, both of which were in Kensington Gardens; and a map was
pub[lis]hed, accompanying their Report, showing those two sites; but for
the [p]rudential reasons which I have given, the other site was only
ge[ner]ally referred to. In consequence of that recommendation Sir
Cha[r]les Wood, the then Chancellor of the Exchequer, entered into
neg[o]tiations for the purchase of the Gore House Estate, whereby the
nec[es]sity of taking any part of Kensington Gardens for the purpose
wou[ld] be avoided. Those negociations, from some cause or other, were
brok[en] off. Just at this time the Exhibition Commissioners found
them[s]elves in the possession of large surplus funds arising from the
Exh[ib]ition, and took into consideration the question of the disposal of
tha[t s]urplus. The result was the elaboration of the scheme set forth in
thei[r] Second Report to the Crown, dated November 1852, in which they
prop[o]sed the purchase of a large tract of land for the purpose of concen-
tra[tin]g the different institutions connected with Science and Art, and so
on. But at the time when this site was originally negociated for by the
Gove[r]nment, so far from the Exhibition Commissioners having anything
to do with it, it was not even known that they would have a surplus
rema[i]ning from the Exhibition. It was in August 1851 that the Report
of th[e] Duke of Somerset's Commission was published. It is obvious
that i[n] the general scheme proposed by the Exhibition Commissioners,
the [N]ational Gallery would very properly occupy a space, assuming it
to be decided that the National Gallery should go to the site purchased
by [th]em. Accordingly, in their Report, they enumerated different
insti[tu]tions, &c., which might be with advantage placed upon the site,
and [o]bserved, hypothetically, that if it were determined to put the
Natio[n]al Gallery there, it might be appropriately erected on the north
side [o]f the estate, adjoining Hyde Park. The observation was made in
that [h]ypothetical way. The next step was a vote by Parliament of
150,[00]0l. towards the expense of purchasing the estate, after the Com-
miss[ion]ers' Report had been placed before the public. The possibility of
remo[vin]g the National Gallery to this site was distinctly spoken of in
the d[eb]ate on that occasion, and the formal Resolution of the House of
Comm[o]ns approving the vote, mentioned the erection of a new National
Galle[r]y on the site as being one of the objects contemplated in its purchase. This was at the end of the year 1852. Then early in the year
1853, the whole subject of the management of the National Gallery, in-
clud[in]g the question of its site, was referred to Colonel Mure's Com-
mitt[ee]. That Committee recommended, as this Commission will re-
memb[e]r, the adoption of the site belonging to the Commissioners for
the E[x]hibition of 1851. The war shortly after that broke out, and the
whole matter remained in suspense till last year, when the Government

Bowring. took into consideration the Report of Colonel Mure's Committee, and concurred in the conclusion at which it had arrived in favour of that site. A Bill was accordingly brought in by them to give effect to this decision on their part. This was followed by Lord Elcho's motion, which was carried against the Government, and the result has been the reference of the whole subject to this present Commission. I think this short sketch of what has passed will show plainly that, so far from the Exhibition Commissioners having attempted to force this site upon the public, they merely followed in the wake of others who had gone before them. It so happened that their proposals accorded with these other proposals; but it is an historical fact, that the first proceedings on the subject took place, as I have stated, in 1850 and 1851, and that the Commissioners took no steps till 1852. I trust that I have shown that they have occupied a natural position in the matter; and that having possession of the Kensington Gore Estate, it was offered by them to the country for the purposes of a National Gallery, if it thought fit to accept it, it being entirely for the country to decide whether or not it would do so.

2842. Have you considered any of the objections which have been made to the site, and particularly owing to its distance from the centre of London?—Yes. I have made a point of getting a good deal of information on that very subject. When I was examined in 1853, I was aware that that was the main objection raised to the adoption of any site at or near Kensington, namely, the so-called distance from the heart of London. Of course the only way to arrive at an unprejudiced opinion on that question was, by examining all the evidence bearing upon it that could be collected. In 1853 I gave some statistical evidence upon the subject. I have continued the statistics then produced down to the present time, and am now in a position to submit the results to the Commission. I laid a table before Colonel Mure's Committee, showing the number of visitors in various years to the chief places of public amusement, both in and out of London, brought down to the end of the year 1852, which was the latest date then known. The places selected as being well-known place of public resort were the British Museum, the National Gallery, and the Vernon Gallery, those constituting what might be called the exhibitions in London, and the Zoological Gardens, Kew Gardens, and Hampton Court Palace, as being places of recreation out of London, and requiring a certain amount of exertion to visit them, in fact, places to which the objection of *distance* would apply. The figures then laid before that Committee showed that the tendency of the number of visitors to the exhibitions in London was to decrease, whereas there was a constant tendency to increase in the number of visitors to the more distant places; and I showed that even in the year 1852 the

APPENDIX A.

number of visitors to the Zoological Gardens, which are further from this part of London than the Kensington Gore Estate, and where there is a charge for admission of a shilling (with the exception of one day a week, when it is sixpence), was very nearly as many as the total number of visitors to the National Gallery itself, in the very heart of London, and where there is no charge whatever for admission. The conclusion which that seemed to point to was, that if you gave a sufficient inducement to people to go a little way, they did not at all mind the extra trouble and the extra distance, and that the mere difficulty of distance was in reality no serious bar to the masses visiting these places.

2843. Did that inference of your's apply as well to artists as to the general public?—It related to the general public. This was an inference founded entirely upon the statistics of the number of visitors to these places. Four years have elapsed since that time, and I have now been able to continue that table down to the end of the year 1856.

2844. Will you have the goodness to give us the result?—The results are so remarkable, that I am desirous of laying them before this Commission. To some extent these returns are rather thrown out by the fact of 1851, the year of the Great Exhibition, having been an exceptional year, and also by the breaking out of the war in 1854, and the additional taxation it involved, having led to the people's diminishing their expenditure and not going so much to places of amusement.

2845. *Dean of St. Paul's.*] Another excitement, in short?—Yes, but that argument applies equally to all places of public resort, and the comparative results remain unaffected. I have now got the figures complete for all these six places, for the years 1850 to 1856 inclusive. In the case of the British Museum they are as follows (leaving out the odd hundreds): In 1850 the number of visitors was 1,098,000; in 1851, the year of the Exhibition, 2,527,000; in 1852 the number fell off to 507,000; in 1853 it increased again to 661,000; in 1854 it fell off to 459,000; in 1855 it fell off again to 334,000; and in 1856 it slightly recovered to 361,000; the result showing in 1856 an increase of eight per cent. as compared with 1855, but a decrease of as much as 45 per cent. as compared with the year 1853, which I have taken as being the most normal year of the whole series, and the one least affected by exceptional causes. It was before the war broke out, and after the excitement of the Exhibition was over, and it therefore seemed the most appropriate year to take. In the case of the National Gallery, the number of visitors in 1850 was 575,000; in 1851, 1,005,000; in 1852, it fell off to 352,000; in 1853, it rose again to 627,000; and in 1854, fell off to 446,000; in 1855, it fell off again to 381,000; and, lastly, in 1856, it fell off once more to

BOWRING.

E

BOWRING.   208,000,* showing a decrease in 1856, as compared with 1855, of no less than 45 per cent.; and a decrease in 1856, as compared with 1853, of as much as 66 per cent. The next is the Vernon Gallery. In the year 1850 there were 61,000 visitors; in 1851, 253,000; in 1852, 155,000; in 1853, 249,000; in 1854, 248,000; in 1855, 228,000; and in 1856, 227,000. I had a note from Mr. Wornum, who gave me these figures, to state that there had been a great decrease in the number of visitors to the Vernon Gallery in 1856, until nearly the end of the year, when the Turner pictures were first exhibited. There was an extraordinary rush of visitors to see those pictures, and but for that unexpected excitement the falling off would probably have been as great as at the National Gallery itself. As it was, the decrease in 1856 as compared with 1855 was merely nominal, viz., ½ per cent., and as compared with 1853, 9 per cent. I now come to the series of places out of London, headed by the Zoological Gardens. In 1850, the number of visitors was 360,000; in 1851, 667,000; in 1852, 305,000; in 1853, 409,000; in 1854, 407,000; in 1855, 315,000; and in 1856, 344,000, showing an increase of 9 per cent. as compared with 1855, and a decrease of 16 per cent. as compared with 1853. But the decrease in the case of the National Gallery in 1856 as compared with 1853, has been already shown to have been 66 per cent., and in that of the British Museum 45 per cent. Then with regard to Kew Gardens. In the year 1850 the number of visitors was 179,000; in 1851, 327,000; in 1852, 231,000; in 1853, the number increased to 331,000, I believe chiefly owing to the Gardens being then opened on Sundays for the first time; in 1854 it was 339,000; in 1855, 313,000; and in 1856, 344,000; showing an increase in 1856 over 1855 of 10 per cent., and over 1853, of 4 per cent. Last in the list is Hampton Court Palace. In 1850 the number of visitors was 221,000; in 1851, 350,000; in 1852, 173,000; in 1853, 180,000; in 1854, 203,000; in 1855, 141,000; and in 1856, 161,000, being an increase of 14 per cent. over 1855, but a decrease of 10 per cent. as compared with 1853. These figures exhibit the remarkable fact, that whereas the number of visitors to the National Gallery formerly exceeded those to the Zoological Gardens and Kew Gardens put together, they have now fallen off to less than one-third of the number visiting the two put together, as in the first comparison. The information in every case has been obtained by me, either from published Parliamentary papers, or from the heads of the different departments—from the Office of Works, for instance, for Hampton Court, Sir William Hooker for Kew Gardens, the Secretary to the

* Although these figures were supplied to the witness by the Keeper and Secretary of the National Gallery himself, and although that gentleman certified to the correctness of a similar return published in Appendix III. to the Report of the Commission, he subsequently stated that he had discovered a most serious error in the figures, and that the correct number was 608,000.

APPENDIX A.

Zoological Gardens for those Gardens, Mr. Wornum for the National Gallery and the Vernon Gallery, and Mr. Panizzi for the British Museum. The conclusion which seems to me to be derivable from these figures is, that the tendency with regard to the exhibitions in London has been to a remarkable falling off in the number of visitors in the last few years, while, with regard to those out of London, where the objection of distance applies, and which, therefore, practically test that objection, so far from falling off the tendency has been the other way. Hence I arrive at the conclusion that the proposed removal of the National Gallery would not entail that falling off in the number of visitors which some apprehend, and which constitutes the most serious objection to such removal.

2846. Mr. *Cockerell.*] You have no distinction of the classes of visitors? —No.

2847. You are quite aware that in times of prosperity the working classes are very willing to enjoy themselves beyond the limits of London streets?—Certainly.

2848. But the classes who might be supposed to visit a National Gallery with advantage would be distinct and very different, would they not, from those classes of workmen-holiday folks?—There would be all classes; and the convenience of the working classes should assuredly not be the least of all consulted, as I presume that one of the most important objects of a National Gallery is to elevate the taste of the masses. But if the National Gallery were on any site in the neighbourhood of Kensington, my impression is, that the visits of the working classes would be greatly increased by the additional distance they would have to go, however paradoxical it may appear. Those classes do not visit places of this character without first making themselves clean, and probably taking half a day's holiday for the purpose, while they take their wives and families with them, and, in short, attempt to make such an occasion a source of rational enjoyment and improvement. So far from their objecting to the National Gallery being removed to Kensington, the enjoyment of the half-holiday taken by them for the purpose of visiting it, with its accessories of ornamental gardens, fountains, &c., would be greatly increased by the walk across the green sward of the parks, where they breathe a purer and more exhilarating air than they are accustomed to in their everyday life; whereas a visit to a National Gallery in the midst of the smoke of London does not afford them this desirable relief. Mr. Cubitt gave decisive evidence on this subject, before the Committee of 1853, founded on his long practical experience of the habits of the working classes. I may, perhaps, observe, with regard to the great falling off in the visitors to the National Gallery in 1856, that if that falling off had occurred subsequently to its removal to Kensington, it would have been assumed, as a matter of course, that it was entirely owing to that circumstance. This allegation, at any rate, cannot now be made.

APPENDIX A.

The witness delivered in the following paper:—

STATEMENT of the Number of Visitors admitted to visit the British Museum, the National Gallery, the Vernon Gallery, the Zoological Gardens, Kew Gardens, and Hampton Court Palace in each year, from 1850 to 1856 inclusive.

Years.	British Museum.	National Gallery.	Vernon Gallery.	Zoological Gardens.	Kew Gardens.	Hampton Court Palace.
	No.	No.	No.	No.	No.	No.
1850	1,098,863	575,005	61,560	360,402	179,627	221,119
1851	2,527,216	1,005,705	253,152	667,243	327,900	350,848
1852	507,973	352,220	155,013	305,203	231,010	173,391
1853	661,113	627,740	249,992	409,076	331,210†	180,753
1854	459,262	446,641	248,466	407,676	339,164†	203,990
1855	334,089	381,897	228,095	315,002	313,816†	141,420
1856	361,714	208,270	227,720*	344,184	344,140†	151,752
1856 compared with 1855	Increase 8 per cent.	Decrease 45 per cent.	Decrease ¼ per cent.	Increase 9 per cent.	Increase 10 per cent.	Increase 14 per cent.
1856 compared with 1853	Decrease 45 per cent	Decrease 66 per cent.	Decrease 9 per cent.	Decrease 16 per cent.	Increase 4 per cent.	Decrease 10 per cent.

2849. Professor *Faraday*.] Can you give us any information with relation to the attendance of students in art apart from the general public?—I am able to state it generally, in the case of the Department of Art.

2850. What are the students to whom you refer?—Quite recently the whole of the Government Schools of Art have been removed from Marlborough House to the Kensington Gore Estate.

2851. Do you consider that the Government Schools of Art are of such a character that they can give us useful information with regard to the case of a National Gallery; are the two objects so far alike, that what is the fact and the result with one may be supposed, to a certain extent, to be the fact and the result with the other?—I consider that there is that analogy. It was expected by the Department of Science and Art that the immediate result of the removal to Kensington would be a very considerable falling off in the number of students attending the schools, because the very same objection would apply in their case that is urged against the removal of the National Gallery to the same neighbourhood, namely, the distance of the site from the heart of London, and its inaccessibility.

2852. Are these students voluntary students?—They are the regular Government students.

---

* The exhibition of the Turner pictures at the end of 1856 led to a very large increase in the number of visitors at that time. There had been a serious falling off in the number in the greater part of the year, as compared with former years.
† Including Sundays.

2853. Do they come under the class of people who are at liberty to do as they like?—They are entirely voluntary students, and need not join the schools unless they like.

2854. *Dean of St. Paul's.*] Do they expect to derive any advantage from what are called the Government schools?—Merely in so far as the fact of their having been trained at the Government schools is of great advantage to them in obtaining employment in after-life. They get no direct advantage from Government, except in the case of students in training for local masterships, who, like the students in the diocesan and other training schools, receive an actual subsidy in aid of their subsistence.

2855. Therefore it is no test as respects the general mass of the public?—It is a test, as far as it goes, as to the extent to which people can be induced to go to such a distance.

2856. Then they have the further inducement of the advantages which they expect to derive from being students?—Yes, in the respect I have just mentioned.

2857. Professor *Faraday.*] But they would have that in London, too?—Yes.

2858. Therefore that makes no difference with regard to the distance from London?—No; but my object was to show that the removal to a certain distance from London, instead of having led to a very great falling off, has not done so.

2859. Have you any figures on that point?—I have not the exact figures, but they can be given by the officers of the Department. I merely state the fact, that the immediate result of the removal a few months ago was expected to be a very great falling off in the number of students. The number has, however, already virtually recovered itself, and the Department of Science and Art is quite surprised at the early success of the removal in this point of view.

2860. Mr. *Richmond.*] How many hours a day are the students employed?—There are different classes; some of them work till late at night.

2861. Some go for the whole day?—Yes; it depends upon the classes which they attend.

2862. Professor *Faraday.*] Do the circumstances of the schools just now, as far as you can judge, appear to indicate that there is any additional difficulty, which would be evident to you, in their having to come so far to the schools?—There appeared to be that difficulty at first, but it has now vanished. The students have returned; and I believe I may safely state that there are nearly as many now as before.

2863. Mr. *Cockerell.*] But not more?—Mr. Cole, or any of the officers of that Department, can give the precise figures; I only know the general fact.

BOWRING.

2864. My experience is against that result. I find that students, whom I should gladly have sent, have not been able to go to the School of Design because of the distance, the sacrifice of time and cost—cost if you travel by omnibus, time at all events ?—That is probably counterbalanced, then, by an increase from other causes, for I have ascertained that there is not that falling off which your remark would lead one to expect. I may also mention another point bearing slightly upon this question of site. Gore House has been for a considerable time occupied by the Government for one of its branch schools, and it has just been closed in consequence of the removal of the whole of the Department of Science and Art to the south-eastern part of the Kensington Gore Estate, and the house has been given back to our Commissioners. I understand that a remonstrance has been made by the students attending that school against its being closed, the site being so convenient to them.

2865. *Chairman.*] Do the students wish the removal back to Gore House ?—Yes ; the students who have been hitherto at Gore House have, I understand, remonstrated against that school being shut up.

2866. *Dean of St. Paul's.*] Where is that school removed to ?—It is now amalgamated with the main school at the south end of our estate.

2867. Professor *Faraday.*] It has been removed from the north to the south end ?—Yes.

2868. Mr. *Richmond.*] Is the difference of distance a quarter of a mile? —It is a long way ; it is more than half a mile.

2869. *Chairman.*] That seems to militate rather against your inference ; that distance does not deter visitors ?—These students were, I believe, Kensington students, and they would have to go further.

2870. Mr. *Richmond.*] The present schools are held in buildings which are really nearer to the metropolis than Gore House ?—Considerably nearer ; but to these students probably further.

2871. They may be Kensington students to the west, but the present site is considerably nearer to the east ?—Yes. The site of the present schools is, in fact, exactly opposite the site of the Exhibition Building of 1851. With regard to the question of distance, I need scarcely remind this Commission of the immense number of visitors that went the same distance in the year 1851. We had upwards of six millions of visits paid to the Great Exhibition in less than six months. Since that time, there is also the experience of the Crystal Palace at Sydenham, which, in the short period of 18 months after its opening, was visited by two and a half millions of persons, although eight miles from London. That plainly shows that if you give sufficient attraction, people will come the necessary distance.

2872. *Chairman.*] Will you state shortly what means of access there would be, supposing the National Gallery were removed to the site you

APPENDIX A. 71

allude to?—In the first place, these great roads (*showing them*) have been made all round the estate since the period of my former evidence. I also understand that it has been proposed to make a road from the south-east corner of the estate across to Belgravia, which will at once give a short and easy approach to the estate from the whole of that part of London, Westminster, Lambeth, &c., without the necessity of going round by the Parks. Again, if Prince Albert's Road were prolonged a very short distance, the estate would be brought into immediate and direct communication with the Thames at Battersea bridge, and with the vast traffic which might be brought by the river. In addition to that, I may mention that even already, I understand, the omnibus proprietors are anxious to make some arrangements whereby they may give the public every facility for visiting the exhibition which is about to be opened permanently on the estate at South Kensington; and a scheme of "correspondence" is, I believe, at this very moment in contemplation, by which the public will be brought, at a single fare, from all parts of London to visit the Sheepshanks Gallery and the Museums of the Department of Science and Art, now erected on the estate.

Bowring.

2873. I see by the evidence which you gave in 1853, that it was contemplated to place not only the National Gallery, but a great many other national institutions, upon this Kensington Gore Estate. They were all to be together?—They were all to be on the estate; the offer was made, at least, in case the public liked to avail themselves of it Amongst other institutions, the present Department of Science and Art was mentioned. The removal of that Department to the estate has now actually taken place. Then, in addition to that, we proposed to give facilities to private bodies and societies to come to the estate, and there are already many indications of an anxiety on the part of these private bodies to come to this neighbourhood.

2874. *Dean of St. Paul's.*] What private bodies do you mean?—I may instance the Architectural Museum, which it has been recently determined to remove permanently to this estate. The removal has, in fact, just taken place. The Sculptors' Institute of London has also recently come to the determination of exhibiting there. The Academy of Music has also applied for a site.

2875. *Chairman.*] Is there any fresh building appropriated to the Academy of Music?—No; that question is not yet decided, but an application for a site has been made, and a Committee has been appointed to consider the question, but no decision has been yet come to. It has been regarded as premature.

2876. Professor *Faraday.*] What part of the estate do these applications refer to which are now made to you for localities? The southern part of the estate?—The same part as the Science and Art Museum.

Bowring. 2877. Mr. *Richmond.*] That is the south-eastern part?—The south-eastern part.

2878. Professor *Faraday.*] What part, according to your knowledge, was intended for the National Gallery?—The whole estate was offered to the public, to choose any part they liked. All the Commission proposed was that the main buildings should be within the great square.

2879. What intention is there of building ordinary houses within that large square?—None whatever.

2880. There would not be the power of covering such parts with houses as were not covered with public buildings?—We have no power to do so, even if we wished it. The Treasury have a lien upon the estate, which puts it quite out of our power to build any private houses on the estate.

2881. Is every part of the estate in the same condition?—Every part of the estate is in the same condition, and none can be appropriated to private dwellings without the consent of the Government. A question was put to me, as to any particular society asking for any particular site. The Architectural Museum and the Sculptors' Institute, to which I have referred, have applied to be admitted to exhibit in the great Museum building which has just been completed.

2882. Have any opportunities arisen yet, of observing what is the subsoil of the whole of that estate?—I have here a map showing the whole character of the soil of the estate. It was prepared by Mr. Mylne, and was referred to by me, when I gave my evidence before the Committee in 1853.

2883. What is the main subsoil?—Gravel is the main subsoil.

2884. From north to south, and pretty nearly from east to west?—The whole estate is gravel with a single exception, which I will point out. This (*showing the map*) is a section of the estate, exhibiting the nature of the soil.

2885. A section from north to south?—Yes; the dark colour represents the London clay, and the light yellow represents the gravel, and it is only on this small portion (*indicating it*) that the London clay comes to the surface; with that exception, the whole of the soil is a gravel soil.

2886. *Chairman.*] In what exact position is that exception?—Some little way at the rear of Gore House. Gore House itself appears by this map to be upon the gravel. It is just at the back of Gore House, at an elevation, I think, of 40 feet above the Trinity House datum; Gore House has an elevation of about 60 feet.

2887. Professor *Faraday.*] Is that section correctly made, with regard to inclination?—It does not appear to be intended to show the inclination.

APPENDIX A.

2888. What is the inclination of the London clay, an ascent or descent?—The London clay disappears as you go south. The only object of this section was to show generally the character of the soil.

2889. But it does not tell me the position of a building on this clay, with regard to draining from north to south?—The whole of the slope is southward; there is no slope northward.

2890. It does not show the slope of the clay under the gravel?—I am afraid that it will not help in considering the question of drainage; it was not prepared with reference to that. I may add, that when we excavated the ground at the south end of the estate, for the purpose of erecting the Museum Building, the Sheepshanks Gallery, and the other buildings now standing there, it was found to consist entirely of excellent gravel; and I can state positively, that there is no portion of the estate, whether gravel or clay, that presents any difficulty in respect to the drainage.

2891. *Chairman.*] Can you give us shortly a summary of what you consider to be the advantages of this estate, for the purposes of a National Picture Gallery. We are not talking of the other Institutions, which you have before alluded to?—In the first place, I may, perhaps, mention that one obvious advantage is, that if this estate is employed, there is no purchase of ground necessary. To that extent there would be a saving of public money. I find from Mr. Pennethorne's evidence in 1853, that he estimated the cost of acquiring the additional ground necessary for enlarging the present National Gallery, at 160,000*l.* The next obvious advantage is, that it makes it unnecessary to interfere in any way with any of the public parks. The jealousy of the public, with regard to interference with the parks is quite proverbial; and we had practical experience of this in 1850, when we proposed for only a few months to occupy a small piece of one of the parks (which piece was previously hardly used at all) for the purposes of the Great Exhibition. The Commissioners may probably recollect that this difficulty was nearly fatal to the whole scheme. A similar case occurred many years ago within my knowledge, when the late Mr. Cubitt proposed to form a very handsome entrance into London from the west, whereby we should have had the finest entrance from the Kensington side that can well be conceived; I mean on the space extending from the Duke of Wellington's statue through Knightsbridge. His proposal was, I believe, to build a row of first class houses, similar to those erected by him in Belgravia, and extending the whole length of the distance in question. It would have been necessary that a small piece of Hyde Park, lying behind the railing, and never used, should be given up for the purpose, he on the other hand giving up a corresponding piece on the other side, so that the public would have been in no respect losers. But the then Government —that of Sir Robert Peel—felt how unpopular it would be to take away

BOWRING.

even this very small section of the Park; and on that single ground, the whole of this great scheme of public improvement fell through, and it has now become impracticable. Then another advantage which would seem to be obtained by a site of this character is, that no destruction of existing buildings is rendered necessary. You have a site entirely free and unencumbered, instead of, as in the case of various other suggested sites, a piece of ground already occupied by public buildings or palaces. That is, of course, an advantage which I need not comment upon. Then there is the question of space. By choosing a large open site, like the Kensington Gore Estate, which contains within the roads a space of 56 acres, or, if the roads are included, 68 acres, an area within which there is no possibility of private buildings interfering with your arrangements, you have room for indefinite extension of the National Gallery hereafter, if found necessary. One of the great difficulties hitherto experienced in all Government buildings has been, that after the buildings have been finished, it has been found necessary to enlarge them, and there has been the constant fresh expense of buying more ground, as has happened at the British Museum. In this case you have the additional ground already, and if you want hereafter to extend your National Gallery, you can do so without one farthing's outlay in obtaining land for the purpose. And I may here remark, that we have no idea at present of the vast extent to which the National Gallery might be increased by gifts and bequests of valuable pictures, if the present possessors were assured that if they gave them to the nation, there would be room for them, or means of making room for them. Then, another point, with reference to this especial site, which has been very little noticed, is the effect of any such building as the National Gallery, if built on this estate, when seen from the lower or south end. All the remarks hitherto made in the discussions respecting it, have had special reference to it as seen from Hyde Park, or the north side only, and not sufficient importance has been attached to seeing it from the south side coming up from Chelsea, and that part of London. In the first place, these great roads (*showing them on the map*), have already been formed, which have at once made an opening to the south; and if the further schemes of new roads to which I have alluded are carried out, the probability is, that the south approach to the estate, which will be the shortest, in point of distance, for a large part of London, will be also a very popular approach. Therefore, it is of great importance to have a site which, when seen from the south, does not present any unfavourable effect, and the configuration of the ground, in that respect, is highly favourable.

2892. *Dean of St. Paul's.*] Of course that supposes that the architectural front of the whole building is to the south?—Yes; or rather I should say an architectural front each way, to the north as well as to the south. This would seem in all respects desirable. Then there is the

APPENDIX A.

question of the adjacency to the Government Schools of Art, which are now permanently established on this estate. As far as it goes, I presume it would be an advantage to have the National Gallery of Pictures and the Art Galleries generally within reach of the students. It is possibly a minor point, but of course as far as relates to the students themselves, and the progress of art in this country as affected by those schools, it would be an advantage to have the National Gallery in their neighbourhood.

2893. Mr. *Cockerell.*] It will remain to be seen how in future time the position of the School of Art at such a distance from the central part of the town and from the east and north will answer?—Precisely; we have very little experience now, but such experience as there is is favourable, and in a very few weeks more we shall have practical experience as to how far the public at large will visit this very site. The Sheepshanks Gallery, and other collections intended to be exhibited on the estate are now on the point of completion, and I believe that before the end of the first fortnight of June the whole is expected to be open to the public.

2894. *The Chairman.*] Where will it be open?—This exhibition will be opened on the south-eastern part of the estate.

2895. Professor *Faraday.*] From Brompton?—The Brompton end.

2896. Mr. *Richmond.*] As I understand you it is your belief, founded upon authoritative statement, that the number of students now attending the classes of the Schools of Practical Art in the south-eastern portion of that estate is as great as when those classes were accommodated in Marlborough House at the end of Pall Mall?—So I understand, as nearly as possible the same; at any rate the great falling off which, as a matter of course, at first took place owing to the removal has been recovered.

2897. Mr. *Cockerell.*] The number ought to be greater, because there surely has been an increase of interest in this country of late years upon the whole matter of design, and of learning the art of design and drawing?—I believe the Department of Science and Art quite expects an increase, but there has really hitherto been no time for it, the removal having only just taken place.

2898. Mr. *Richmond.*] A removal will always disturb the arrangement of any school or classes. How long have the classes been removed from Marlborough House?—A very few months, and everything was thrown into confusion by the removal.

2899. The arrangements are not yet complete?—They are scarcely complete even now.

2900. Mr. *Cockerell.*] You have given us the gross amount of visitors, many of whom undoubtedly are popular visitors, holiday-makers. Have you considered professional visitors to a National Gallery, such as lawyers, such as architects, and professionals of all descriptions, who desire to take an occasional opportunity of visiting these noble masterpieces, and of deriving that consolation and elevation of mind which naturally proceed from the contemplation of such fine works? Those are persons who address us on all occasions with deep interest upon the position of the National Gallery, persons who cannot really spare any extra time to go to visit these objects, but who take them as they can catch an opportunity, and who derive very great advantage from them. Have you formed any opinion upon that question?—I am afraid that there are no means of obtaining any statistics on that point; we can only get the figures in the gross, and I scarcely see how it is possible to give more than an individual opinion. Taking myself, for instance, as one of the working public, my time is occupied in London for many hours every day, in Whitehall, within half a mile of the present National Gallery, and I am sorry to say that I do not find myself inside it as often as once a year. I have very little doubt that if it were at Kensington, I should be there very much oftener, and I know that the same is the case with many others. However paradoxical it may seem, one does go more to places at a little greater distance, and which it may require a little more effort to reach, than to those close at hand, which one may see at any time.

2901. Professor *Faraday*.] Experience, I suppose, would tell both ways in that respect?—Very probably so.

2902. It may be so with you, but many drop in because they can drop in, and would not go any distance?—I have no means of giving a general opinion.

2903. Mr. *Cockerell*.] How are we to account for the constancy of exhibitions in all parts of Pall Mall, and the success of publishers in the neighbourhood of Pall Mall, such as Colnaghi and Graves? It is true it is a matter of opinion, but how are we to account for the success of these establishments in that neighbourhood rather than at a great distance? It is quite clear that none of them could succeed if they were at Kensington.—So far as the higher classes who visit those exhibitions, and form the best customers of those establishments, are concerned, I should assume that it would make very little difference to them whether they went to Kensington or to Pall Mall to see these exhibitions of pictures, and so on. Certainly, in 1851, a site immediately adjoining the Kensington Gore Estate was the place where all the fashionable classes went in numbers beyond all precedent.

2904. That was a special occasion?—Doubtless. But quite irrespectively of any such consideration, the fact does remain that the number of visitors to the National Gallery on the present site, which has every advantage of centrality that you can possibly desire, has for several years continued to decrease in a very remarkable manner. I gather

APPENDIX A.

Bowring.

from a question asked before the National Gallery Committee by one of the members, that he considered the normal number of visitors to the National Gallery to be about 700,000 a year.* The number has now fallen off to 200,000; and the conclusion I draw is, that the best means of effecting a restoration of the normal number would be that very removal of the site of the gallery which some have deprecated, and the erection elsewhere of a new National Gallery in all respects worthy of the nation.

2905. Mr. *Richmond.*] I suppose a very large proportion of that 200,000 is of a class which was pleasantly called, I believe by Mr. Ford, "æsthetic idlers"?—Doubtless so; and I can vouch for there being a great number of nursemaids and children among them.

2906. With respect to the soil of this Kensington Gore Estate, have you any information to give the Commissioners upon that subject?—There has been some difference of opinion as to what the soil is. The soil generally is a gravel soil, with the exception of a piece within this zone (*pointing it out on the map*), where the London clay comes to the surface.

2907. How far deep does that extend on the northern side of the estate; how far into the estate?—It is only this small zone (*indicating it*).

2908. What depth of feet is that from the road?—Immediately adjoining the road, the soil appears to be gravel. It is in the Gore House garden, in fact, where this piece of clay soil appears.

2909. But the character of the soil is gravel, for the most part?—Yes; the whole of the lower part is exclusively gravel. We have had a great deal of building operations there, when this was clearly shown.

2910. There are some brooks running through it, I believe?—There is a very little brook, into which the drainage runs, at the bottom.

2911. *Dean of St. Paul's.*] A little brook went along Gore-lane?—Yes.

2912. Mr. *Richmond.*] Have you any further information to give the Commissioners?—I may, perhaps, make an observation with regard to the Kensington Gore Estate occupying a spot in the south-western part of London. It has this important advantage of position with respect to atmospheric influences: inasmuch as the wind blows from between the south and west for the greater part of the year, it is obvious that it reaches this property before it is contaminated by the London smoke; while, on the other hand, when the wind blows from the other quarters, the north and east, which, I believe, are considered objectionable quarters in respect of the influence on pictures, it is true that it has passed across the smoke of London before it arrives at the estate, but it has been largely diluted and cleared from the impurities contracted in its passage across London, inasmuch as there has been a large and open

---

* See Question No. 8678, p. 613, of Report of Committee of 1853.

Bowring. expanse of park and pleasure ground intervening after leaving the London smoke; therefore, in those two respects, an estate situated in the south-west part of London has advantages peculiar to itself. I may, perhaps, mention to the Commissioners that a model has been prepared by the Department of Science and Art, and is now on the point of completion, showing the whole configuration of the estate, and the adjoining parks, most accurately and minutely, on the large scale of 20 feet to the mile.

2913. *Chairman.*] When will it be finished?—It is virtually finished now, if the Commissioners would wish at any time to see it.

2914. Where is it?—In the Museum Building at South Kensington. To give an idea of the extent of the Commissioners' property, which is mentioned as containing 86 acres, (including the portion devoted to roads,) I may state, that it is much larger than the Green Park, and exceeds by several acres the total area of St. James's Park. The total fall from end to end of the property is about 40 feet, over a total length of 2,500 feet.

2915. Professor *Faraday.*] From north to south?—From north to south; therefore, if it were made a hanging level, it would be a fall of about 1 in 60; at present the fall is confined to the upper half, and is about 1 in 30—something like the fall in St. James's Street.

2916. Mr. *Richmond.*] At what distance is the most southerly point of the estate from the river, as the crow flies?—Considerably less than a mile.

2917. *Dean of St. Paul's.*] Battersea Bridge would be the nearest point?—Yes.

2918. Mr. *Richmond.*] Do you know the exact distance which it is from Hyde Park Corner to the south-east portion of the estate?—It is within a mile; the milestone is beyond.

2919. Mr. *Cockerell.*] The river turns off south?—The river turns off suddenly south, near Battersea Bridge. It is rather more than three-quarters of a mile from the south end of our estate to the river, in a direct line.

2920. Mr. *Richmond.*] It is very nearly a mile from Hyde Park Corner?—Yes; but not quite so much as the crow flies. It is just a mile from Exhibition Road, at the West Side of the new buildings, to Hyde Park Corner. Gore House is a little farther from Hyde Park Corner.

2921. Do any of the students live at the east end of London, so far as you know, who now attend Gore House?—I do not know how that is, but I presume that most of the students living in the east of London would attend the Spitalfields branch school rather than the main school at South Kensington.

2922. *Dean of St. Paul's.*] You have not got Lord Auckland's property at present?—No. That plan shows two pieces of land within the main square as not belonging to the Commissioners. The one is Lord Auckland's property (Eden Lodge), and the other is covered by the 12 houses called Kensington Gore, to which I have referred during my evidence.

BOWRING.

III.—EVIDENCE OF PROFESSOR DONALDSON.

DONALDSON.

3194. *Chairman.*] You are Foreign Secretary to the Royal Institute of British Architects, I believe?—I am.

3195. Has your attention been particularly called, at any time, to the question of the site for the projected National Gallery?—Frequently. I attended once at the Board of Works some years since by invitation of the Chief Commissioner, to advise upon the subject, with Mr. Cockerell, Sir C. Barry, Mr. Hardwick, and one or two other architects, who were also there.

3196. Has the Government ever called upon you for a decisive opinion upon the subject?—We were called into the room together, to confer with the Chief Commissioner upon the subject, who asked us a few questions upon various sites.

3197. Will you have the goodness to state what was the principal result of the opinion you gave?—I was not prepared for the question now put to me, and I do not remember exactly the result. I know that our opinions were asked upon various sites, but I am not able now to state what our different opinions were, for there was no general result arrived at; only each gentleman gave his opinion to the Chief Commissioner.

3198. There was no positive opinion as to preference of site?—No decision was come to at that time.

3199. What was your own opinion upon the question?—My own opinion was that it was desirable, certainly, to remove the National Gallery from Charing Cross.

3200. Professor *Faraday.*] What is your judgment now?—It is the same now.

3201. *Dean of St. Paul's.*] May we ask for what reasons you formed that opinion?—I think, first of all, that sufficient space could not be procured on that spot, equal to what would be necessary for the purposes of a National Gallery in point of extent.

3202. Do you include in that the adjacent property, which has been suggested, including the barracks, the workhouse, and the baths and washhouses?—Yes, I do not think that if you got the barracks, the workhouse, and so on, there would be an extent sufficient for a complete National Gallery. From what I know of it, I do not think there is space large enough conveniently to admit of a complete collection.

3203. *Chairman.*] Supposing that the National Gallery should not embrace sculpture as well as painting, would there not be for pictures alone a sufficient space for the erection of an adequate gallery?—For pictures alone there might be room.

3204. Professor *Faraday.*] Would that include a National Gallery of Portraits?—I think there might be room; but I do not think it would be desirable on account of the light, otherwise it would be a convenient site.

3205. *Dean of St. Paul's.*] That which is necessary, as we are informed, to be included in the area occupied by the National Gallery, is—first, a collection of the ancient pictures which we at present possess, with such augmentation as we may fairly expect by purchase, by gift, or by legacy; secondly, the collection of modern pictures now at Marlborough House, with any accessions which may be made to that; thirdly, the whole collection of Turner's pictures and drawings; and fourthly, the proposed Gallery of British Portraits, even if there were not others of the sculptural or architectural collections which it might be expedient to put there. Do you think that there would be sufficient space, including that accession, by embracing the barracks, &c., for all those purposes comprehended under the National Picture Gallery?—For what we at present possess, I am pretty sure there might be sufficient space; but in looking prospectively to what we may reasonably look forward to, taking into consideration also the fact that there should be a combination of other objects to render such collection complete in every department, I do not think there would be at all sufficient space.

3206. Have you ever thought about what space, either in area or square feet, would be requisite for the Gallery?—For the building of the Gallery alone, about 1,000 feet by 500 would afford ample space for a central court.

3207. *Chairman.*] It has been stated that the site is, as regards position, the very finest in the metropolis; is that your opinion?—That, I think, was the opinion of Sir Robert Peel. He mentioned it, I presume, as being architecturally fine. There can be no doubt that that is the position for an architectural monument. From the space from which it could be viewed, and from the ample area and fall in front, it is one of the finest that could be possessed.

3208. Do you still think that to be the case?—It is a very noble site for a public monument.

3209. Do you know any in the metropolis that is finer?—No, I do not think that there is any site equal to it.

3210. Professor *Faraday.*] The mere circumstance of being an architectural ornament has nothing at all to do in particular with a National Gallery?—No.

APPENDIX A.

3211. Is there any other reason which occurs to you that is connected with its position as a National Gallery which makes it a good site?—To a certain extent, I think it is a very good position for a National Gallery of Pictures. It is the centre of traffic, and in many other respects is also adapted for the purpose.

3212. Do you mean for access or for the preservation of the pictures? —For access. Being in a thoroughfare, it is accessible for ordinary visitors. I do not think it is the best position that might be taken for the National Gallery, but I think it a good position.

3213. Mr. *Cockerell.*] What is the best position that you could suggest for the National Gallery?—My opinion, having thought upon the subject a good deal, is, that the Kensington Gore site is certainly one of the best positions in the metropolis.

3214. Would you call that in the metropolis?—I think it is sufficiently attached to the metropolis to be called a part of it.

3215. Professor *Faraday.*] What are your reasons for preferring that site?—First of all, there is ample area for admitting the National Gallery. It is sufficiently distant from all other buildings to be viewed from all parts; it is also sufficiently clear not to be annoyed by the chimnies of adjoining buildings. I think there is a pure air there. It is in the district where I have the appointment of district surveyor. I am, therefore, well acquainted with the spot. It would be to me a considerable loss if not covered with building houses. My opinion, therefore, in its favour may be considered impartial. But, irrespective of that, I think that, being free from houses, it would be open to the public view, and would afford a fine opportunity for displaying its architectural features, and, in my opinion, also, it is not so remote from the metropolis that the distance would at all hinder students from going there for the purposes of study or visitors. I have not much opinion of visitors who usually go in for five minutes to the National Gallery. I would rather that they made up their minds to a visit of an hour or two hours, and inspected it seriously.

3216. Would you rather they did not come at all?—No; I would rather they should have five minutes than none at all.

3217. Mr. *Cockerell.*] Would not you consider it the duty of every individual to be informed upon the question of the National Gallery?— Yes; as to the distance, I may say that the young men who attend my own classes come from Clapton, Clapham, Camberwell, Highbury, and so on a distance of three or four miles walk in the evening, and go back.

3218. *Dean of St. Paul's.*] Are not they obtaining professional instruction?—Yes, exactly; and I am considering the National Gallery also as a place of study for students.

3219. Professor *Faraday.*] Have you any other reasons for preferring Kensington Gore?—I think it is desirable that the National Gallery

DONALDSON should be comprehended at least within three stories in height; a basement partially sunk, an entrance floor, and a first floor. And I think that would afford ample space for galleries and rooms, with skylights and without, as also for courts within, to afford a complete thoroughfare of air for ventilation.

3220. *Dean of St. Paul's.*] Is not that higher than the present National Gallery?—I think it is somewhat higher than the present National Gallery.

3221. If the present National Gallery were raised to the height you propose, would not it afford much more accommodation than it does at present?—Yes; but you could not afford the accommodation in the metropolis that you could in a building which is at a distance from any other. The light is only obtained at a high inclination, to which you are obliged to confine yourself in the metropolis; but if you have a palace, or any other building in the midst of a park, you find the light enters all round for the rooms of the lower floors.

3222. *Mr. Richmond.*] If you have a free area round the building, you can have side lights?—Yes. It would reduce the inconvenience of a lower story or floor considerably.

3223. *Dean of St. Paul's.*] Have you considered the inclination of the ground at Kensington Gore? Does not it fall very much to the south?—Yes; but that would be no objection at all, because the entrance floor could be rendered level with the upper ground to the north by a terrace at the lower end to the south.

3224. Would it not almost seem necessary that the main entrance should be towards the south?—One of the fronts would be towards the south.

3225. Then the chief access would be through Knightsbridge?—Yes; for both fronts.

3226. Would it not be very remote from the other parts of the town, for instance, from Tyburnia, and from all the north of the town from Westbourne Terrace, from the Regent's Park, and from the whole of that district, unless you had a road through the Park?—Yes; unless there were a road through the Park.

3227. You would think that necessary?—I should think it so for carriages.

3228. *Professor Faraday.*] Is not there a road through the Park already?—Yes; but it is private now.

3229. *Mr. Richmond.*] Do you think there would be much advantage on the score of light at Kensington Gore?—I think the light is much clearer. I have been frequently there when I have seen the metropolis in a dense atmosphere. It has been very light at Kensington Gore when I have observed over the whole of Westminster and the upper part of Piccadilly a thick fog.

APPENDIX A.

3230. *Dean of St. Paul's.*] Have you not often seen the Park, and Kensington Gore especially, enveloped in a dense fog, when the other parts of London were comparatively clear ?—It does not occur to me to remember that.

3231. Professor *Faraday.*] Do not you know Kensington Gore well ? —Yes; I am there officially two or three days in the week.

3232. Can you speak positively as to the relative atmospheres of Kensington Gore and Trafalgar-square, whether one is better than the other or both are alike ?—I should think Kensington Gore superior, being higher and clear.

3233. Is it more or less smoky ?—Less smoky a great deal.

3234. Mr. *Cockerell.*] Is not there building rapidly going on to the south and west of Kensington Gore ?—Yes; there are large houses building to the west, but to the south it is already covered.

3235. *Dean of St. Paul's.*] Does not the smoke come thither from the river from Wandsworth, and all that part ?—No; I may add, that those parts are very well drained, and that has produced great good in that respect.

3236. Professor *Faraday.*] What is the soil of the Kensington Gore ? —It is a sandy gravelly soil, the most beautiful soil that there can be for buildings.

3237. Is there any clay ?—There is very little clay; the sand is so pure that they make it up for their mortar, it is a very clear sharp sand.

3238. Have you looked at the sections of the Kensington Gore Estate ?—Yes.

3239. Do you consider it unexceptional for building ground ?—I have no objection whatever.

3240. As an architect, what do you think of the place in relation to its level with Kensington Gardens, and that part which is to the north ? —Kensington Gardens are higher.

3241. Would not that be detrimental to the site at Gore-lane ?—Not at all; the damp would be intercepted by sewers; it is very well drained.

3242. Would not you look down upon the building ?—I should think the building would be kept up.

3243. *Dean of St. Paul's.*] That would suppose a considerable elevation of ground to the south ?—Yes; there would be a terrace and garden ground, and fountains, and other like features, and you could throw that back, say 500 feet, from the present road, as there is ample space from the number of acres it contains.

3244. Professor *Faraday.*] Have you any recollection of the average wind at Kensington Gore ?—I have not, I do not know.

3245. *Dean of St. Paul's.*] Both Hyde Park and Kensington Palace have been suggested; should you think the Kensington Gore site equally eligible with those ?—The question, in my mind, would be merely one of distance; and I think that, after a certain distance, it would be better not to be half a mile more remote, if you have arrived at a sufficient site within that extent.

3246. Every half mile you consider of importance?—I think it desirable not to be very far off.

3247. *Chairman.*] Do you think Kensington Gore sufficiently accessible ?—I should think so.

3248. Even with reference to distance ?—Even with reference to distance; attention has already been directed with respect to the accessibility of those parts. Only the other day a scheme came forward to have a railway level with the roads, which would take people there in a few minutes.

3249. Mr. *Richmond.*] Might not the river be made a means of access ?—Yes; it is within a mile of the river.

3250. If you were called upon to provide a place for public exhibition for precious and costly works, which easily collected dirt, and which when dirty, could never be cleaned without risk or injury, would not your first care be to select a site as clear and as free from smoke as you could obtain ?—Quite so.

3251. Does any other site occur to you about London, at an equal distance from what we may call the metropolis, which combines these advantages as they are combined at Kensington Gore ?—London is getting covered over so much, that it is difficult to find sites of that nature. Kensington Palace was one of the sites mentioned to us when I waited upon the Chief Commissioner of Public Works. It is an admirable site, and the only question between Kensington Gore and Kensington Palace would be the half-mile distance. I think that Kensington Palace, if it were as near London as the other, would be preferable, from its being more elevated. There can be no doubt that greater elevation is advantageous.

3252. Should you consider the inner circle of Regent's Park a desirable place ?—I think it would be very bad.

3253. Will you favour us with your reasons for that opinion ?—A clay soil produces damp. I have been constantly applied to, professionally, for my advice as to living there, and I always recommended my clients not to do so, on account of the dampness.

3254. Do you think it cannot be drained ?—It is difficult to say that it is not to be drained; I could not say positively, but from present circumstances, I may say that I should not advise people to go there. Even the front of the houses, particularly on the western side, is damp.

APPENDIX A.

I went with a friend the other day, and we found vegetable matter growing up in the areas, and under the porticoes, and, therefore, I could not advise a Picture Gallery, above all things, to be in such a situation as that.

3255. Would you infer that that results from a condition of the soil that cannot be altogether remedied ?—It seems very difficult to do so, as the clay goes there to great depth.

3256. Mr. *Richmond.*] Is not the clay there 40 feet deep ?—I believe it is; I do not know that there is any gravel below it found at all, it goes to such a depth that I do not think it is remediable. As to other points, it is a very fine situation.

3257. *Dean of St. Paul's.*] Supposing the building were upon a sort of arched plateau, would not that raise it above the bad effect ?—No, I do not think it would; it retains the damp upon the surface, it does not sink away as it does in sandy or gravelly soil.

3258. Professor *Faraday.*] Does not that mean that the soil gives the character to the lower stratum of air above, and that again gives a character to the air above it ?—Yes; and all the air round is influenced by the clay.

3259. Mr. *Richmond.*] You would wish to see the new National Gallery insulated as far as you could by a wide area about it ?—Entirely insulated.

3260. That is on account of the light partly, and on account of what other reasons ?—On account of the light and air. It is necessary to get a good circulation of air completely round, and to keep the building, its rooms and galleries, as dry as possible. I think the state of the air has very much influence upon all such objects of the Fine Arts.

3261. Professor *Faraday.*] If the National Gallery were removed from its present site, would you object to put it in a space enclosed by other houses, such as the site of Burlington House ?—I think Burlington House in a very fine position. I think I was asked about it by the Chief Commissioner, and that the only objection was that it was too closely surrounded by houses, and could not be seen from a distance.

3262. A building there would make no ornament to the metropolis ?—It would make an ornament, but it could not be appreciated to the same extent as a building at Charing Cross. If there were a wide street from Pall Mall to Burlington House, it would be as fine a site as the other.

3263. Would not that meet your objection ?—It would.

3264. *Chairman.*] What do you think of the site now occupied by St. James's Palace and Marlborough House, and one or two contiguous buildings running along the Park ?—I think it is very bad.

3265. Why do you think it is very bad ?—I think that the lowness is a great objection; it is very low indeed; I think it is hardly above the level of high tide.

APPENDIX A.

3266. *Dean of St. Paul's.*] It is much below the site of the present National Gallery?—It* is below that, I should apprehend. It is very difficult to detect it by casual observation of the eye unless at night. Carlton House Terrace rises up considerably from Pall Mall. I was Commissioner of Sewers for the district of Westminster and part of Middlesex for 10 years, and I think there were some difficulties with respect to discharging the sewers, and getting the proper depth for them beneath the houses there, so that we might relieve them from their tidal water, and take it into the Thames. The Parade has been under water from overflowing of the Thames.

3267. Mr. *Cockerell.*] Have you considered Devonshire House as a site for the new National Gallery?—It is much upon the same level as Burlington House. I should suppose that there is hardly space enough in front for the elevation there. If you had wings upon each side, it would leave a very narrow court in the centre, supposing that you had galleries 40 and 50 feet wide.

3268. You are acquainted with the habits of professional men engaged both in architecture and in law. Is not there a large class who look to the National Gallery as a most desirable place to visit frequently, and who, therefore, value its vicinity very much?—Yes; I was speaking the other day with my brother, who is a solicitor, upon the subject: he said, " I go several times in the year to the National Gallery at Charing Cross; I should be sorry if it were removed, because in my way from Westminster I often look in at the National Gallery for a half-hour, to enjoy the pictures, which I could not be able to do if they were removed to Kensington." I replied, " I would rather that you made a more serious study of your visit, and gave a half-holiday to it instead of a half-hour."

3269. Theoretically, as Professor of Architecture, would you say that a great metropolis should have, as it were, in equal vicinity, a Temple, a Public Library, a National Gallery, and a Theatre sufficiently near to the Forum and the places of public resort and access?—I think the site of the British Museum certainly would be a fine site for the National Gallery. There is good soil and a good air, and it is central. But then, I object on account of its being surrounded with houses. Hitherto this district has been under the shade of two breweries. However, those are nuisances which will be much reduced; but it is difficult to get rid of the smoke of houses, and to keep the houses sufficiently distant.

3270. Have you not less smoke there than you have elsewhere, because you have several great squares there?—Yes; there is a point near, where you can see seven or eight squares at once, and the soil is excellent; but you have now houses in close contiguity.

---

* The Ordnance Map gives the relative levels of Pall Mall at St. James's street and these points, as follows:—14 feet below the road in front of the National Gallery; 11 feet below Carlton Terrace; 3 feet 9 inches above Charing Cross at King Charles I.'s statue.

APPENDIX A.

DONALDSON.

3271. Speaking as to general estimation, would not 50,000*l.* an acre be necessary to provide a site in London?—Yes; that is the lowest estimate.

3272. Mr. *Richmond.*] Do not you think that the ground to the west and south of the Kensington Gore site will, in twenty or twenty-five years, be very thickly built over?—The south is pretty well occupied now by buildings—it is completely covered—the west at present is free.

3273. And to the west is not that ground also doomed for building?—I cannot say, but I do not think it will be within twenty years.

3274. Within what time will it be built upon?—One cannot tell; it is impossible to say there is any limit to the metropolis. I should think that, having the space which you have there secured to you, you have so large an area that you are protected as much as possible from those contingencies that might arise. I do not see any other spot where you could get it, and if you were to go too far off, you would throw it too much out of the area of London for freedom of access.

3275. Professor *Faraday.*] Would there not be power of enlargement, supposing it were needed?—Yes, quite so, it is a very ample space.

3276. Mr. *Richmond.*] Do you think there is space there for almost a fabulous extension of building without forfeiting the condition which you desire now, of having a spacious area about it?—Yes; and then you have the Park, near which is another open space; and all the houses which are built there have large gardens behind or in front, leaving spacious open areas.

3277. Do you think it is important to have first-class houses in your neighbourhood, rather than third-class houses?—I think so.

3278. Why is that?—The stream of smoke is not so low as in third-class houses; and it is much better to have a free space of garden than a space covered with houses.

3279. Is it not also the fact that those houses are not inhabited all the year round?—Certainly.

3280. Professor *Faraday.*] Taking a certain area of ground covered with large houses, and the same area covered by smaller, which, according to your experience, sends out the greater quantity of smoke?—It is difficult to say. The advantage of large houses is, that the smoke is carried higher; it is carried 70 feet, whereas, perhaps, it is only 30 or 40 feet in the smaller houses.

3281. Which produce the most smoke?—I suppose, perhaps, the larger houses. There would be more economy of fuel in the smaller houses.

3282. Mr. *Cockerell.*] What are the best exemplars in your experience of National Galleries, in point of disposition and lighting, that you have met with in your experience?—I think that, as the Louvre has been recently improved, it approaches very near to what could be expected of a perfect gallery, and admirable light has been introduced into the

APPENDIX A.

DONALDSON. ceilings. For a large class of pictures, I think it is as near perfection as possible.
3283. *Dean of St. Paul's.*] Have you seen the Dresden Gallery?—No.
3284. Or the Munich Gallery?—I know very little of Germany; but Bologna was the best Picture Gallery I saw in Italy. Florence is very good. There is a charming one at Venice, a circular one like the Pantheon at Rome; and the effect also of the recent building at the Paris Exhibition was very pleasing. It was admirably disposed, and the light came in extremely well.

APPENDIX B.

CORRESPONDENCE between HER MAJESTY'S COMMISSIONERS and the LORDS COMMISSIONERS of HER MAJESTY'S TREASURY, in reference to the KENSINGTON GORE ESTATE.

I.—HER MAJESTY'S COMMISSIONERS to the CHANCELLOR of the EXCHEQUER.

SIR,   Palace of Westminster, May 1, 1858.

I AM directed by Her Majesty's Commissioners for the Exhibition of 1851 to acquaint you, that they have had under their serious consideration the question of their position in connexion with the Kensington Gore Estate.

It will be in your recollection that this estate was purchased by the joint contributions of Parliament and the Commissioners, and is accordingly the joint property of the Government and the Commission, the legal title to the estate being, however, vested in the latter, in pursuance of the arrangements laid down in the Treasury Minute of the 15th February 1853.

A reference to the terms of that Minute will serve to show the complicated nature of the tenure of the property rendered necessary by its divided ownership, and the peculiar circumstances under which the estate was acquired. It is there stated that the arrangements which the Minute proposes have it in view "to secure for the Crown that superintendence and control which is always necessary when monies are granted by Parliament for public purposes." Accordingly it is provided that the Commissioners should hold the estate, "subject to such directions of appropriation as shall from time to time be issued by the Treasury in respect to such part, not exceeding one moiety, as shall, by agreement between the Treasury and the Royal Commissioners, be set apart for such institutions connected with Science and Art as are more

APPENDIX B.

immediately dependent upon and supported by the Government from funds voted by Parliament; and subject also, with respect to the other parts thereof, to such general superintendence by the Lords of the Treasury as may be necessary to secure that the appropriation proposed to be made, and all the arrangements in relation thereto as regards buildings to be erected thereon, shall be in conformity with some general plan which shall be adopted as applicable to all parts of the property, whether such buildings shall be erected from public monies or by private subscription."

Her Majesty's Commissioners have accordingly continued to hold the estate up to the present period, subject to the above conditions; and although it cannot be denied that the double authority provided for therein must, from its very nature, tend to interfere with the active prosecution of any one uniform plan for the appropriation of the estate, the Commissioners freely admit that, under the circumstances of the case, and considering the large amount of public money invested in the purchase of the estate, it was necessary that the Treasury should lay down stipulations of some such nature for the protection of the public interests before making advances out of the sums voted by Parliament towards the purchase; and the Commissioners accordingly at that time gave their ready assent to the various proposals contained in the Treasury Minute.

Her Majesty's Commissioners having been solely actuated in effecting the purchase of this property by an earnest desire to promote the interests of Science and Art, by making it available for such purposes, it is unnecessary for them to observe that they have been at all times ready to entertain favourably any proposals having those objects in view, and they may mention that they accordingly placed a considerable portion of the estate unreservedly at the disposal of the Department of Science and Art some time ago, on an application being made to them to that effect, and that they understand that that Department has already derived much advantage from the enlarged space now available for its operations, as compared with the accommodation formerly possessed by it, and that its sphere of usefulness has been proportionately increased. The erection of the Sheepshanks Gallery, and of the South Kensington Museum, on the same part of the estate, has also been highly appreciated by the public, as shown by the large number of persons by whom they are constantly visited.

Her Majesty's Commissioners cannot, however, conceal from themselves, that, as respects the appropriation of the main part of the estate, the position occupied by them in relation to the Government, as already mentioned, has tended seriously to interfere with the prosecution of their plans for the advancement of Science and Art as originally set forth. It is now more than five years since the joint purchase was effected; and the absence of any decision on the part of Her Majesty's Government with respect to the national institutions for which sites were to be provided on the estate has precluded the Commissioners from taking any active steps themselves. The Commissioners have at the same time been serious sufferers, in a pecuniary point of view, from the large sum invested by them in the purchase of the estate remaining idle for so lengthened a period, instead of the income which might be derived from it being made available for the promotion of the objects for which they are incorporated.

The Royal Commissioners feel that, being responsible to the public for the administration and application of what must be considered as a popular fund, they are bound to represent the injurious consequences of a continuance of the present state of things. They do not presume to anticipate the views and intentions of Her Majesty's Government with regard to the national institutions already referred to, but if it should appear that the Government have arrived at the conviction that it is no longer advantageous to carry out the original plan by means of a joint partnership with the Commission, Her Majesty's Commissioners have come to the conclusion, after mature deliberation, that it would be right for them to offer to relieve the Government from any existing embarrassment, by taking upon themselves the entire execution of their own plans for the promotion of Science and Art in the manner that may appear to them best adapted for the purpose, and in conformity with the principles and objects set forth in their Second Report.

Should Her Majesty's Government concur in this opinion, I am directed to express to you the readiness of Her Majesty's Commissioners to repay to the Government the whole of the sums that have been advanced by Parliament towards the purchase of the Kensington Gore Estate, amounting to 177,500*l*., together with a moiety of the net rents that have been received from the estate (after deducting payment for taxes, &c.) during the time that it has remained the joint property of the Commissioners and the Government, and which moiety amounted on the 31st March last to 3,879*l*. 4*s*. 2*d*., the whole of the estate being made in return the absolute property of the Commissioners, in whose name the title, as previously observed, is already vested.

I am to request that Her Majesty's Commissioners may be favoured with an early reply to this communication.

I have &c.

EDGAR A. BOWRING.

The Right Hon.
   The Chancellor of the Exchequer.

APPENDIX B.

II.—The SECRETARY to the TREASURY to HER MAJESTY'S COMMISSIONERS.

Treasury Chambers,
May 11, 1858.

SIR, MY LORDS, and GENTLEMEN,

I AM directed by the Lords Commissioners of Her Majesty's Treasury to acknowledge the receipt of your Secretary's letter of the 1st instant, representing the evils which arise from the complicated nature of the tenure of the Kensington Gore Estate, rendered inevitable by its divided ownership, and the peculiar circumstances under which the estate was acquired ; and stating that the Royal Commissioners, feeling that they are responsible to the public for the administration of what must be considered as a popular fund, are bound to represent the injurious consequences of a continuance of the present state of things, and to offer to relieve the Government from any existing embarrassment, by taking upon themselves the entire execution of their own plans for the promotion of Science and Art, in the manner which may appear to them best adapted for the purpose, and to be in conformity with the principles and objects set forth in their Second Report.

With this view the Royal Commissioners express their readiness to repay to the Government the whole of the sums which have been advanced by Parliament towards the purchase of the Kensington Gore Estate, amounting to 177,500*l*., together with a moiety of the net rents which have been received from the estate (after deducting payments for taxes, &c.) during the time that it has remained the joint property of the Commissioners and the Government, the whole of the estate being made in return the absolute property of the Commissioners, in whose name the title is already vested.

My Lords are fully sensible of the inconvenience, delay, and even pecuniary loss which have arisen from the relations which the arrangement of the 15th February 1853, between the Government and the Royal Commissioners, has rendered inevitable ; and they concur with the Commissioners in the opinion that the double ownership and authority of Her Majesty's Government and the Royal Commissioners offer serious impediments to the active prosecution of any one uniform plan for the appropriation of the estate to the important purposes connected with the promotion of Science and Art, to which the Commissioners are desirous of devoting it.

Under these circumstances, my Lords, after a careful consideration of the subject, have arrived at the conclusion that the objects which Parliament had in view in making grants of public money, as well as the interests of Science and Art, will be most effectually promoted by adopting the proposal contained in your Secretary's letter ; and my Lords trust that the Royal Commissioners will thus be enabled to pursue with greater facility the important objects for which the Commission was instituted, and which must always command the earnest solicitude of Her Majesty's Government.

I am desired to add, that my Lords will defer to a future occasion the consideration of the measures which may be necessary, with reference to the position occupied by the Department of Science and Art on the estate of the Commissioners.

I am, &c.

The Royal Commissioners for the GEO. A. HAMILTON.
Exhibition of 1851.

III.—HER MAJESTY'S COMMISSIONERS to the SECRETARY to the TREASURY.

SIR, Palace of Westminster, May 14, 1858.

I AM directed by Her Majesty's Commissioners for the Exhibition of 1851 to transmit to you herewith, for the information of the Lords of the Treasury, a copy of a Memorandum recapitulating the circumstances which originally led to the connexion that has hitherto united Her Majesty's Government and the Commissioners as joint owners of the Kensington Gore Estate, and explaining the reasons for the proposed dissolution of that connexion.

I have, &c.

The Secretary to the Treasury. EDGAR A. BOWRING.

MEMORANDUM.

Now that it is proposed to dissolve the connexion which has hitherto united the Government and the Royal Commissioners for the Exhibition of 1851 as joint owners of property purchased by them at Kensington, it may be useful shortly to recapitulate the circumstances which originally led to this connexion and to the purchase of this property, as well as to point out the relative position, throughout these transactions, of the Government and the Commissioners.

At the close of the Great Exhibition of 1851 the Royal Commissioners found themselves in possession of a large disposable surplus, which, according to the provisions of a supplemental charter then conferred upon them, they were bound to appropriate in furtherance of objects connected with Art and Science.

In their Second Report, dated November 11, 1852, they point out the large sum (amounting annually, from private as well as public sources, to little short of a quarter of a million) expended upon national and other institutions connected with Science and Art; and state, that while "the fact shows that much effort, both on the part of the State and of the public, is made for the promotion of Science and Art, it makes it the greater subject of regret that, owing to a want of unity and combination, they produce comparatively small direct benefit to industry."

APPENDIX B.   93

The cause of this they attribute to a "want of system and want of space;" the want of space in which to develop it rendering the adoption of any harmonious system impossible. They trace this effect through all the four divisions of industry into which the Great Exhibition was divided.

It is not necessary here to follow the Commissioners in their remarks on the first three divisions—those, namely, of "Raw Materials," "Machinery," and "Manufactures," in each of which they point out the advantages which would result from a concentration of the efforts made for their advancement, were space only afforded in which such a concentration might be effected. It is to the fourth division—that of the Fine Arts (though all were equally the objects of the Commissioners' care)—that it is now sought to draw particular attention.

In none did the want of space make itself more felt; in proof of which the Commissioners cite more particularly "the National Gallery, the Galleries of Sculpture in the British Museum, and the Department of Practical Art, including the Schools of Design."

Of the former, they say that an "arrangement" (that is, of its pictures, in a systematic order, according to schools and periods), "with a view to schools and the progress of Art, is impracticable, for want of room." While of the two latter, and the collections in each that would be valuable for instruction, they express their opinion that "by a union in one locality of these different means of instruction, with the *advantage of not being far from the National Gallery*, the public taste would be educated in the most efficient way, and the history of Art, as applied to useful purposes, practically exemplified."

That this connexion between the National Gallery and the Schools might be brought about, were "space" afforded for the development of a well-arranged plan, the Commissioners had every reason to hope, from what had already taken place on the subject of the former.

In 1848 a Committee of the House of Commons, consisting of Lord John Russell, Sir Robert Peel, Mr. Hume, Lord Morpeth,* Mr. Goulburn, Mr. B. Wall, Mr. Charteris,† Lord Lincoln,‡ Sir B. Hall, Lord Granby,§ Mr. Tufnell, Mr. Wakley, Mr. Disraeli, Mr. Vernon Smith, and Mr. Bankes, reported in favour of the present site for the National Gallery, as one for which "perhaps it would be difficult to find a parallel in our own or any other capital."

But another Committee, appointed in 1850, in which all the members above enumerated again served, with the exception of Lord Morpeth, Mr. Charteris, Mr. Hume, Lord Lincoln, and Mr. Tufnell, for whom Lord Seymour, ‖ Mr. S. Herbert, Mr. H. Hope, Sir R. Inglis, and Colonel Rawdon were substituted, reported that "in reviewing the evidence collected by them," they could not "recommend that any expenditure

---
* Now Lord Carlisle.　　† Now Lord Elcho.　　‡ Now Duke of Newcastle.
§ Now Duke of Rutland.　　‖ Now Duke of Somerset.

should be at present incurred for the purpose of increasing the accommodation of a National Gallery upon the existing site."

They also report, that they "are not prepared to state that the preservation of the pictures, and convenient access for the purpose of study and the improvement of taste, would not be better secured in a Gallery further removed from the smoke and dust of London; but being in ignorance of the site that might be selected, the soil on which it might stand, and the expense which might be incurred, they cannot positively recommend its removal elsewhere."

The question of site was accordingly referred, in 1851, to a Royal Commission which was appointed to "consider the question of a site for a new National Gallery" (the Commissioners being Lord Seymour, Lord Colborne, Mr. Ewart, Sir R. Westmacott, and Sir C. Eastlake), who reported in August 1851 in favour of Hyde Park and Kensington, because "these large open spaces afford a present security against the inconveniences to which the National Gallery is exposed, and are the only grounds which remain safe for future years, amidst the growth of the metropolis."

They further reported, that "from 15 to 20 acres of land, with a frontage to the Park, might yet be obtained at a reasonable price, which would afford a space for the construction of a Gallery on an eligible site."

The Government had accordingly (while Sir C. Wood was Chancellor of the Exchequer) entered into negociations for the purchase of such a property, comprising $21\frac{1}{2}$ acres, belonging to Mr. Aldridge, and known as the Gore House Estate.

This negociation, however, was not carried to any result, and when, in 1852, the Royal Commissioners for the Exhibition of 1851 came (under the conditions of their new charter) to consider the question of the appropriation of their surplus, the property in question was still unbought.

Influenced, therefore, by the considerations above stated, of the necessity, in the first instance, of obtaining space on which a well-arranged scheme for bringing the national institutions for the promotion of Art and Science into connexion with each other might be developed; and bearing in mind the recommendation of the Royal Commission on the National Gallery as regarded a new site for it; having, further, reason to believe, that while advancing their own plans for the promotion of Science and Art, they were also assisting the views of the Government, by securing the possession of the property for which the Government had been in negociation, with a view to giving effect to the recommendation of the National Gallery Commission as above mentioned; bearing all these considerations in mind, the Royal Commissioners for the Exhibition of 1851 determined at once to apply a portion of their surplus to the purchase of the property in question, in the intention (afterwards carried into execution) of offering it to the Government as a site for the proposed

APPENDIX B.

new National Gallery, and as a main feature of the further plans which they hoped themselves to develop.

The purchase was accordingly effected for 60,000*l.*

It is now that the immediate connexion between the Government and the Commissioners commences.

The site of the National Gallery was the affair of the Government, and this would be provided for in the manner already contemplated by them, if they should accept the offer now made to them by the Commissioners, to place at their disposal for the purpose, under certain conditions, the property thus purchased.

These conditions embraced the co-operation of the Government with the Commissioners in making further purchases of land in the same neighbourhood, where the Schools of Art and other kindred institutions might be brought into juxtaposition with the National Gallery and each other, and a fuller development thereby given to their means of instruction and usefulness.

The Government (Mr. Disraeli being now Chancellor of the Exchequer) entered warmly into these views; and the Commissioners engaging to contribute the sum of 150,000*l.* in all, out of the surplus funds at their disposal, towards a joint purchase of land at Kensington, a vote for the same amount was proposed to the House of Commons, and agreed to, without a division, on the 6th of December 1852.

The resolution affirming this vote is recorded as follows in Hansard :—

"That a sum not exceeding 150,000*l.* shall be granted towards defraying in 1852–53 the purchase of land at Kensington Gore for a new National Gallery, and institutions connected with Science, in aid of the sum already contributed thereto by the Commissioners for the Exhibition of 1851."

In the course of the same session, namely, in March 1853, a Select Committee was appointed to inquire generally into the management of the National Gallery, and, amongst other matters, into the best site for a new building.

This Committee, of which Colonel Mure, Mr. Labouchere, Lord Elcho, Mr. Stirling, Mr. Raikes Currie, Mr. Monckton Milnes, Mr. Marshall, Lord Seymour, Mr. Vernon, Lord Brooke, Mr. Goulburn, Mr. Ewart, Mr. Baring Wall, Sir William Molesworth, Mr. Hardinge, Lord William Graham, and Mr. Hamilton, were members, decided, as regarded the question of site, by a majority of ten to one (Mr. B. Wall being the sole dissentient), "that the site of the present National Gallery is not well adapted for the construction of a new Gallery."

It was next resolved, by a majority of six to five, the minority being composed of Lord Elcho, Mr. B. Wall, Sir William Molesworth, Lord William Graham, and Mr. Hamilton, "that the estate at Kensington Gore, purchased by the Royal Commissioners for the Exhibition of 1851, and by them offered to the nation, presents many of the advantages recommended by the witnesses before your Committee. The position, which has been suggested at the entrance of Kensington Gardens, would afford a better guarantee for the future protection of the works of art there collected; . . . . but your Committee are fully aware that the acquisition of such a site is attended with difficulties which they see no adequate means of removing, and, in consequence, they are prepared to recommend the acceptance of the offer of the Commissioners."

Another motion having been made by Mr. B. Wall, to "recommend that the selection of the exact site of the new Gallery be entrusted to a Royal Commission," was negatived by eight to three ; Lord Elcho, Lord W. Graham, and Mr. B. Wall constituting the minority.

The Committee having next recommended, by a majority of seven to four (the minority being Lord Seymour, Sir W. Molesworth, Mr. Vernon, and Mr. Hamilton), "that the question of combining the various artistic and archæological collections in the British Museum with the National Gallery be referred to a Royal Commission," a final resolution was carried by a majority of six to one (Mr. B. Wall being again the only dissentient), "that no time should be lost in obtaining the decision upon the above question, in order that the new National Gallery should be commenced with all convenient speed."

This Report was laid on the table of the House of Commons on the 4th of August 1853.

In September following, the Commissioners having pointed out that a further sum of money would be required to complete the necessary land purchases at Kensington, towards which they were willing themselves to contribute 15,000*l*., the Chancellor of the Exchequer (then Mr. Gladstone), in a Minute dated the 28th October 1853, states his approval of a further advance by the Government for the purpose named, of 25,000*l*. This was subsequently increased to 27,000*l*. On the 7th July 1854 a resolution was accordingly moved, in Committee on the Miscellaneous Estimates, "that sum not exceeding 27,500*l*. be granted to Her Majesty for the year ending the 31st day of March 1855, towards the purchase by the Commissioners for the Exhibition of 1851 of certain additional lands at Kensington Gore, necessary for the purpose of the new National Gallery, and other institutions connected with Science and Art."

This resolution, after some opposition, based chiefly on the argument that it appeared to preclude Parliament from again entertaining the question of the best site for the National Gallery, was carried by a majority of 169 to 48.

In the course of the same session an Act was also passed empowering the Commissioners to form roads, and to take other steps for the improvement of the property which had been thus purchased.

In the exercise of the powers thus conferred on the Commissioners, new roads were immediately commenced, and have now been completed, at a total expense, exclusive of what was contributed by neighbouring

APPENDIX B.

proprietors, of upwards of 14,000*l.*; the principal of which, 80 and 100 feet wide respectively, enclose a quadrangle containing 56 acres, within which it was proposed that the scheme developed by the Commissioners in their Second Report should be carried into effect; the upper portion of the quadrangle, as being that originally contemplated by the Government for the site of a new National Gallery, and as standing on the highest part of the ground, with a frontage to Hyde Park, being reserved for that institution.

In 1853 the Government having, in furtherance of the objects which, in common with the Commissioners, they had in view, constituted a new Department, under the Board of Trade, for the general superintendence and direction of all matters connected with Science and Art, the Commissioners (in whom the title to the Kensington Estate had been vested) placed freely at the disposal of that Department, and without demanding more than a nominal rent, Gore House, the rental of which had been valued at from 600*l.* to 800*l.* a year.

And further, when it became necessary to remove from Marlborough House the schools and museums which had been temporarily established there, the Commissioners gave up to the use of the same Department, and equally free of rent, an outlying piece of ground near the Brompton-road, from the houses on which, now occupied as offices by the Department, they had previously drawn rents amounting in the aggregate to about 450*l.* annually.

On the ground thus given up to them, the new Department, while waiting for the adoption by Government of a permanent and general scheme to be developed within the main quadrangle, erected temporary iron buildings, for which a vote of 15,000*l.* was obtained from Parliament; but that sum proving insufficient, the Commissioners did not hesitate to contribute from their own funds a further sum of near 3,000*l.* which was required for their completion.

Besides this, they erected exclusively at their own expense, and with the like view of promoting the objects of the new Department, an exhibition and refreshment rooms, which, when completed at a cost of 2,000*l.*, they made over as a free gift to the Department, which now derives a certain profit from them, by letting the refreshment rooms to a contractor.

In the buildings thus erected, not only have the schools and collections formerly kept at Marlborough House been established on a widely-extended scale, but the Patent and Educational Museums have also found space for exhibition there, which they could not obtain elsewhere; and a most interesting Collection of Animal Produce, formed by the Commissioners themselves at an expense of about 4,000*l.*, has been made over by them gratuitously to the Department, and forms not the least attractive part of the Museum.

APPENDIX B.

The establishment thus formed, with the assistance of the Commissioners, by the new Department of Science and Art at Kensington, has been eminently successful. The numbers visiting it have increased beyond all expectation, and amount, from the day of its opening on the 22nd June 1857 to the beginning of May 1858, to no less than 427,797. The students under instruction during the last session were 396, which number might be considerably increased, did space allow of a compliance with the many applications for admission.

In all the steps they had hitherto taken, and in the further measures which they contemplated as necessary to the full development of their plan (of which, as has been seen, the removal of the National Gallery to the new site was a main feature), the Commissioners were justified in thinking that they were acting, and would continue to act, in conjunction with the Government.

The expectations, however, which the Reports of the different Committees and Royal Commission appointed to consider the subject in 1850, 1851, and 1853, and the subsequent votes of the House of Commons, had been calculated to excite, were again placed in doubt by the proceedings in the House of Commons in 1856. In the course of that session Sir George Lewis, who had succeeded Mr. Gladstone as Chancellor of the Exchequer, obtained leave to bring in a Bill respecting the site of the National Gallery, with a view to giving effect to the recommendations of the above-mentioned Committees. But on the second reading of the Bill, on the 27th June 1856, an amendment was moved by Lord Elcho, and carried against the Government by a majority of 153 to 145, to the effect that " an humble Address be presented to Her Majesty, praying Her Majesty to be graciously pleased to issue a Royal Commission to determine the site of the new National Gallery, and to report on the desirableness of combining with it the Fine Art and Archæological Collections of the British Museum, in accordance with the recommendation of the Select Committee on the National Gallery in 1853."*

After some delay (caused perhaps by the difficulty of finding fit persons to sit upon the Commission, the great majority of those who would otherwise have been naturally selected for such an inquiry being ineligible, from the fact of their being already members of the Commission for the Exhibition of 1851, or who had otherwise expressed strong opinions on this subject), it was finally constituted under the presidency of Lord Broughton, and consisted, besides himself, of the Very Rev. the Dean of St. Paul's, Mr. Faraday, Mr. C. R. Cockerell, and Mr. G. Richmond. This Commission reported in 1857 against the removal of the National Gallery from its present site, and the whole

---

* That Committee had decided, however, by a majority of eight to three, against referring the question of site to a Royal Commission.

APPENDIX B.

question was thus thrown back into the position in which it stood in 1851.

It is true that Sir G. Lewis considered the Report to be so little satisfactory, being only that of three of the Commission (one having opposed the Report, and another declining to vote), that he gave notice, at the commencement of the session of 1858, that he would again move for the appointment of a Select Committee to reconsider the subject. This intention was prevented by the change of Government; nor does it seem that much prospect exists of Government being enabled at an early period to take any effectual steps for putting an end to the state of uncertainty that has so long existed.

The Commissioners have, therefore, found themselves compelled seriously to consider their own position, and they find that whilst the Government and general public have derived the advantages above mentioned, from a purchase originated by them, and towards which they have themselves so largely contributed, they have themselves obtained no return whatever for their outlay beyond the few reserved rents for houses on the estate still in the occupation of tenants, for the grazing of the land, &c.; and while waiting for the decision of the Government on the subject of the National Gallery, and the other institutions under Government control, they have been precluded from all independent action, or from carrying into execution any plans of their own.

This state of things has now lasted for upwards of five years.

The Commissioners are as earnest as ever in their desire to co-operate with the Government in carrying into execution the plans for the development of which the joint purchase of land was made in 1852. But it does not appear to them desirable or advantageous that the present state of uncertainty and inaction should be further prolonged; and should the Government, from whatever cause, still find itself unable to give a solution to those questions for a decision upon which the Commissioners have been so long waiting, the only alternative appears to be that which has been suggested, namely, that they should be allowed to make such arrangements as may be in their power for repaying to Government the whole of the advances made by it, and, by thus becoming themselves the sole owners of the Kensington property, place themselves in a position to give effect, without further hindrance or delay, to such plans as may appear to them best calculated to effect the objects for which they are incorporated. By so doing they may hope to free themselves from any blame which the public might not unnaturally be disposed to attach to them were the advantages to Science and Art which they have been led to expect from a judicious appropriation of the funds at the disposal of the Commissioners to be still indefinitely postponed.

APPENDIX C.

ACT of PARLIAMENT (21 & 22 Vict. c. 36.) for releasing the LANDS of the COMMISSIONERS for the EXHIBITION of 1851, upon the REPAYMENT of MONIES granted in aid of their FUNDS.

[*Royal Assent, 12th July* 1858.]

WHEREAS the Commissioners for the Exhibition of 1851 have purchased lands at Kensington Gore with a view to secure adequate space in the metropolis for institutions connected with Science and Art: And whereas in aid of the funds of the said Commissioners, arising from the said Exhibition, which were applied to such purchases, two several sums of one hundred and fifty thousand pounds and twenty-seven thousand five hundred pounds were granted by Parliament in the sessions holden in the sixteenth and seventeenth and in the seventeenth and eighteenth years of Her Majesty, and it was agreed, on the issue of such sums, that the lands purchased as aforesaid should be held subject to such directions of appropriation as should from time to time be issued by the Treasury in respect to such part, not exceeding one moiety, as should by agreement between the Lords of the Treasury and the said Commissioners for the Exhibition be set apart for such institutions connected with Science and Art as were more immediately dependent upon and supported by the Government from funds voted by Parliament, and subject also, with respect to the other part thereof, to such general superintendence by the Lords of the Treasury as might be necessary to secure that the appropriation proposed to be made, and all the arrangements in relation thereto, as regards buildings to be erected thereon, should be in conformity with some general plan, which should be adopted as applicable to all parts of the property, whether such buildings should be erected from public monies or by private subscription: And whereas the said Commissioners have proposed to repay the sums granted by Parliament as aforesaid, together with a moiety of the net rents received by the said Commissioners up to the thirty-first day of March last, amounting to three thousand eight hundred and seventy-nine pounds four shillings and twopence (making, together with the sums granted as aforesaid, the sum of one hundred and eighty-one thousand three hundred and seventy-nine pounds four shillings and twopence), upon having the said lands released from the trusts or obligations created in respect of the sums granted as aforesaid: And whereas it is expedient that the said proposal should be accepted, subject to such provision as is herein-after contained with reference to a part of the said lands of which the possession may be retained for the purposes of the Department of Science and Art: Be it therefore enacted by the Queen's most Excellent Majesty, by and with the advice

APPENDIX C.

and consent of the Lords Spiritual and Temporal, and Commons, in this present Parliament assembled, and by the authority of the same, as follows:

I. Upon payment by the Commissioners for the Exhibition of 1851 of a sum or sums amounting together to the said sum of one hundred and eighty-one thousand three hundred and seventy-nine pounds four shillings and twopence into the receipt of the Exchequer in such manner as the Commissioners of Her Majesty's Treasury may direct, the Commissioners for the said Exhibition, and all the Lands purchased or to be purchased by or in the name of such Commissioners, shall be absolutely released and discharged from the agreement herein-before recited, and from all trust, obligation, control, claim, and demand to which such lands may be subject in respect of the sums granted by Parliament as aforesaid: Provided always, that if such payment be not made within six months from the passing of this Act, there shall be added to the said sum a further sum equal to one half of the net rental which shall accrue to the time when such payment shall be made. *[margin: Lands purchased by Commissioners for the Exhibition of 1851 to be released on repayment of Parliamentary Grants and moiety of rents.]*

II. Provided always, that it shall be lawful for the Commissioners of Her Majesty's Treasury to require that part of the said lands now in the occupation of the Department of Science and Art, that is to say, the piece of land containing twelve acres or thereabouts, bounded on the west by Exhibition-road and on the south by Cromwell-road, with the museum, gallery, and other buildings thereon, shall be retained in the occupation and for the use of Her Majesty's Government for purposes connected with Science or the Arts, so long as the said Commissioners of the Treasury think fit, with liberty to erect, add to, or alter any buildings on the said piece of land, and, if such Commissioners of the Treasury think fit, to cause to be taken down, removed, and disposed of all or any of the buildings which have been already erected or which may hereafter be erected thereon; and it shall be lawful for the Commissioners of the Treasury to direct that the payment of such portion of the said sum of one hundred and eighty-one thousand three hundred and seventy-nine pounds four shillings and twopence as they may think fit, nor exceeding what may appear to them to be the value of the said piece of land, may be postponed so long as such piece of land is so retained as aforesaid; and upon payment in manner herein-before mentioned of the residue of the said sum of one hundred and eighty-one thousand three hundred and seventy nine pounds four shillings and twopence, after deduction of the amount of which the payment may be so postponed, the said Commissioners of the Treasury shall, by warrant under the hands of two of such Commissioners, declare that the residue of the said lands shall be absolutely released and discharged from the said agreement, and all such trust, obligation, control, claim, and demand as aforesaid, and the same shall be released and discharged accordingly. *[margin: Land occupied by the Department of Science and Art may be retained for such Department.]*

Monies paid to be carried to the Consolidated Fund.

III. All monies paid into the receipt of the Exchequer under this Act shall be carried to and form part of the Consolidated Fund of the United Kingdom.

APPENDIX D.

DEED of GIFT by JOHN SHEEPSHANKS, Esq., of his COLLECTION of PICTURES and DRAWINGS, in trust, to form the Nucleus of a National Gallery of Art in connexion with Her Majesty's Department of Science and Art,

AND

MINUTE of the PRESIDENT of the BOARD OF TRADE thereon.

MINUTE.

At the Council Chamber, Whitehall, the Sixth Day of February 1857. By the Right Honourable the Lords of the Committee of Privy Council appointed for the Consideration of all Matters relating to Trade and Foreign Plantations.

My Lords take into consideration the Deed of Gift by which Mr. Sheepshanks transfers to the President of this Board his valuable collection of pictures and drawings, in order to found a Gallery of British Art in connexion with the Schools of Art under this Board.

The President has accepted with much gratification the trusteeship created by this deed, under the conditions therein described.

My Lords are sensible of the great value of the magnificent gift thus presented to the nation during the lifetime of the donor, and they desire to express their admiration of the very liberal spirit in which it has been made.

My Lords admit the reasonableness of the condition that the deed of gift shall only take effect when a suitable gallery shall have been provided in an airy situation near the gardens or public parks at Kensington, and they have given directions, with the consent of the Treasury, for the erection of such a gallery without delay.

Their Lordships direct that a letter should be written to Mr. Sheepshanks, thanking him, on the part of the Government, for his munificent gift to the nation, and for the open character of the conditions under which it has been made; and stating, that, whilst the liberality of these conditions has greatly enhanced its value to the nation, they are well calculated to realize the disinterested object of the donor to found a Gallery of British Art.

APPENDIX D.

DEED OF GIFT.

To all to whom these presents shall come, I, John Sheepshanks, of Rutland Gate, Knightsbridge, in the County of Middlesex, Esquire, send greeting.

WHEREAS I desire that a collection of pictures and other works of art, fully representing British Art, should be formed, worthy of national support, and have the advantage of undivided responsibility in its management, instead of being subject to the control of any body of trustees or managers: And whereas I conceive that such a collection should be placed in a gallery in an open and airy situation, possessing the quiet necessary to the study and enjoyment of works of art, and free from the inconveniences and dirt of the main thoroughfares of the metropolis: And whereas I consider that such a gallery might be usefully erected at Kensington, and be attached to the Schools of Art in connexion with the Department of Science and Art now established there: And whereas, with the view to the establishment of such a collection, and in the hope that other proprietors of pictures and other works of art may be induced to further the same object, I have determined to make such a conditional gift of the original pictures and drawings (the productions of British artists) which I possess, as herein-after expressed. And I do, therefore, hereby transfer the pictures and drawings belonging to me specified in the schedule hereto, and the property and proprietorship thereof unto, and do declare that the same shall remain vested in, the Right Honourable Edward John Stanley Baron Stanley of Alderley or other, the member of Her Majesty's Government for the time being charged with the promotion of Art education now undertaken by the Department of Science and Art as the ex-officio Trustee thereof, upon the following terms and conditions, viz. :—

1. The said Right Honourable Edward John Lord Stanley, as the first and present ex-officio Trustee, shall sign a memorandum of his acceptance of the trusteeship hereunder at the foot hereof.

2. A well-lighted and otherwise suitable gallery, to be called "The National Gallery of British Art," shall be at once erected by Her Majesty's Government, and be attached or near to the public buildings built or to be built for the Department of Science and Art on the estate purchased by Her Majesty's Commissioners for the Exhibition of 1851, or the public parks or gardens at Kensington.

3. The said pictures and drawings shall be deposited in such gallery with any other pictures or other works of art that may be subsequently placed there by other contributors, as it is not my desire that my collection of pictures and drawings shall be kept apart, or bear my name as such.

APPENDIX D.

4. The right of property and possession in the said pictures and drawings shall be solely in the ex-officio Trustee for the time being, but subject to the conditions herein expressed; and the said pictures and drawings shall always remain under his sole care and control, and he shall be the sole arbiter of any question that may arise touching the management or disposition thereof under these presents.

5. The said pictures and drawings shall be used (as the primary object) for reference and instruction in the Schools of Art now or hereafter placed under the superintendence of the said Department, and subject thereto, shall be exhibited to the public at such times as shall not interfere with the arrangements of the said schools, and under such regulations as the ex-officio Trustee shall prescribe; and so soon as arrangements can be properly made by him for that purpose, the public, and especially the working classes, shall have the advantage of seeing the collection on Sunday afternoons, it being, however, understood that the exhibition of the collection on Sundays is not to be considered as one of the conditions of my gift.

6. None of the said pictures and drawings shall ever be sold or exchanged, or be dealt with contrary to the true spirit and meaning of the disposition and control thereof herein prescribed; but this condition shall not restrict the temporary loan of any of them, upon terms sanctioned by the ex-officio Trustee, to any place in the United Kingdom where any School of Art exists in connexion with the Department of Science and Art, or generally where there is any safe and proper place for their reception and public exhibition.

7. The ex-officio Trustee shall be advised and assisted on matters connected with the preservation of the said pictures and drawings by William Mulready, Esquire, R.A., or, failing him, by Richard Redgrave, Esquire, R.A., or failing him, by some one other R.A. of London, to be selected by the ex-officio Trustee for the time being, as the professional adviser of the ex-officio Trustee.

8. That the ex-officio Trustee may sell the right to engrave or reproduce any of the said pictures or drawings, upon such terms as he may think proper, but the engravings and reproductions shall be approved by the artist of the picture or drawing engraved or reproduced before publication, and such artist shall be paid whatever sum may be received by the ex-officio Trustee for the sale of such right.

9. The said pictures and drawings, or the conditional gift of them hereby made, shall not be subject to the provisions of the Act of the 19 & 20 Vict. c. 29, intituled "An Act to extend the Powers of the Trustees and Directors of the National Gallery, and to authorize the Sale of Works of Art belonging to the public," or to any future enactment of the Legislature, which, but for this declaration to the contrary, shall have the effect of placing the said pictures and drawings under any

other care or ordering than is herein prescribed, or would otherwise alter or interfere with the disposition thereof hereby made. And in case of such interference on the part of the Legislature, or if the terms and conditions as herein expressed be not strictly adhered to, then the conditional gift hereby made of the said pictures and drawings, in favour of a National Gallery of British Art, the Schools of Art, and the public generally, shall wholly cease, and the ex-officio Trustee for the time being shall thereupon hold the said pictures and drawings in trust for the University of Cambridge, to be added to, and for ever thereafter form part of, the Fitzwilliam collection in the said University.

 Witness my hand and seal, this second day of February One thousand eight hundred and fifty-seven.

      (Signed) JOHN SHEEPSHANKS. (L.S.)

Signed, sealed, and delivered by the
above-named John Sheepshanks,
in the presence of
 WILLIAM COWPER,
  17, Curzon Street, London.
 RICHARD REDGRAVE,
  18, Hyde Park Gate, South Kensington.
 HENRY COLE,
  24, Onslow-square.

I, the above-named and under signed Right Honourable Edward John Stanley Baron Stanley of Alderley, do accept the trusteeship created by the above deed.

      (Signed) STANLEY OF ALDERLEY.
LYON PLAYFAIR, witness.

APPENDIX E.

CORRESPONDENCE between HER MAJESTY'S COMMISSIONERS and HER MAJESTY'S GOVERNMENT on the SUBJECT of the ANIMAL PRODUCE MUSEUM.

I.—HER MAJESTY'S COMMISSIONERS to the LORD PRESIDENT of the COUNCIL.

MY LORD,   Whitehall, 16th December 1857.

I AM directed by Her Majesty's Commissioners for the Exhibition of 1851 to call your Lordship's attention to the Trade Collection, the property of the Commissioners, now being exhibited in the South Kensington Museum, under the Science and Art Department of the Committee of Council on Education.

APPENDIX E.

The enclosed statement, constituting the preface to the catalogue of the Animal portion of that Collection, that has recently been published by the Commissioners, will suffice briefly to explain to your Lordship the circumstances attending the original formation of the Collection, and to show in what manner it has been gradually brought into its present condition, originally with the zealous assistance of the Society of Arts, as represented by Professor Solly, and subsequently by the Commissioners themselves, aided by the liberal contributions of many exhibitors, and under the immediate superintendence of Dr. Playfair, the very valuable nature of whose services (which the Committee of Council on Education were good enough to authorize on the occasion) it affords the Commissioners much gratification to take this opportunity of recognising.

To the particulars contained in the accompanying statement the Commissioners have only to add, that the original numbers of Contributors to the Collection in 1851 (exclusive of drawings,) was 2,035, of whom 1,020 were British, 212 Colonial, and 803 Foreign. The commercial value of the articles then presented was estimated at between 8,000l. and 9,000l. But while, on the one hand, the subsequent determination of the Commissioners to retain permanently only the Animal Section of the Collection, and to distribute amongst the various public institutions of the country the Vegetable and Mineral sections of it, has, of course, effected a corresponding reduction in the value of the articles permanently preserved, on the other hand a very considerable expenditure has been incurred by the Commissioners in bringing the Collection of Animal Products into its present state, and in providing the necessary fittings, &c.; which, added to the voluntary contributions of individual exhibitors since the removal of the Collection to the South Kensington Museum, has resulted in the formation of a Collection of great pecuniary value in itself, but which value bears no proportion to the real value of the Collection as an aid to industrial and technical instruction, and an illustration (although as yet incomplete) of the present state of commercial manufacturing enterprise in this great section of industry.

The experience derived from the few months during which the South Kensington Museum has been open to the public has sufficed to show the remarkable manner in which this particular department of the Museum is appreciated, especially by the industrial classes, to whom it is so important to impart an accurate knowledge of the various processes on which depend the industries in which they are severally engaged. The crowded state of the gallery containing the Collection of Animal Products on those days and nights when the Museum is thrown open to the public free of charge, and which shows that it excites an interest at least equal to that felt in any other collection in the Museum, has been a source of much satisfaction to the Commissioners.

APPENDIX E.

Having now brought the Collection to its present state of comparative completeness, and made arrangements whereby its gradual development may be relied upon, Her Majesty's Commissioners feel that the time has arrived when the public may not unreasonably be supposed to be desirous of becoming the possessors of a Collection which has now for the first time been brought together in this country, and the Collections corresponding to which in the Vegetable and Mineral Kingdoms have already been formed at considerable expense to the nation, and are now established as the property of the public, in the Museum of Economic Botany at Kew, and the Museum of Practical Geology in Jermyn-street, respectively; and I am accordingly directed to offer to present the entire Collection as an absolute gift to the Department presided over by your Lordship, on the sole condition that measures shall be adopted for its permanent preservation and exhibition, and for its future further development as opportunities may offer.

Should the Committee of Council on Education be prepared to accept this proposal, the Commissioners feel assured that they will have the goodness to complete the distribution amongst the public institutions of the country of the Vegetable and Mineral portions of the original Trade Collection, on the principles and in the manner already commenced by the Commissioners, as indicated in the enclosed statement, for which purpose every assistance will be afforded by their officers.

I am to add that, in order to facilitate the proposed arrangement in a financial point of view, Her Majesty's Commissioners will be prepared to defray as heretofore the whole expense of the Staff, &c., required for the custody of the Collection until the close of the present financial year on the 31st March next. They will also be happy to hand over to the Department their property in the two catalogues published by them, and on which they have incurred a considerable outlay.

In submitting for the consideration of your Lordship the proposal set forth in this letter, in making which the Commissioners are solely actuated by a desire to promote the public interests, I am to request that they may be favoured with an early intimation of the decision which may be arrived at by Her Majesty's Government in respect of it, in order that they may make the necessary arrangements accordingly.

I have, &c.

The Right Hon. the
Lord President of the Council.

EDGAR A. BOWRING.

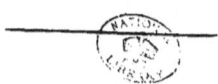

II.—The SECRETARY to the DEPARTMENT of SCIENCE and ART to HER MAJESTY'S COMMISSIONERS.

Science and Art Department, South Kensington,
SIR,   London, W., 18th January 1858.

I AM directed by the Lord President of the Council to acknowledge your letter of the 16th ult. by which the Royal Commissioners for the Exhibition of 1851 offer to present the entire Collection of Animal Products, now in the South Kensington Museum, as an absolute gift to the public through the Science and Art Department, on the sole condition that measures shall be adopted for its permanent preservation and exhibition, and for its future further development as opportunities may offer.

Considering the great value of the Animal Collection in promoting industrial instruction, and the remarkable interest which has been manifested in it by the general public, my Lords have pleasure in accepting the liberal offer of the Royal Commissioners with the conditions annexed to it; and their Lordships will also be prepared to complete the distribution of the Vegetable and Mineral portions of the original Trade Collection among public institutions of the country, on the principles and in the manner already commenced by the Commissioners. Their Lordships have issued directions that this Department shall take charge of the Collection at such time as the Commissioners may arrange; and will be prepared to recommend to Parliament to defray all expenses connected therewith on and after the 1st of April next.

I have, &c.
E. A. Bowring, Esq.   HENRY COLE, Secretary.

III.—HER MAJESTY'S COMMISSIONERS to the SECRETARY to the DEPARTMENT of SCIENCE and ART.

SIR,   Whitehall, 26th January 1858.

WITH reference to your letter of the 18th inst., announcing the acceptance by the Lord President of the Council on behalf of Her Majesty's Government of the Collection of Animal Products belonging to the Commissioners now exhibited in the South Kensington Museum, I am directed to acquaint you, for the information of his Lordship, that the Commissioners propose that the formal transfer of the Collection to the Department of Science and Art shall date from Monday next the 1st February.

Her Majesty's Commissioners have instructed their Financial Officer to make the necessary arrangements for the payment of the salaries, &c., of the officers employed on the Collection between that date and the 31st

APPENDIX F. 109

March next, in accordance with the intimation conveyed in their letter of the 16th ult.

I have, &c.

Henry Cole, Esq., C.B.   EDGAR A. BOWRING.

APPENDIX F.

REPORT of the SELECT COMMITTEE of the HOUSE OF COMMONS appointed in 1860, to inquire and report concerning the SOUTH KENSINGTON MUSEUM.

YOUR Committee, looking to the terms of the reference, have limited their inquiries, as far as possible, to the South Kensington Museum, and have not thought it their duty to enter at any length upon the many large and important subjects involved in the Institutions for promoting Science and Art; namely, the School of Mines, the Geological Museum and Geological Survey, the Museum of Irish Industry, the Royal Dublin Society, the Industrial Museum of Scotland, the 12 Navigation and Science Schools, and the 80 Art Schools, throughout the United Kingdom, all of which are under the Science and Art Department. The general superintendence of and pecuniary grants to these institutions are administered by the Lord President of the Council and the Vice President of the Committee of Council on Education, at South Kensington; but these institutions did, and might, exist quite independently of the South Kensington Museum itself, which indeed was added to them as late as 1857. The Art Schools, however, have direct relations with the Museum, in respect of the collections and books of Art; and Your Committee have accordingly investigated these relations.

1. Your Committee proceeded, in the first instance, to ascertain the nature, cost, and uses of the objects deposited in the South Kensington Museum, and the reasons why they had been placed in that locality. They find that the collections consist of—1. Objects of Ornamental Art, as applied to Manufactures, with an Art Library; 2. British Pictures, Sculpture, and Engravings; 3. Architectural Examples; 4. Appliances for Scholastic Education; 5. Materials for Building and Construction; 6. Substances used for Food; 7. Animal Products; 8. Models of Patented Inventions; and, 9. Reproductions by means of Photography and Casting.

2. It is on behalf of the Ornamental Art Collections of various kinds that the State has made the principal outlay. The system of purchase commenced as early as 1838, in accordance with the recommendation of a Committee of the House of Commons of 1835-6.

APPENDIX F.

A sum of 10,000*l*. was voted in 1840 to purchase examples of Art for the Schools of Design ; 5,000*l*. was voted to buy examples from the Exhibition of 1851; and in 1855 Parliament granted 20,000*l*. to buy specimens from the Bernal Collection. It appears that the State has expended during the last 22 years on purchases of Art specimens and books, now in charge of the South Kensington Museum, nearly 50,000*l*. Mr. Cole produced an inventory which shows the classes of objects which have been deposited in this department of the Museum. They illustrate various manufactures, pottery, glass, metal-working, furniture, woven fabrics, and the like; and their date extends from the 12th century to the present time. The Committee of the House of Commons, in 1836, recommended that "specimens from the era of the revival of arts, everything in short which exhibits in combination the efforts of the artist and workman, should be sought for in the formation of such institutions. They should also contain the most approved modern specimens, foreign as well as domestic." This recommendation has been carried into effect by the South Kensington Museum.

The system by which purchases are made was fully described by various witnesses. It is the duty of Mr. Robinson, the Superintendent of the Art Collections, to find out and select suitable specimens, which, after consultation with the Inspector General for Art, Mr. Redgrave, R.A., and the Secretary and General Superintendent, Mr. Cole, are submitted to the Lord President or the Vice-President. If they are approved, a Minute is made either for an absolute or conditional purchase. If the purchase be conditional the object is exhibited in the Museum, pursuant to a Minute passed by Mr. Henley, President of the Board of Trade, in 1852, and public criticism is invited upon it. All purchases are registered, and an inventory of them is published and sold, which enables the public to know the history, the date, and the price which has been paid for each article. The objects are well arranged for public instruction as far as the limited space allows. Every article is fully labelled in the Museum, so that the visitors are not obliged to refer to a catalogue. The collection seems to have been economically made. Sir Francis Scott, chairman of the Birmingham School of Art, and a collector himself, considers that the objects would fetch from seven to ten per cent. more than has been paid for them. Mr. Webb would "like to give double the price paid for many things." Mr. Cole produced a letter written by Mr. Hope, which stated, "that if Government is inclined to speculation, it will realize a handsome profit on the sums originally expended."

3. Your Committee have investigated a complaint often made against the South Kensington Museum and British Museum, to the effect that the officers of these institutions compete with each other at public sales. After examining Mr. Panizzi, the officers of the South Kensington Museum, and Mr. Webb, the agent who buys for both institutions, your

APPENDIX F.

Committee find not only that such competition has never occurred, but that a concerted action has been always taken between both institutions, by the employment of one buyer for the two to prevent any such competition. The report appears to have originated from the fact, as stated by Mr. Webb, that the British Museum and the Ordnance Department once competed for a suit of Greek armour, the British Museum being in entire ignorance that the Ordnance Department contemplated such a purchase for the Tower of London.

4. Evidence was produced to your Committee showing the great extent to which the public are disposed to co-operate with the State in assisting exhibition. Exclusive of the Koh-i-noor Diamond, and the British Pictures, the liberality of the Queen and of private individuals, during the last seven years, has given the public the benefit of loans and gifts of Ornamental Art, which have been estimated at a value exceeding 460,000*l*.

5. The objects have not been merely exhibited in the metropolis, but a system of circulation first recommended by the Committee of 1836, has been matured, and very successfully carried into effect by means of a travelling museum, the exhibition of which offers many advantages to schools and museums in provincial towns.

Her Majesty has been pleased to allow objects of great value and very fragile nature, such as Sevres porcelain, to be circulated in this manner; and Her example has been followed by many private gentlemen, benefactors to the Museum. It is remarkable that although the collection has travelled through the United Kingdom, and been packed and unpacked 56 times, not a single article has been lost or broken.

Alderman Dunn, Chairman of the Sheffield School of Art; Sir Francis Scott; Mr. Minton Campbell, Chairman of the Stoke (Potteries) School of Art; Mr. Thomas Fairbairn, Chairman of the late Art Treasures Exhibition at Manchester, and several other witnesses testified to the public importance of the principle of circulation, by which Public Collections are not circumscribed to a merely metropolitan use, but are rendered national. Your Committee are glad to find that the Trustees of the National Gallery are willing to permit the circulation of national pictures which may not be necessary to the Central Collection.

The Fine Arts Committee of the House of Commons expressed, in 1841, an opinion that, "independently of the beneficial and elevating influence of the Fine Arts upon a people, every pecuniary outlay, either for the purpose of forming or extending collections of Works of Art in this country, has been directly instrumental in creating new objects of industry and of enjoyment, and therefore in adding at the same time to the wealth of the country." Evidence, illustrated by actual specimens, was brought before your Committee, which proved the soundness of these views, and showed how by a judicious cultivation of the taste of purchasers and manufacturers, and by their action on each other, new branches of Ornamental Manufactures had been created within the last few years.

The Art Collections when first formed were placed in Somerset House, then transferred temporarily to Marlborough House, and were removed to South Kensington, when it became necessary to give up Marlborough House for the residence of the Prince of Wales.

6. The Collection of British Pictures at South Kensington was commenced by Mr. Sheepshanks, who in giving them to the nation stipulated that his pictures must be kept either in the immediate neighbourhood of Kensington in a suitable building, or, failing this, at Cambridge. This gift of some of the choicest pictures of the British School has been valued at 52,595*l.* It has lately been followed by a gift of Water Colours by Mrs. Ellison, valued at 2,996*l.*, and other gifts to the nation are in prospect if Parliament is disposed to find room to receive them. Mr. Sheepshanks approved of the building erected from Captain Fowke's design to receive his pictures, which are admirably displayed in it, both by day and night. He also expressed his desire that the local Schools of Arts should derive some benefit from his pictures, and some of the drawings of his collection are now in circulation. The specimens of British Sculpture are valued at 7,130*l.*, and have been entirely contributed by gift or loan. The Collection of Engravings and Etchings has also been formed by gift or loan, without expense of purchase to the public.

7. Other British pictures are exhibited to the public at South Kensington. They form part of the collections belonging to the Trustees of the National Gallery, and consist of the bequests of Messrs. Vernon, Turner, Jacob Bell, and others, together with the British pictures purchased with the Angerstein Collection. They were first exhibited in the basement of the National Gallery in Trafalgar-square, and were then removed to Marlborough House. When it was necessary to give up possession of Marlborough House to the Prince of Wales, it was proposed to fit up the old Riding School at Carlton-terrace, and to remove the pictures to this building, which was not fire-proof. It was held to be a better plan to erect fire-proof buildings of a plain and very economical character at South Kensington, and this was done at a cost less than would have been incurred by a provisional arrangement at Carlton-terrace, if the value of the land on that site be taken into consideration. The transfer of these pictures from Marlborough House to South Kensington has been attended with increased facilities to the public for seeing them; they are now open to view by day, every day in the week, and also on three evenings.

8. The collections illustrating Architecture are partly the property of the public and partly belong to the Architectural Museum Committee. The collections of that Committee are valued at 3,000*l.*, and were brought from some lofts in Cannon-row to commence a National Gallery of

APPENDIX F. 113

Architecture. These collections, for want of room, are at present ill arranged and crowded. They are much consulted by artisans employed in architecture. The same want of room has hitherto prevented the Department from taking possession of the architectural casts obtained as models for the Houses of Parliament, purchased by the public at 7,000*l.*, and now costing the Office of Works 492*l.* a year for house room at Thames-bank.

9. The Collection of Books, Maps, Diagrams, Models, and Apparatus used in primary education both at home and abroad has been made chiefly by private liberality. This collection was begun by the Society of Arts, and first exhibited at St. Martin's Hall in 1854, and at the close of the exhibition numerous objects were presented to the Government to form the nucleus of an Educational Museum. The collection remained for some time afterwards unexhibited for want of room, and was sent to South Kensington. It has cost the public 2,101*l.*, whilst the value of the gifts and loans is estimated at 5,085*l.* It is now chiefly supported by the producers of educational works, who voluntarily send them for exhibition. The catalogue of the collection shows its comprehensive and practical nature. It excites great interest among the visitors, and is attended by clergymen and others especially interested in schools. Your Committee regard it as a highly useful collection.

10. The Collections of Materials for Building and Construction, Food, and Animal Products, have been almost wholly made by private individuals without cost to the State. The greater part of them were given to the Commissioners of the Exhibition of 1851 by Exhibitors, and for several years were packed away in Kensington Palace, until space was provided at the Kensington Museum to receive them. Whilst the State has purchased objects of the value of 371*l.*, the public has supplied objects valued at 14,290*l.* These collections greatly interest the public, and are useful to commerce. The Rev. W. Rogers states that they especially attract the notice of the working classes, and your Committee consider that they are well worth preserving. Whenever sufficient space is provided for the Natural History Collections belonging to the public, it may be worthy of consideration if the Animal Products Collection ought not to be united with them.

11. The Collection of Models of Patented Inventions under the Commissioners of Patents, is placed in a portion of the iron building at South Kensington, and is much cramped for room.

12. The Collections of Reproductions by Photography and Casting have been made primarily to furnish models for the use of the 80 Art Schools in connexion with the Department of Science and Art; they are obtained from public collections at home and abroad. After providing for the Art Schools, it has been thought right to give the public at large the benefit of the photographs at cost price, for the promotion of general

H

Art education. The Science and Art Department express a desire to avoid any competition with professional photographers by limiting their sales to photographs taken from Government Collections, to which, except in rare and special cases, the trade is not admitted; but it has been objected by one commercial firm, enjoying peculiar privileges of admission to collections, and by Mr. Fenton, a photographer of eminence, that even such a limited sale by the Department is an improper interference with private enterprise.

There is an obvious distinction between copying and photographing pictures and works of art belonging to the public. Copying is attended by no very serious inconveniences, while photography almost invariably requires the removal of the object, deprives the public of the exhibition of it, exposes it in the light to the risks of breakage, rain, &c., which can only be guarded against by great vigilance, requires a special apparatus of considerable bulk, and uses chemicals which are always unpleasant and often dangerous. Mr. Panizzi shows that the only fire ever known at the British Museum was caused by the negligence of a photographer. Under such circumstances all the witnesses agree that a general right to photograph cannot be conceded to all like the right to copy. Mr. Fairbairn stated that at the Manchester Art Treasures Exhibition the photographic professors were pests, and that it was found absolutely necessary to limit the privilege to one person. In order to execute photographs in public collections there must be a monopoly somewhere. If it be proposed to grant this privilege to a limited number of competent persons, as was at one time the practice at the British Museum, the difficulty arises which was felt by the Trustees, of deciding who is competent. Mr. Panizzi considers it "a very difficult thing to determine who is competent," and the Trustees were forced to say, "We will only admit our own photographer." For a Public Department to attempt to determine this question in the case of every application, would lead to constant difficulties and heart-burnings. Moreover, the favoured persons having the monopoly among them might league among themselves to make the public pay an unfair toll for the use of their own property. These objections would apply all the more strongly to the appointment of a single private individual or firm, as the monopoly would be all the closer. The experience obtained at the British Museum, as well as at the South Kensington Museum, has led to the conclusion that the only feasible course for public interests is to employ one responsible public officer; and by harmonious co-operation between these two departments, one photographer is employed for both. A tariff of moderate prices is published, at which the public may obtain negatives, and print positives for themselves. Any publisher may thus produce and publish, at his own prices, any object in the British Museum or the South Kensington Museum.

APPENDIX F.

As respects "positives" of public objects, the sale of them by the Department to the public is limited to objects in public collections which it is not permitted to private enterprise to photograph, and to a price only covering the cost of production. Your Committee consider that there is no other course so free from objections or so good for the public at large as the present system of the Department. The printing of photographs stands on the same footing as the printing of Parliamentary papers, and the publishers might, as well as the photographers, complain of the low price at which they are sold. If the price were increased, there is no doubt that the sales would be greatly diminished, and the spread of knowledge of Parliamentary proceedings arrested. The Trustees of the British Museum attempted to supply the public with photographs of objects in the British Museum, at the same time allowing their photographer the privilege of publishing, but they abandoned the system after considerable losses.

Your Committee have investigated fully a complaint of Mr. Scott, in respect of the photographs taken by him from Raffaelle's cartoons. Mr. Scott complains that Mr. Caldesi was obstructed by the officer of the Department of Science and Art in taking his photographs, and that he has been undersold by the Department; but Mr. Redgrave proved that Messrs. Caldesi would have been unable to have produced any satisfactory photographs unless the Department had permitted them to have the benefit of the removal of the cartoons by their officer, and that as the sale of the cartoons by the Department cannot yet be said to be in operation, the apprehension of being undersold is at least premature. At any rate the public have no reason to regret that Mr. Scott's suggestion of vesting in his firm an absolute monopoly of the photographs of the cartoons has not been complied with. The arrangement by which a private was joined to an official photographer, was almost sure to lead to disputes, and should not be repeated.

13. Your Committee find that the total cost of the South Kensington Museum in its collections, land, and buildings has been 167,805*l*. This amount is exclusive of the annual cost of management, which so far as it can be separated from the cost of the general administration of the Science and Art Department and the cost of the Art Training Schools, exclusive of the supply of furniture, and postage, and official stationery, is estimated at about 7,000*l*. a year.

14. Your Committee are informed that above one million and a half of visitors have inspected the Museum during the first three years since its opening, on the 22nd of June 1857. Such a result, in so short a time, proves that the Museum has met a public want. This success is clearly due to the great care taken to meet the convenience of the public, especially by admission in the evening. The returns show that very nearly half the number of visitors attended in the evening, although the hours

H 2

for admission in the evening are less than one-fourth of those in the daytime. Much cost for lighting and vigilant superintendence arises from opening in the evening; but as the arrangement makes the Museum accessible to labouring men and their families, who would otherwise scarcely be able to visit it, your Committee consider the money well laid out, and the experiment deserving of imitation. The success of the Museum has also shown that an institution, although it may be situated in the suburbs, may be rendered so attractive as to compete in point of the number of visitors with other institutions nearer the centre of the metropolis.

15. So vast is the metropolis, and so ready are the people to avail themselves of every convenient opportunity for intellectual improvement and recreation, that similar institutions, if properly managed, in other parts of London, hold out fair prospects of a similar success; and it would be within the means of the South Kensington Museum to facilitate the formation of such institutions by loans of objects, made on a principle similar to that of the Circulating Museum.

16. The principles upon which the administration of the Museum is conducted have been explained fully to your Committee, and documentary details are given in the Appendix. Authority for every measure is obtained direct from the Lord President of the Council, or the Vice-President of the Committee of Council on Education. The accounts certified by the Vice-President are sent monthly to the Audit Office. The rules for the appointment of officers are calculated to exclude incompetency. Finally, a full annual Report of proceedings has been always submitted to Parliament.

17. Having arrived at the opinion that the South Kensington Museum, in respect of its action, as well throughout the United Kingdom as in the metropolis, is exercising a beneficial influence, and that it is fully deserving of continued Parliamentary support, your Committee next turned their attention to the state of the buildings at South Kensington.

18. The South Kensington Museum is situate on a plot of ground consisting of about 12 acres, which under the Act 21 & 22 Vict. cap. 36, have been reserved by the Treasury for the use of the Science and Art Department, at the original cost, namely, 5,000*l*. an acre. The land has therefore cost the country 60,000*l*. The land is at present occupied by various buildings, the nature and uses of which are shown by different colours on a plan attached to this Report.

In 1855 Parliament voted 15,000*l*. for the erection of a temporary iron structure to receive various collections presented to the public. The object in view was to obtain the greatest amount of covered space at the least possible cost. So large a building of iron, applied for the first time to such purposes, was altogether a novelty in this country, and expe-

APPENDIX F.

rience has shown, both in this case and at the Art Treasures Exhibition at Manchester, that an iron building, owing to its variations in temperature and the difficulty of keeping it water-tight, is not suitable for the preservation of Works of Art. Mr. Braidwood, also, does not consider it secure from fire. Much expense is required to keep it in good order. The officers of the Department report that the more delicate and valuable Works of Art suffer from cold, heat, damp, and the leakiness of the roof, and ought to be removed out of it as soon as possible.

In 1856 Parliament voted 10,000*l.* to remove the Offices of the Science and Art Department and the Art Training Schools, the latter built of wood, from Marlborough House to South Kensington, and this amount was expended, as well on this object as in rendering four old houses useful for class rooms and official residences.

The wooden schools are not secure from fire, and a fire has recently occurred in them. If they were not public property they would be condemned under the Building Act. The old houses are dilapidated, full of dry rot, and built in such a way as to be extremely liable to fire; one of them was on fire a few weeks ago, owing to the presence of a wooden beam in a chimney; another has had a story removed to save it from falling. They should be taken down without delay.

In 1857 Parliament voted 3,500*l.* to erect a permanent building to receive Mr. Sheepshanks' gift of British pictures, and in 1859 a sum of 8,198*l.* was voted for fireproof buildings to afford accommodation for the Vernon and Turner pictures, which it was necessary to remove from Marlborough House. These are solid and convenient buildings, and have been erected as part of a general plan which was laid before your Committee by Captain Fowke, and is appended to this Report.

It results from the account above given of the state of the iron building that additional space for the accommodation and exhibition of the Art collections should be provided at once. Captain Fowke states that the cheapest mode of obtaining this space would be to complete the quadrangle of brick buildings which was commenced by the Sheepshanks, Vernon, and Turner Galleries; and to glaze it over. He estimates that this might be done for 17,000*l.*, and by doing so the Art collections now in the Iron Museum would be placed in safety, others not properly shown would be efficiently exhibited, whilst space would be provided in the Iron Museum to receive and exhibit the architectural casts procured as models for the Houses of Parliament, which at present lie unexhibited in buildings at Thames-bank, costing an annual rent of 490*l.*

The danger arising from the use of the wooden schools and dilapidated houses renders it equally necessary to remove these buildings, and instead of them to provide at once safe buildings for official residences and the Art Training Schools. The cost has been approximately estimated by Captain Fowke at 27,000*l.*

Your Committee recommend these works as matters of extreme urgency, the completion and covering in of the quadrangular court as a means of rescuing much valuable public and private property from a receptacle quite unfit for it, the removal of the wooden schools and the dilapidated houses from considerations of safety and therefore of real economy. The iron building and the temporary brick buildings your Committee see no occasion to disturb at present; they can be usefully employed, and may well be allowed to stand for some years to come.

Your Committee are by no means anxious to involve the revenue in large expenses for mere ornament. The Museum is yet in course of formation, and they think it unwise to commit the country to a heavy expense in anticipation of its wants. The Committee recommend that any plan which may be adopted for the buildings to be erected should be capable of being worked into a general plan which would at once fully occupy the ground, and be susceptible of a proper amount of decoration. Such a plan has been laid before the Committee by Captain Fowke.

APPENDIX G.

AGREEMENTS between HER MAJESTY'S COMMISSIONERS and the HORTICULTURAL SOCIETY for the LEASE to the SOCIETY of a PORTION of the COMMISSIONERS' ESTATE at KENSINGTON GORE, together with the NEW CHARTER granted to the SOCIETY.

I.—ORIGINAL AGREEMENT.

ARTICLES OF AGREEMENT made this 24th day of July in the year of our Lord 1860, between the Commissioners for the Exhibition of 1851 (herein-after referred to as "The Commissioners"), of the one part, and the Horticultural Society of London (herein-after referred to as "The Society"), of the other part. Whereas the Society being desirous of obtaining a suitable area in or near the metropolis for an ornamental garden, in which they may exhibit and display the progress of Horticulture, and to which they propose to admit not only their members and the holders of transferable tickets to which certain life members are and will be entitled, and also the holders of such debentures as are herein-after mentioned (without any payment), but other visitors on payment (by such visitors) of fees for admission, have applied to the Commissioners for a lease for that purpose of a portion of their estate at Kensington Gore herein-after described; and the Commissioners, being satisfied that the intended operations of the Society will extend the influence of the Science and Art of Horticulture upon productive industry, and that the formation of the said garden will be beneficial to their neighbouring property, have agreed to

APPENDIX G.

grant such lease on the terms herein-after appearing. And whereas it has been agreed that certain earthworks for altering the levels of the land to be demised, as well for the permanent improvement thereof as for facilitating the operations of the Society, and certain arcades on the boundaries of the said land which as to some of them or some part or parts thereof shall be leased to the Society as herein-after mentioned, and as to others or other part or parts of such arcades, shall or may be used by the Society as herein-after mentioned, and may be available for other improvements on the estate of the Commissioners, and which may be connected with buildings which the Commissioners may hereafter cause or allow to be erected on their estate, should be formed and erected at the expense of the Commissioners, and that the other works upon the ground to be demised should be constructed and done at the expense of the Society. And whereas the land proposed to be demised as aforesaid is that piece or parcel of land at Kensington Gore, in the county of Middlesex, containing 20 acres or thereabouts, the abuttals and boundaries of which, and the sites of the proposed erections thereon or connected therewith, are particularly delineated on the plan hereunto annexed, and the Commissioners have caused to be commenced the earthworks herein-before mentioned. And whereas the Society, for the purpose of defraying the expense of the works to be done by them on the premises to be demised, have entered into engagements for raising the sum of 40,000l. by debentures, the residue of the sum of 50,000l. (the amount agreed to be expended by the Society) having been obtained by them by donations and fees on the admission of members for life. Now it is hereby mutually covenanted and agreed between the Commissioners and the Society, each covenanting for all matters and things to be done and forborne by them respectively as follows :—

1. The Society shall, immediately after the execution of the earthworks which have been commenced as aforesaid, enter upon the said land for the purpose of laying out and constructing, and will forthwith lay out and construct an ornamental garden, with walks, trees, shrubs, terraces, steps, fountains, band-houses, statues, and vases, and in addition thereto with a conservatory or winter garden at the north end. The Society may also erect on the said land such offices and other buildings as may be necessary and convenient for the carrying on the affairs and business of the Society. The whole of the above-mentioned works to be done to the satisfaction and subject to the approval of the Commissioners; and the said ornamental garden, with the works connected therewith, to be in a state fit for opening to visitors within six months after the Commissioners shall have finished the arcades herein-after referred to. The Society will expend in laying out and constructing the said garden, with the works and buildings aforesaid, a sum of not less than 50,000l.

APPENDIX G.

2. The Commissioners, simultaneously with the progress of the works hereby undertaken by the Society, will at their own cost enclose the said ground with arcades of an architectural character, as indicated in the said plan. As respects the upper arcades coloured orange in the said plan, such arcades shall be substantial and finished buildings. But as respects the central and lower arcades, coloured blue and yellow in the said plan, the same may be of a more temporary nature. The Commissioners will expend the sum of 50,000*l*. in and upon such earthworks as aforesaid, and in erecting the said arcades.

3. If the Society shall complete the works undertaken by them as expressed in the first clause of this agreement, the Commissioners will grant to the Society a lease of the land and the garden and of the erections to be made or built thereon by the Commissioners and the Society respectively, as after-mentioned, for a term of 31 years, to be computed from the 1st day of June 1861, on the terms and conditions following.

4. The buildings to be included in the lease shall be all such as are to be erected by the Society, and also the said upper arcades, except the parts coloured green in the said plan. The said excepted parts of the upper arcades, and the central and lower arcades, shall not be so included, but shall remain the absolute property of the Commissioners, subject to a right of way or promenade therein or thereunder during the continuance of the said lease, to be allowed to the Society and their visitors in such mode and to such extent nevertheless as respects the lower arcades as not to prejudice or prevent the erection or letting of stalls in such lower arcades by and for the benefit of the Commissioners, which privilege, and the granting to the occupiers of stalls (but not to strangers, unless by payment by or for them to the Society of the usual charge for the admission of strangers to the gardens on the day on which such right shall be enjoyed,) right of way thereto by such access as may from time to time be appointed by the Society, the Commissioners expressly reserve to themselves; and the Commissioners also reserve to themselves the monies received from such occupiers in respect of the stalls; and such monies are not to be considered for the purposes of the provisions herein-after contained as receipts from the garden, but shall belong wholly to the said Commissioners. And the said Society is not, without the consent of the Committee herein-after mentioned, in any of the arcades to be demised to them, to let any part thereof for stalls or the sale of any matters, except refreshments. And with respect to the sale of refreshments, the sale thereof in the arcades to be demised to the Society shall continue only until suitable permanent arrangements for the supply of the refreshments shall (with the consent of the Society) have been made by the Commissioners.

5. It is understood that the Commissioners or their assigns are to have

full power to arch over, if they should think fit, all or any part of the entrances or ways into the garden, for the purpose of erecting over the space thereof any buildings, and to erect for the purposes of the arches, or of the superstructure, piers or columns on any part of the ground appropriated to such entrances or ways, so far as the same may be done without obstructing the convenient access to the garden so far as respects the entrance on the west side; and in regard to that on the east side, so far as may not interfere with the meeting rooms and offices proposed to be erected there by the Society; and the demise and grant of rights to the Society, of or in respect of the arcades, is not to prejudice the right of the Commissioners to erect, or allow to be erected, any superstructure on or building connected with the arcades, (except that no superstructure shall be erected on the demised part of the upper arcades), or to take down any of such arcades for the purpose of erecting others of a more substantial or different character, and to suspend, so far as may be necessary, during the progress of such works the right of promenade, and use by the Society of such arcades.

6. No buildings shall be erected by the Society during the said lease without the sanction of the Commissioners, except strictly temporary buildings.

7. The Society shall keep in good repair all buildings to be included in the said lease, and all other the buildings which may be erected on the land to be demised, except the excepted parts of the upper arcades and the central and lower arcades, and the buildings by the Commissioners mentioned in Clause No. 5, which last-mentioned arcades and buildings shall be kept in good repair by the Commissioners; and the Society shall, at the end of the term, give up such buildings, except as aforesaid, in good repair, together with all the Statues and Works of Art which may be placed or put up in the gardens, and with all fixtures, including conservatories, greenhouses, and other erections at any time put up on the ground, and with all shrubs, trees, and plants that may be growing thereon: Provided that the Society be at liberty to remove all statues and works of Art, temporary conservatories, greenhouses, and other temporary structures put up by them, or with their consent, and paid for out of their own funds, after the commencement of the said term (except in the cases where the payments for such statues or works, conservatories, greenhouses, or other structures, shall have been allowed to them out of, or as part of, the current expenses of the said garden, by the Committee herein-after mentioned).

8. The Society shall use the demised premises for the purpose for which they have applied for the lease of the same as herein-before expressed, and for no other; and if, in the management or dealings with the demised premises, the Society do or propose any act, matter, or proceeding which, having regard to the terms and stipulations of these presents, shall, in the

judgment of the Commissioners, be unreasonable or prejudicial to the demised premises, or the other property of the Commissioners, or to their rights, the Commissioners shall have full power to prohibit the act, matter, or proceeding in question, and the Society shall abstain or forthwith discontinue the act, matter, or proceeding so prohibited.

9. The Society shall insure from loss by fire all such of the buildings to be erected on the premises demised as the Society is under Clause No. 7 bound to repair.

10. The Society shall not assign, underlet, or otherwise part with the lease to be so granted, or the premises to be so demised, except with the consent in writing of the Commissioners.

11. All monies received from Fellows of the Society, who have already signified their intention of compounding, and who have paid or shall pay such composition, and all sums received from new life-members elected prior to the 1st day of June 1861, shall be considered capital, and belong to, and may be invested or used by the Society for the purpose of redeeming outstanding debentures, or otherwise.

12. The Society shall cause to be kept an account of all monies received by them in respect of the admission to the gardens, and of all monies received by them from members for annual subscriptions (not compositions from Fellows nor life-memberships) received or subscribed for subsequent to those which are included in the amount of 50,000*l.* mentioned in the recital to these presents, and all monies paid or to be paid for admission of any person to the Society on terms conferring any right of entering the gardens, all which monies and such proportion or annual sums from time to time as herein-after mentioned, of or in respect of the monies received for compositions from Fellows who shall, after the execution of these presents, signify their intention of compounding, and for life-memberships of Fellows elected after the said 1st day of June 1861, are to be considered and are herein-after referred to, as "receipts from the Gardens," and such accounts shall be rendered, and the rents herein-after stipulated for, so far as they can be ascertained, paid half-yearly to the Commissioners.

13. With respect to monies received for compositions from Fellows, who, after the execution of these presents shall signify their intention of compounding, and for life-membership of Fellows elected after the said 1st day of June 1861, the same shall be accounted for and disposed of in manner following (viz.), the annual receipts of the Society from such compositions from Fellows and from such life-members as last aforesaid, shall be taken in making out the account above referred to according to the number of such Fellows and members respectively in existence at the commencement of each financial year, and at the rate for each of such Fellows and members respectively, of one fifteenth of the sum which he may have paid for composition, or in lieu of annual payments, or for

admission (*i.e.*) at the rate of 2*l*. 16*s*. for each Fellow or member who may have paid 42*l*., and at the rate of 1*l*. 8*s*. for each Fellow or member who may have paid 21*l*., and the Society shall be charged in such financial year with such "annual receipts" as part of the "receipts from the gardens;" and subject to the stipulation in the present clause, all sums of money paid to the Society for the composition of annual payments by Fellows, and for the admission of Fellows as life-members, may be applied and disposed of as part of the general funds of the Society, or in such manner as the Society shall think fit.

14. Out of the gross amount of the "Receipts from the Gardens" there shall be first retained by the Society such a sum as shall from time to time be allowed by the Committee herein-after mentioned, in respect of the expenses of the Chiswick garden, or other garden in lieu thereof, to be kept up for experimental or scientific purposes, the reasonable expenses of the management of the Society, including the expenses of the exhibition in the demised grounds (or elsewhere, with the consent of the Commissioners) of flowers, fruits, and other articles; bands, police, and other general and necessary expenses; and also sums to be given for medals or prizes for competition for articles shown at such exhibitions; and further in respect of the current expenses of the gardens, to be laid out and constructed under these presents, including the repairs to be done by the Society, costs of insurance, and any structural or other improvements or ornaments which the Committee may think fit, which allowance shall from time to time proceed and be made upon a fair and reasonable basis, and so as to keep and maintain the said gardens and all the buildings, improvements, and ornaments upon and belonging thereto in thoroughly good order and condition. 2ndly. There shall be then retained by the Society out of such receipts, the amount which may be from time to time payable by the Society in respect of interest, not exceeding 5 per cent. on the sum of 40,000*l*. which they have borrowed on debentures as aforesaid, or on so much of the said sum of 40,000*l*. as may remain unpaid or undischarged; and, 3rdly. There shall then be paid by the Society to the said Commissioners as rent, the yearly sum of 2,145*l*., if the receipts shall be adequate for such payment after retaining to the Society the sums authorized to be retained by them under the 1st and 2nd heads of the present clause, but otherwise such a sum only as shall be equal from year to year to the residue of the receipts over and above the sums so in precedence. And if there shall remain any surplus over and above the said several payments herein-before directed to be made or retained out of the "Receipts from the Gardens," there shall be paid to the Commissioners for their own use and as additional rent yearly, a sum equal to half such surplus.

15. For the purpose of regulating the amount to be retained by the Society in each year for expenses, a Committee shall be appointed

APPENDIX G.

annually, which Committee shall consist of six persons, three of whom shall be appointed by the Commissioners, and three by the Society, and any three of such Committee shall form a quorum, so as one at least shall be a person appointed by the Commissioners, and one a person appointed by the Society. Seven days' notice of every meeting of the Committee shall be given in writing to each member of the Committee by a letter to be sent by the post. As vacancies may occur in each year by death, incapacity, or resignation, such vacancies may be filled up respectively by the Commissioners or the Society according as the original appointments were made by them respectively.

16. The Committee shall from time to time select one of those committeemen who have been appointed by the Commissioners as Chairman of such Committee, which Chairman shall have the power of voting on all occasions equally with the other committeemen for the time being, acting; and such Chairman, in case of equality, to have a casting-vote in addition; and the Committee shall have power to make bye-laws for their own government in the execution of the duties confided to them.

17. The Society shall devote and apply towards the liquidation of the debt of 40,000*l*. (being the amount which they have so raised by debentures as herein-before recited), three-fifths of the money actually received by them from time to time in respect of the "Receipts from the Gardens," after the payments directed to be retained out of the said receipts for expenses and interest by the Society, and the rent to the Commissioners.

18. In case it shall happen, after the expiration of the first five years of the lease, that the sum or sums payable thereunder to the Commissioners as rent, shall fail in every one of any five consecutive years subsequent to the first five years to be equal to the sum of 2,145*l*. per annum, then, and in any such case, it shall be lawful for the Commissioners to re-enter upon the said demised premises, and to resume full and absolute possession thereof, with all improvements therein, and all erections thereon, and with all the plants, shrubs, and trees in and about the same, and out of whatever fund the same may have been paid for, and that without making any compensation whatsoever to the Society. Provided always, that the right of re-entry shall not arise if the Commissioners, from the commencement of the term, have, under the aforesaid provisions, received such a sum of money for rent as would, reckoning from such commencement to the expiration of the last year in which such continued deficiency shall occur, amount to an average sum of 2,145*l*. per annum.

19. The Society shall not require the lessor's title to be deduced, nor shall any objection be made on the ground that a part or the whole of the ground to be demised is on mortgage, and that the mortgagees do not concur.

20. The Society shall have the right of giving to the Commissioners, two years before the expiration of the term of 31 years (provided such lease shall not have been previously determined or become subject to be determined under the proviso for re-entry herein-before mentioned or contained), a notice in writing calling upon the Commissioners to renew the lease to be so granted for a further term of 31 years, to commence at the expiration of the first term of 31 years, subject to all and every the terms and conditions on which the original term is to be granted, except the right of renewal, and except as herein-after appears. And in case of such notice being given, the Commissioners (provided the original term shall not have become liable to forfeiture after the giving of such notice) will either grant a renewal in accordance with such notice and these presents, or, at their option, may decline to grant such renewal on the terms and conditions of their taking upon themselves at the end of the original term of 31 years, the payment of such amount of the original debenture debt of 40,000*l.* as may remain unpaid and undischarged at the expiration of that term, provided such amount do not exceed 20,000*l.*, or upon condition of taking upon themselves the payment of 20,000*l.*, part of such debt, if there remain owing a larger sum than 20,000*l.* at the expiration of such term, which sum of 20,000*l.* so to be paid by the Commissioners shall be applied in discharge or satisfaction of the unpaid debentures for the time being rateably and without preference or priority. If, on the other hand, the debenture debt shall at the expiration of such term be less than 15,000*l.*, or in case there should be no part of the said debenture debt then owing or unpaid, the Commissioners, in the former case, shall pay to the Society such a sum as when added to the amount of debenture debt, then owing or unpaid, shall constitute a total sum of 15,000*l.*; and the Commissioners shall in the latter case pay to the Society the full sum of 15,000*l.*; and the Commissioners shall make their election to renew or take upon themselves such payment within six calendar months from the receipt of the notice requiring a renewal. If the Commissioners elect to renew, a renewal shall take place accordingly, but the proviso for re-entry shall be so framed as to operate immediately and without a suspension of the first five years of the renewed term.

21. If the Commissioners elect not to renew, they shall give a bond under their common seal to the Society, to secure the due performance of the obligation which they are to undertake in respect of the portion of debt of the Society, not exceeding 20,000*l.* remaining unpaid, or of the payment of the sum not exceeding 15,000*l.* as aforesaid, as the case may be, in which bond some certain day, not being more than 12 months from the date thereof, shall be named for the principal sum of money thereby conditioned to be paid, and in the meantime interest at the rate of 5*l.* per cent. per annum shall be payable thereon.

22. The costs of the original lease and counterpart, and of any renewal, and of these presents shall be paid by the Society.

23. If either of the parties hereto shall differ as to the construction of the terms and provisions herein contained, or the mode in which this present agreement is to be executed, or as to the provisions to be contained in any lease to be granted in pursuance of these presents, then all questions in difference shall, on the application of either party, be determined by an arbitrator to be named in writing by Her Majesty's Attorney-General for the time being; and the decision of such arbitrator in writing, within the time, and as shall be directed by the said Attorney-General, shall be binding on all parties. In witness, &c.

II.—Supplemental Agreement.

ARTICLES OF AGREEMENT made this 20th day of November in the year of our Lord 1860 between the Commissioners for the Exhibition of 1851 (herein-after referred to as "The Commissioners") of the one part and the Horticultural Society of London (herein-after referred to as "the Society") of the other part. Whereas by certain articles of agreement bearing date the 24th day of July 1860, and made between the Commissioners of the one part and the Society of the other part, it hath been convenanted and agreed between the Commissioners and the Society that certain works shall be done and executed by the Commissioners and the Society respectively in and upon a piece of land part of the estate of the Commissioners at Kensington Gore, which piece of land is agreed and intended to be used as an ornamental garden in which may be exhibited the progress of Horticulture, and which land is herein-after referred to as "the gardens," and that on certain terms and subject to certain conditions therein specified a lease of the gardens should be granted by the Commissioners to the Society renewable as therein mentioned. And whereas the intended works are now in progress; and whereas the Society require for purposes connected with their said undertaking the use of some additional land adjoing or near "the gardens," and the Commissioners have allowed the Society to take and have possession for such purposes of certain land adjoining the gardens which is shown on the plan hereunto annexed and specified by a red colour, and which land is hereinafter referred to as "the additional land," but the Commissioners have declined to include such land in the lease to be granted, as they may require to resume possession of the same for other purposes; and whereas an access to the gardens is at present afforded by means of a lane or path shown on the said plan and marked with the colour brown, but the Commissioners have declined to include in the lease the use of such way, as it might interfere with other arrangements to be made by them of and concerning other parts of their estate at Kensington Gore; and whereas

APPENDIX G.

with the view to the mutual convenience of the Commissioners and the Society, it hath been agreed to make and enter into this agreement as supplemental to the said recited agreement of the 24th day of July 1860: now it is hereby mutually covenanted and agreed between the Commissioners and the Society, each covenanting for all matters and things to be done and forborne to be done by them respectively as follows, viz. :—

1. The Society shall have and continue to hold possession of the additional land, viz., of all that piece of ground shown in the plan hereto annexed and marked with the colour red, as tenants thereof from year to year under the Commissioners, such tenancy to be held and understood as commencing on the 24th day of June last, until the Commissioners shall think fit to resume possession of the same, which they shall be at liberty to do at any period of the year without reference to that on which the tenancy commenced, on giving six calendar months' notice in writing of their intention so to do, and subject to the stipulations and conditions herein-after contained; or the Society may give up the same on six months' notice at the end of any current year of their tenancy.

2. The Society shall build thereon a gardener's house, an engine house, tanks, and other buildings required for the purpose of the said undertaking, with the necessary works and appliances, but no other erections or buildings whatsoever, and all such buildings, except strictly temporary buildings, shall be erected in accordance with plans previously submitted to and approved by the Commissioners, and shall be completed to their entire satisfaction, or otherwise the Society shall not be entitled to the benefit of this agreement; and the said additional land shall be used only for the purposes of the said undertaking, and shall not be underlet or assigned by the said Society to any person or persons whomsoever, and shall not be so used as to allow the public or any other person or persons to obtain any rights or easements over the same that can or may in any way interfere with the use thereof by the said Commissioners for any purposes or purpose whatsoever; and the Society will, at the request of the Commissioners, do and allow to be done all acts and things the Commissioners may think necessary to prevent any such rights or easements being obtained.

3. Until the Commissioners shall resume possession of the said additional land under the provisions in that behalf herein-before contained, the Society will yearly pay to the Commissioners the rent of 1s. as an acknowledgment of the tenancy of the said land and of the use of the easement herein-after agreed to be granted to them, the first yearly payment to be made on the 24th day of June 1861.

4. The Society shall, so long as the Commissioners think fit, have a right to use the road or way specified by the colour brown on the said plan as an access to the gardens, and the Commissioners shall not stop up or interfere with such right unless and until they shall provide another

road for the use of the Society in lieu thereof; and in case the Commissioners think fit to stop the said access to the said gardens, the said Commissioners shall find and provide some other fit access to such gardens, which access they shall be at liberty nevertheless from time to time to alter as they shall think fit.

5. In case the Commissioners shall desire to resume possession of the additional land, and the Society shall continue at the time of the service of the six months' notice entitled to the lease agreed to be granted to them under the said agreement of the 24th day of July 1860 (such lease not being forfeited or liable to forfeiture), the Commissioners shall, before the expiration of such notice, appropriate for the use of the Society as tenant from year to year, and subject to like provisions to those herein contained, some portion of their estate at Kensington Gore convenient for the purposes for which it is intended to use the additional land: And also that they the said Commissioners shall and will within the period of six months after service of such notice, and at their cost and expense, reinstate upon the land to be so appropriated as aforesaid the buildings and works as nearly as possible in the same condition as the buildings and works erected on the additional land.

6. All land to be substituted for the additional land shall be held by the Society, subject to all the stipulations herein contained, particularly the right of the Commissioners again to resume possession thereof on terms similar to those herein specified as regards the additional land, and nothing herein contained shall give to the Society any lien or claim on the whole or any particular portion of the estate of the said Commissioners, so as to prevent them doing as they may think fit with their said estate.

7. The Commissioners shall have full power and absolute right to take and resume possession, without paying any compensation whatever, of all the additional land for the time being appropriated for the purposes of the said Society as aforesaid, and all erections and buildings thereon, in case the Society shall do or commit any act or default which would be or amount to a forfeiture of the lease agreed to be granted to them by the said agreement of the 24th day of July 1860; and in the event of such forfeiture such possession may be taken without the six months' notice; and they may also in the event of the Society doing or committing any such act or default stop up the aforesaid access altogether without any such notice.

8. The Society shall, so long as any tenancy shall continue under this agreement, either as regards the land, the immediate subject matter thereof or any other land to be appropriated in lieu thereof, pay all rates and taxes payable in respect of such land, and keep the same in good order and condition, and shall insure and keep insured all buildings and erections thereon, and shall keep such buildings and erections in

good and tenantable repair, and generally in all cases not hereby expressly provided for, the said land hereby agreed to be let and any land to be substituted for it shall be used and dealt with as if comprized in the agreement of the 24th day of July 1860, or in the lease to be granted pursuant thereto.

9. If either of the parties hereto shall differ as to the construction of the terms and provisions herein contained, or the mode in which this present agreement is to be executed, or as to what might or ought to be done or forborne in pursuance or by virtue of or under the terms and stipulations herein, or in reference to any other matter or thing arising under these presents, then all questions in difference shall, on the application of either party, be determined by an arbitrator to be named in writing by Her Majesty's Attorney-General for the time being, and the decision of such arbitrator in writing within the time and as shall be directed by the said Attorney-General shall be binding on all parties. In witness, &c.

III.—SECOND SUPPLEMENTAL AGREEMENT.

ARTICLES OF AGREEMENT made the 1st day of March in the year of our Lord 1861 between the Commissioners for the Exhibition of 1851 (herein-after referred to as "The Commissioners") of the one part, and the Horticultural Society of London (herein-after referred to as "the Society") of the other part. Whereas by certain articles of agreement bearing date the 24th day of July 1860, and made between the Commissioners of the one part and the Society of the other part, it was mutually covenanted and agreed between the Commissioners and the Society that certain works should be done and executed by the Commissioners and the Society respectively in and upon a certain piece of land, part of the estate of the Commissioners at Kensington Gore, which piece of land is agreed and intended to be used as an ornamental garden, and is in the now reciting agreement, as well as herein-after, referred to as "the gardens;" and that, on certain terms and subject to certain conditions therein specified, a lease of the gardens should be granted by the Commissioners to the Society for the term of thirty-one years, computed from the 1st day of June 1861, renewable as therein mentioned. And whereas it was by Clause 1 of that agreement provided that the Society should expend in laying out and constructing the said gardens, with the works and buildings in the said agreement in that behalf specified, a sum of not less than 50,000*l.* ; and it was by Clause 2 of that agreement provided that the Commissioners, subject to the conditions therein mentioned, should expend the sum of 50,000*l.* in and upon the works by them to be done in accordance with the said agreement. And whereas it is provided by Clause 14 of the said agreement that out of the gross amount of the receipts from the gardens certain expenses therein mentioned should be retained by the Society; and, secondly, that there should be then retained by the Society the amount which might be payable by the Society in respect of interest not exceeding 5l. per cent. on the sum of 40,000l., which it appears by the recitals therein contained they had borrowed or arranged to borrow on debentures, or on so much of that sum as might remain unpaid or undischarged; and, thirdly, there should be paid by the Society to the Commissioners, as rent, the yearly sum of 2,145l., if the receipts should be adequate for such payment after retaining to the Society the sums authorized to be retained by them under the first and second heads of that clause, but otherwise such a sum only as should be equal from year to year to the residue of the receipts over and above the sums so in precedence, and if there should remain any surplus over and above the several payments therein-before directed to be made or retained out of the receipts from the gardens, there should be paid to the Commissioners for their own use, and as an additional rent, yearly, a sum equal to half such surplus. And whereas Clause 17 of such agreement provides that the Society shall devote and apply towards the liquidation of the debt of 40,000l. three fifths of the money actually received by them from time to time in respect of the receipts from the gardens after the payments directed to be retained out of such receipts for expenses and interest by the Society, and the rent to the Commissioners; and it is by the 18th Clause of such agreement provided that the Commissioners shall have a right of re-entry in certain events in case of such continued non-payment of the rent of 2,145l. as therein mentioned. And whereas it is provided by the 20th Clause of such agreement that the Society shall have a right to give such notice as therein mentioned, calling for a renewal of the lease to be granted to them, and the Commissioners may either grant such renewal or decline to grant it, on the terms and conditions of their taking upon themselves at the end of the original term of thirty-one years the payment of such amount of the original debenture debt of 40,000l. as should remain unpaid and undischarged at the expiration of that term, provided such amount do not exceed 20,000l., or upon condition of taking upon themselves the payment of 20,000l., part of such debt, if there remain owing a larger sum than 20,000l., with a provision that if the debenture debt shall be less than 15,000l., or in case no part of the debenture debt shall be then unpaid, the Commissioners would pay a sum of 15,000l. in manner and for the purposes in that clause mentioned. And whereas the Society and the Commissioners are each desirous of respectively having the right of increasing the outlay by them respectively undertaken to be made by the said agreement, to any amount not exceeding as to each of them the sum of 10,000l. over and above the respective sums of 50,000l. by them respectively undertaken to be laid out as aforesaid, and of acquiring such rights and privileges as herein appear in respect of such additional outlay, if made. Now, it is hereby mutually covenanted and agreed between the Commissioners and the Society, each covenanting for all matters and things to be done and forborne by them respectively, as follows :—

1. That the Society may at any time before the 1st day of January 1864, if they think fit (but they are not hereby required so to do, notwithstanding any additional outlay that may be made by the Commissioners) borrow and take up on their debentures or other securities, any sum or sums not exceeding in the whole the sum of 10,000*l.*, in addition to the sum of 40,000*l.* in the agreement mentioned as having been borrowed, or for the borrowing of which arrangements had been made, and may within the like period lay out and expend the sum or sums so borrowed in addition to the original sum of 50,000*l.* therein mentioned in and about such works and things as are in the 1st Clause of the said recited agreement undertaken to be done by them, and in and about which the original sum of 50,000*l.* is required by that clause to be expended, such additional sum or sums nevertheless being laid out and expended in such mode, and the works on which the same shall be expended to be subject to the like approval, as in that clause provided in respect of the sum of 50,000*l.* as therein mentioned.

2. That the Commissioners may, if they think fit at any time before the 1st day of January 1864, (but they are not hereby required so to do, notwithstanding any additional outlay that may be made by the Society,) lay out and expend such sum or sums of money as they may think fit, not exceeding in the whole the sum of 10,000*l.* in addition to the original sum of 50,000*l.* in Clause 2 of the said agreement mentioned, in and about such works, matters, and things, as by that clause are undertaken to be done by them, and in and about which the sum of 50,000*l.* is required by that clause to be expended by them.

3. In case both or either of the parties hereto think fit to make any such outlay, such parties respectively or party shall have no claim or demand against the other of them or against the gardens or against the receipts from the gardens save and except as herein-after mentioned, viz., that with a view to compensate such parties respectively or party in some degree for such additional outlay, the following alterations shall be made in the said recited agreement, and in the lease to be granted pursuant thereto, viz.

4. The 14th Clause of the said recited agreement shall be altered and amended as follows, viz., out of the gross amount of the receipts from the gardens there shall be first retained by the Society such a sum as shall from time to time be allowed by the Committee mentioned in Clause 15 of the said agreement in respect of the expenses of the Chiswick Garden, or other garden in lieu thereof, to be kept up for experimental or scientific purposes, the reasonable expenses of the management of the

Society, including the expenses of the Exhibition on the demised grounds (or elsewhere with the consent of the Commissioners,) of flowers, fruits, and other articles, bands, police, and other general and necessary expenses, and also sums to be given for medals, or prizes for competition for articles shown at such Exhibition, and further in respect of the current expenses of the gardens to be laid out and constructed under the said agreement, including the repairs to be done by the Society, costs of insurance, and any structural or other improvements or ornaments which the Committee may think fit, which allowance shall from time to time proceed and be made upon a fair and reasonable basis, and so as to keep and maintain the said gardens, and all the buildings, improvements, and ornaments upon and belonging thereto in thoroughly good order and condition; secondly, there shall be then retained by the Society out of such receipts the amount which may be from time to time payable by the Society in respect of interest not exceeding 5 per cent. per annum on the sum of 40,000l. originally borrowed or agreed to be borrowed by them on debentures as aforesaid, and on any further sum or sums they may borrow and expend in accordance with Clause 1 of this agreement not exceeding 10,000l., or on so much of the original and additional sums as for the time being may have been raised and shall not have been paid off; and thirdly, there shall then be paid by the Society to the said Commissioners as rent the yearly sum or sums herein-after in that behalf mentioned, if the receipts shall be adequate for such payment, after retaining to the Society the sums authorized to be retained by them under the first and second heads of the present clause, but otherwise such a sum only as shall be equal from year to year to the residue of the receipts over and above the sums so in precedence, viz., if the Commissioners shall limit their outlay under Clause 2 of the said recited agreement to 50,000l. then the yearly sum of 2,145l. only, but if under Clause 2 of this agreement they shall expend a larger sum, then an addition shall be made to such rent at the rate of 4l. 5s. for every additional 100l. which the Commissioners shall think fit to expend in accordance with that clause, not exceeding 10,000l. in the whole. And if there shall remain any surplus over and above the said several payments herein-before directed to be made or retained out of the "Receipts from the Gardens," there shall be paid to the Commissioners for their own use, and as additional rent yearly, whether or not they make any additional outlay, a sum equal to half such surplus.

5. The 17th clause of the said recited agreement shall be altered as follows, viz., the Society shall devote and apply towards the liquidation of their debenture debt, whether it amount to the original sum of 40,000l. only, or any increased amount under the authority of clause 1 of this agreement, three-fifths of the money actually received by them from time to time, in respect of the "receipts from the gardens," after

the payments directed to be retained out of the said receipts for expenses and interest by the Society and the rent to the Commissioners.

6. The 18th clause of the said recited agreement shall be altered as follows, viz., in case it shall happen after the expiration of the first five years of the lease, that the sum or sums payable thereunder to the Commissioners as rent shall fail in every one of any five consecutive years subsequent to the first five years, to be equal to the sum of 2,145l. per annum, in case only that sum shall be payable, or to such larger amount as is hereby made payable as rent to the Commissioners, in respect of any additional outlay under Clause 2 of this agreement, if such increased rent become payable, then and in any such case it shall be lawful for the Commissioners to re-enter upon the said demised premises, and to resume full and absolute possession thereof, with all improvements therein and all erections thereon, and with all the plants, shrubs, and trees, in and about the same, and out of whatsoever fund the same may have been paid for, and that without making any compensation whatsoever to the Society ; provided always, that the right of re-entry shall not arise if the Commissioners from the commencement of the term have, under the provisions herein or in the said recited agreement contained, received such a sum of money for rent as would, reckoning from such commencement to the expiration of the last year in which such continued deficiency shall occur, amount either to an average sum of 2,145l. per annum (if only 50,000l. shall have been expended by them), or (in case of an additional outlay by the Commissioners under the 2nd clause of these presents), to an average sum equal to 2,145l. and interest at 4l. 5s. per cent. per annum on the amount of such additional outlay.

7. Provided always that nothing herein contained or to be done under the authority of these presents shall alter or prejudice the rights of the respective parties under Clause 20 of the said recited agreement, save and except that in estimating the debenture debt of the Society for which under that Clause provision or compensation is to be made by the Commissioners, regard shall be had not only to the original debt raised by the Society, but to the increased or additional debt raised by the Society under the authority of these presents ; and in case the aggregate amount of those debts remaining unsatisfied shall exceed 20,000l., the said Clause No. 20 shall be read as if the sum named for defining the ultimate liability of the Commissioners had, in lieu of the sum of 20,000l., been such a sum as would be equal to 20,000l., and in addition thereto one-half of the sum actually raised by the Society by debentures or other securities under the authority of Clause No. 1 herein contained ; and it is hereby expressly declared that the provision in the said Clause No. 20, as to the payment of 15,000l. by the Commissioners in either of the events therein mentioned, shall not be altered or prejudiced by these presents.

8. Nothing herein contained shall prejudice or affect a certain supplemental agreement made between the Commissioners and the Society, and bearing date the 20th day of November 1860, save only that such last-mentioned supplemental agreement shall be held and taken to be an agreement supplemental to the original agreement, as altered by these presents.

Lastly, all costs, charges, and expenses of and incident to this agreement shall be borne and paid by the Society.

In witness, &c.

IV.—NEW CHARTER OF HORTICULTURAL SOCIETY.

VICTORIA, by the Grace of God of the United Kingdom of Great Britain and Ireland, Queen, Defender of the Faith, to all to whom these presents shall come, greeting.

1st. Incorporation of the Society by Letters Patent, 49 Geo. III.

1. Whereas the Horticultural Society of London, herein-after referred to as " the said Society," was incorporated by Royal Letters Patent under the Great Seal of our said United Kingdom, bearing date at Westminster the 17th day of April, in the 49th year of the reign of His late Majesty King George the 3rd, for the purpose of the improvement of horticulture in all its branches, ornamental as well as useful.

2nd. Arrangement between the Commissioners of the Exhibition of 1851 and the Society.

2. And whereas it has been represented to Us that the said Society has sedulously pursued and successfully promoted the objects for which it was incorporated, and it has been also represented to us that with the view of still further promoting such objects, an arrangement was lately entered into between the Commissioners for the Exhibition of 1851 (herein-after referred to as the Commissioners), and the said Society, which is contained in certain Articles of Agreement, dated the 24th day of July 1860, and sealed with the Corporate Seals of the Commissioners, and the said Society respectively, whereby it was agreed (amongst other things), first, that a piece of land at Kensington Gore containing 20 acres or thereabouts, part of the estate of the Commissioners, should be leased to the said Society for a term of years ; secondly, that the said Society immediately after the execution by the said Commissioners of certain earthworks, should lay out and construct on the land an ornamental garden, with walks, trees, shrubs, terraces, steps, fountains, band houses, statues, and vases ; and at the north end of the said land a conservatory or winter garden, and expend not less than 50,000*l*. ; and, thirdly, that the Commissioners simultaneously with the progress of the works of the said Society, should at their own cost enclose the said land with arcades, distinguished as the upper arcades, central arcades, and lower arcades, respectively, and that the upper arcades (except the parts thereof coloured green in the plan annexed to the said Articles of Agreement), and certain rights and easements as to the use or enjoyment of the central and lower arcades, and the excepted parts of the upper

arcades, should be included in the lease of the said land, and that the Commissioners shall expend the sum of 50,000*l*. about such earthworks, and in erecting the said arcades. And it is also represented to Us that under the said Articles of Agreement the sum of 40,000*l*. (part of the 50,000*l*. to be expended by the said Society) is to be raised by debentures (the remainder of the 50,000*l*. having been already raised by donations and fees on the admission of life members), and divers stipulations or agreements are made thereby or contained therein for the application and disposition of the income of the said Society, it being part of such arrangements that the "receipts from the gardens," consisting of and including the moneys and income therein mentioned in that behalf, should be applied or disposed of in the following manner, viz., out of the gross amount of the "receipts from the gardens," such a sum as shall from time to time be allowed by the Committee herein-after mentioned, in respect of the expenses therein mentioned of the said Society, and of carrying on the operations and concerns thereof, is, in the first place, to be retained by the said Society; secondly, there is to be then retained by the said Society out of such receipts, the amount which may be from time to time payable by the said Society, in respect of interest not exceeding 5*l*. per cent. on the sum of 40,000*l*., to be borrowed on debentures as aforesaid, or on so much of the said sum of 40,000*l*. as may remain unpaid or undischarged; and, thirdly, there is then to be paid by the said Society to the Commissioners as rent, the yearly sum of 2,145*l*., if the receipts shall be adequate for such payment, after retaining to the said Society the sums authorised to be retained by them as therein mentioned, for the expenses and for the interest respectively aforesaid, but otherwise such a sum only as shall be equal from year to year to the residue of the receipts over and above the sums so in precedence; and if there shall remain any surplus over and above the several payments herein-before mentioned, out of the "receipts from the gardens," there is to be paid to the Commissioners for their own use, and as additional yearly rent, a sum equal to half such surplus; and further, that by the said Articles of Agreement it is provided or stipulated that for the purpose of regulating the amount to be retained by the said Society in each year for expenses, a Committee shall be appointed annually, which Committee is to consist of six persons, three of whom are to be appointed by the Commissioners and three by the said Society, and any three of such Committee are to form a quorum, so as one at least shall be a person appointed by the Commissioners, and one shall be a person appointed by the said Society; and as vacancies occur in each year by death, incapacity, or resignation, such vacancies are to be filled up respectively by the Commissioners or the said Society, according as the original appointments were made by them respectively; and further, that the Committee is from time to time

to select one of those Committee-men who have been appointed by the
Commissioners as Chairman of such Committee, and he is to have an
equal vote with the other Committee-men for the time being acting, and
in case of equality a casting vote in addition ; and the Committee is to
have power to make bye-laws for their own government in the execution
of the duties confided to them ; and that it is also thereby provided or
stipulated that the said Society shall devote and apply towards the
liquidation of the debt of 40,000*l.*, to be raised by debentures as aforesaid, three-fifths of the money actually received by them from time to
time, in respect of the "receipts from the gardens," after the retentions
and payments aforesaid, from and out of the "receipts from the gardens,"
for expenses and interest by the said Society and the rent to the Commissioners, and divers other agreements or stipulations for carrying into
effect, or consequent on, or relating to the said arrangement are contained
in the said Articles of Agreement.

3. And whereas it is further represented to Us that by a supplemental
Agreement dated the 20th day of November in the year 1860, and made
and entered into in like manner between the said Commissioners of the
one part, and the said Society of the other part (in which the said piece
of land is referred to as "the gardens "), an arrangement has been made
between the said parties for the occupation by the said Society of some
additional land of the Commissioners shown on the plan annexed to
such supplemental Agreement by a red colour adjoining or near "the
gardens " (which additional land the Commissioners had for the reason
therein mentioned declined to include in the lease to be granted under
the first-mentioned Agreement), and for an access to "the gardens" by
means of a lane or path shown on the same plan, marked with the colour
"brown," and by the said supplemental Agreement the interest of the
said Society in or with respect to the said additional land, and the right
of the said Society with respect to such access, with the duties and
rights of the said Society concerning the said additional land and access
respectively are defined (the rent payable by the said Society in respect
thereof being the nominal rent of 1*s.*), and power is reserved to the
Commissioners at any time to resume possession of such additional land,
and also upon providing another road as therein mentioned, to stop up
or take away the said road by or over which there is such access as
aforesaid afforded to "the gardens."

4. And whereas it is further represented to Us that by further Articles
of Agreement, dated the 1st day of March, in the year 1861, made and
entered into in like manner between the said Commissioners of the one
part, and the said Society of the other part ; after reciting the aforesaid
Articles of Agreement of the 24th day of July 1860, and setting forth
divers of the clauses or provisions contained in the same Articles, and
reciting that the said Society and the Commissioners are each desirous

of respectively having the right of increasing the outlay by them respectively undertaken to be made by the said therein recited Agreement, to any amount not exceeding as to each of them the sum of 10,000*l.* over and above the respective sums of 50,000*l.* by them respectively undertaken to be laid out as aforesaid, and of acquiring such rights and privileges as in the said further Agreement now in recital appear in respect of such additional outlay if made, it is thereby mutually agreed between the Commissioners and the said Society (amongst other things) that the said Society may at any time before the 1st day of January 1864 borrow, or take up on their debentures or other securities, any sum or sums of money not exceeding in the whole the sum of 10,000*l.* in addition to the sum of 40,000*l.* in the said therein recited Agreement mentioned as having been borrowed, or for the borrowing of which arrangements had been made, and may within the like period lay out and expend the sum or sums so borrowed in addition to the original sum of 50,000*l.* therein mentioned of the said Society, in and about such works and things as are in the clause in the said Agreement now in recital referred to as the 1st clause of the said therein recited Agreement (being the clause secondly mentioned in the recital herein-before contained of such Agreement) undertaken to be done by them, and in and about which such original sum of 50,000*l.* is required by that clause to be expended, and that the Commissioners may at any time before the 1st day of January 1864 lay out and expend such sum or sums of money as they may think fit, not exceeding in the whole the sum of 10,000*l.*, in addition to the original sum of 50,000*l.* in the clause in the said Agreement now in recital referred to as clause 2 of the said therein recited Agreement (being the clause thirdly mentioned in the recital herein-before contained of such Agreement) mentioned in and about such works, matters, and things as by that clause are undertaken to be done by them, and in and about which the same sum of 50,000*l.* is required by that clause to be expended by them, and further that in case both or either of the parties thereto should think fit to make any such outlay, such parties respectively or party shall have no claim or demand against the other of them or against the gardens, or against the receipts from the gardens, save and except as herein-after mentioned ; *videlicet*, that with a view to compensate such parties respectively, or party in some degree for such additional outlay, the following alterations should be made in the said therein recited Agreement and in the lease to be granted pursuant thereto, *videlicet*, the 14th clause (which provides for the application and disposition of "the receipts from the gardens," as hereinbefore mentioned), shall be altered and amended as follows, viz :—Out of the gross amount of the receipts from the gardens there shall be first retained by the said Society such a sum as shall from time to time be allowed by the Expenses Committee, mentioned in the therein and

APPENDIX G.

said first herein-recited Agreement in respect of the expenses mentioned in the said Agreement now in recital, being the same expenses as in the said therein and first herein-recited Agreement are directed to be first retained by the said Society from and out of "the receipts from the gardens." 2ndly. There shall be then retained by the said Society out of such receipts the amount which may be from time to time payable by the said Society in respect of interest not exceeding 5l. per cent. per annum, on the sum of 40,000l. originally borrowed or agreed to be borrowed by them on debentures as aforesaid and on any further sum or sums they may borrow and expend in accordance with clause 1 of the Agreement now in recital, not exceeding 10,000l., or on so much of the original and additional sums as for the time being may have been raised and shall not have been paid off; and, 3rdly, there shall then be paid by the said Society to the said Commissioners, as rent, the yearly sum or sums therein and herein-after in that behalf mentioned, if the receipts shall be adequate for such payment, after retaining to the said Society the sums authorized to be retained by them under the first and second heads of the present clause, but otherwise such a sum only as shall be equal from year to year to the residue of the receipts over and above the sums so in precedence, *videlicet*, if the Commissioners shall limit their outlay under clause 2 of the said therein and first herein-recited Agreement to 50,000l., then the yearly sum of 2,145l., only, but if under clause 2 of the Agreement now in recital they shall expend a larger sum, then an addition shall be made to such rent at the rate of 4l. 5s. for every additional 100l. which the Commissioners shall think fit to expend in accordance with that clause, not exceeding 10,000l. in the whole. And if there shall remain any surplus over and above the said several payments therein-before directed to be made or retained out of the "receipts from the gardens," there shall be paid to the Commissioners for their own use, and as additional rent, yearly (whether or not they make any additional outlay), a sum equal to half such surplus, and that it is by the said Agreement now in recital also provided (*inter alia*) that the clause (therein referred to as the 17th clause) of the said therein and first herein recited Agreement relating to the application of the three-fifth shares of the said Society towards the liquidation of the said debenture debt of 40,000l. shall be altered as follows; *videlicet*, the said Society shall devote and apply towards the liquidation of their debenture debt (whether it amount to the original sum of 40,000l. only, or any increased amount under the authority of clause 1 of the Agreement now in recital,) three-fifths of the money actually received by them from time to time in respect of the "receipts from the gardens," after the payments directed to be retained out of the said receipts for expenses and interest by the said Society and the rent to the Commissioners, and that certain alterations consequential on

APPENDIX G. 139

the execution of the said Agreement now in recital are thereby made in the other agreements or stipulations contained in the said therein and first herein recited Agreement and herein-before mentioned or referred to.

5. And whereas it is further represented to Us that in consequence of the arrangement and the several Articles of Agreement respectively aforesaid, and in order that the same and the objects thereof may, so far as regards the said Society, be fully carried into effect, it is necessary or expedient that the constitution of the said Society should be in some respects altered, and that the powers of the said Society should be enlarged, and it is also represented to Us that the usefulness of the said Society would be increased thereby, and that the said Society hath consented thereto. Therefore We have been besought to grant unto the persons now composing the Horticultural Society of London, and such other persons as shall be approved of and elected as herein-after mentioned, Our Royal Charter of Incorporation for the purposes aforesaid, and with and under such powers and directions as herein-after mentioned, and it is Our will and pleasure that such Society shall henceforth be called "The Royal Horticultural Society." *The necessity for, and objects of, the New Charter.*

6. Now know ye, that We, being desirous of promoting the objects of the said Society, and of increasing the usefulness thereof, have, of Our especial grace, certain knowledge, and mere motion, given and granted, and We do hereby give and grant, that Our right trusty and well-beloved Henry John, Earl Ducie, Fellow of the Royal Society, Charles Richard, Lord Bishop of Winchester, Prelate of the Most Noble Order of the Garter, John Jackson Blandy, John Clutton, Charles Wentworth Dilke the younger, Charles Edmonds, Septimus Holmes Godson, Henry Thomas Hope, John Lee, Henry Pownall, James Veitch the younger and Robert Wrench, (being respectively some of the persons now composing the Horticultural Society of London,) and all other persons now (with the persons respectively herein-before named), being fellows or members of the said Society, and such others as from time to time shall be appointed and elected in the manner herein-before directed, and their successors, be and shall for ever hereafter continue and be, by virtue of these presents, one body politic and corporate, by the name of "The Royal Horticultural Society;" and them and their successors for the purposes for which the Horticultural Society of London was incorporated by the same Letters Patent, and with and subject to such additions and modifications to or in the same purposes as appear in and by or flow from or are consequent on the said arrangement between the said Commissioners and the said Society, and the said Articles of Agreement of the 24th day of July 1860, and of the 20th day of November 1860, and of the 1st day of March 1861 respectively, We do hereby constitute and declare to be one body politic and corporate, and by the same name *Incorporation of the Members of the present Society, and all Members to be appointed and elected as herein-after mentioned, in confirmation of the existing Society.* *Corporate Name.*

140   APPENDIX G.

Power to hold goods and lands now belonging to the Society, and to purchase and hold other goods and lands.

to have perpetual succession, and for ever hereafter to be persons able and capable in the law, and to have power to hold and to purchase, receive and possess the goods and chattels already vested in or belonging to the Horticultural Society incorporated by the recited Letters Patent, and any other goods and chattels whatsoever, and (notwithstanding the Statutes of Mortmain) to hold and to purchase, hold, and enjoy, to them and their successors, any lands, tenements, and hereditaments whatsoever, including as well the lands, tenements, and hereditaments now vested in or belonging to the said Society, or agreed to be leased to them as herein-before recited, as all other lands, tenements, and hereditaments wheresoever situate, such other lands, tenements, and hereditaments not exceeding in the whole the annual value of 5,000*l*. without incurring the penalties or forfeitures of the Statutes of Mortmain

To sue and be sued.

or any of them, and by the name aforesaid to sue and be sued, plead and be impleaded, answer and be answered unto, defend and be defended in all courts and places whatsoever of Us, Our heirs and successors, in all actions, suits, causes, and things whatsoever, and to act and do in all things relating to the said corporation in as ample manner and form as any other Our liege subjects, being persons able and capable in the law, or any other body politic or corporate in Our said United Kingdom of Great Britain and Ireland, may or can act and do, and also to have and

To use a Common Seal.

to use a Common Seal, and the same to change and alter from time to time as they shall think fit.

Fellows.

7. And We do hereby declare and grant that the several persons who respectively now are as aforesaid Members or Fellows of the first-mentioned Society, shall be or continue Members or Fellows, and shall be and continue subject and liable to all such duties and obligations as they are now subject or liable to as Members or Fellows of the first-mentioned Society, and that all such persons as shall be appointed and elected as herein-after mentioned shall likewise become or be Fellows or Members of the Society hereby incorporated, which is hereafter referred to as "the Society."

Council and officers.

8. And We do further declare and grant, that for the better rule and government of "the Society," and for the better direction, management, and execution of the business and concerns thereof, there shall be henceforth such bodies and officers as are respectively herein after mentioned; that is to say, there shall be for ever a Council, one President, a Treasurer, and a Secretary of "the Society" appointed, and to be elected in manner herein-after mentioned, and with reference to the said Articles of Agreement, dated the 24th day of July 1860, between the Commissioners and "the said Society," and so long as "the Society" shall hold and use or enjoy as aforesaid the said land mentioned in the same Articles of Agreement of the Commissioners at Kensington Gore in pursuance of the said arrangement, there shall be a Committee for

regulating the amount to be retained by "the Society" in each year from "the receipts from the gardens" for expenses. The said Council shall consist of 15 Members appointed and to be elected as herein-after mentioned, whereof any five shall be a quorum. The said Committee shall be appointed as herein-after mentioned. And We do hereby nominate and appoint or confirm Our well-beloved Consort His Royal Highness Prince Albert, K.G., the said Earl Ducie, the said Bishop of Winchester, the said John Jackson Blandy, the said John Clutton, the said Charles Wentworth Dilke the younger, the said Charles Edmonds, the said Septimus Holmes Godson, the said Henry Thomas Hope, the said John Lee, John Lindley, F.R.S., the said Henry Pownall, William Wilson Saunders, F.R.S., the said James Veitch the younger, and the said Robert Wrench (who constitute the present Council of "the Society,") the Council. And We do hereby further nominate and appoint or confirm His Royal Highness the Prince Consort (now being President) the President, the said William Wilson Saunders (now being the Treasurer) the Treasurer, and the said John Lindley (now being the Secretary) the Secretary, of "the Society," (all and each of the aforesaid Councillors and officers to continue in such their respective offices until the second Tuesday in the month of February 1862; and as regards such of the said Councillors as shall not be balloted out from time to time as herein-after mentioned, they shall continue in office until so balloted out). And We do also hereby nominate and appoint and confirm the said Earl Ducie, Bishop of Winchester, John Jackson Blandy, and Charles Wentworth Dilke (being the present four Vice-Presidents) to be the Vice-Presidents of "the Society," until some other persons shall be chosen in their respective rooms in the manner herein-after mentioned. *The Council.* *The Expenses Committee under the arrangement between the Commissioners and the Society.* *Nomination of First Council.* *President. Treasurer. Secretary.* *Vice-Presidents.*

9. And with respect to the said Committee to be appointed for regulating the amount to be retained by "the Society" for the expenses aforesaid from the "receipts from the gardens," We do hereby further declare and grant that such Committee shall consist of six persons, three of whom shall be appointed by the Commissioners and three by the Council of "the Society," as herein-after mentioned, and any three of such Committee shall form a quorum, so as one at least shall be a person appointed by the Commissioners, and one appointed by "the Society." As vacancies occur in each year by death, incapacity, or resignation, such vacancies may be filled respectively by the Commissioners and "the Society" respectively, according as the original appointments were made by them respectively. The Committee shall from time to time select one of those Committee-men who have been appointed by the Commissioners as Chairman of such Committee; which Chairman shall have the power of voting on all occasions equally with the other Committee-men for the time being acting; and such Chairman, in case of equality, shall have a casting vote in addition, and *The Constitution and mode of appointing the Expenses Committee.*

the said Committee shall have power to make bye-laws for their own government in the execution of the duties confided to them."

Annual removal of Members of Council and appointment of other officers.

10. And it is Our will and pleasure also, that the Fellows of "the Society," or any 11 or more of them, shall and may, on the second Tuesday in the month of February in the year 1862, and on the second Tuesday in the month of February in every succeeding year, assemble together at the then last or other usual place of meeting of "the Society," or some other convenient place (which meeting shall be called "the Annual Meeting,") and that at each and every such meeting the Fellows then present shall proceed by method of ballot to put out and remove some three of the Members of the Council of the preceding year, and shall and may, by method of ballot, elect three other discreet persons from amongst the Fellows of "the Society," to supply the places of such three as shall have been so put out and removed (so that one-fifth of the Council shall be yearly removed and renewed by ballot as aforesaid). And it is Our will and pleasure also, that at each and every annual meeting the fellows then present shall and may, in manner aforesaid, elect from among the Members of the Council for the year next ensuing, the President, Treasurer, and Secretary of "the Society" for such ensuing year (each of such offices to be filled by a distinct person,) and also elect, as well in the first instance as annually from time to time afterwards from the members of "the Society," three persons, to form (with the three Committee-men appointed or to be appointed by the Commissioners,) the Expenses Committee aforesaid for the year ensuing; and in case of the death or incapacity from any cause whatever of any of the Members of the Council, or of the President, Treasurer, or Secretary for the time being, or of any of "the Society's" Committee-men aforesaid, either before the first of the annual meetings aforesaid or between any two of such annual meetings, the said Council shall and may nominate or appoint some other discreet person or persons, being a Fellow or Fellows of "the Society," to supply the place or places of the Member or Members of Council and of the President, Treasurer, and Secretary respectively, and of the Committee-man or Committee-men respectively, or any or either of them respectively, so dying or becoming incapable, until the annual meeting next following such nomination or appointment; and such Member or Members of Council, President, Treasurer, and Secretary, and Committee-men or Committee-man respectively so nominated or appointed as aforesaid, shall until and on such next annual meeting be deemed to stand respectively for all purposes in the place of the person or persons respectively, or officers repectively, in or to whose place they respectively shall have been so nominated or appointed or should have succeeded; and further, as regards any Member or Members of Council dying or becoming incapable before the first annual meeting aforesaid, or in the interval between any two such

annual meetings as aforesaid, and whose place or places shall not be supplied by the said Council as aforesaid, the place or places of such Member or Members of Council shall at the first or next annual meeting after the vacancy be supplied from the Fellows of "the Society," by ballot as aforesaid, and in such case the number of Fellows to be balloted out at such meeting shall be proportionately reduced, it being Our will and pleasure that the vacancy or vacancies, by reason of death or incapacity, not supplied by the Council, and actually existing at the time of any annual meeting, shall be treated and supplied as and in lieu of a vacancy by ballot. And it is also Our will and pleasure that any such annual meeting as aforesaid may accept the resignation of, or for incapacity remove, any one or more of the Members of the Council for the time being, and elect in manner aforesaid any person or persons from among the Fellows in the place or places of the Members so retiring or being removed, in addition to the Member or Members which the Fellows present at such meeting are herein-before authorized to elect. And further, that it shall be lawful for any such annual meeting to resolve that the Secretary of "the Society" shall be a paid officer, and, accordingly, that such salary or compensation shall be paid to him as shall be determined by the said meeting, but in such case the Secretary shall be incapable of being a Member of the Council, and such meeting shall in manner aforesaid thereupon appoint a Member of Council in his place. And it shall also be lawful for any such annual meeting to resolve that the three Members appointed by the Society to form part of the Committee for regulating the amounts to be retained by the said Society for the expenses aforesaid shall be paid, and accordingly that such salary or compensation shall be paid to them as shall be determined by the said meeting, but in such case the said Members of such Committee shall be incapable of being Members of the Council, and such meeting shall in manner aforesaid thereupon appoint Members of Council in their place.

11. And it is Our further will and pleasure, that so soon after the elections aforesaid as conveniently may be, the person who shall at any time hereafter be elected to be President of the said Society in manner aforesaid may and shall nominate and appoint four persons being Members of the said Council to be Vice-Presidents of "the Society" for the year ensuing. *Annual appointment of Vice-Presidents by the President.*

12. And it is Our further will and pleasure, that the three persons who shall be appointed by the Commissioners Members of the Expenses Committee shall be appointed simultaneously with or immediately before or after the appointment of the Members of the said Committee who shall be appointed by the Council, and that notice thereof shall be given by the Commissioners to "the Society" at the time of or immediately after the said appointment by "the Society," and that such Committee shall continue for the year ensuing; nevertheless, on the death or inca- *Appointment of the Commissioners' three Members of the Expenses Committee.*

pacity of any or either of the Committee-men appointed by the Commissioners before the expiration of their or his year of office, the place of such deceased or incapable Committee-man respectively, or Committee-man, may be forthwith supplied by the Commissioners, and the person or persons so appointed shall continue in office until the time at which the deceased or incapable Committee-man would have vacated his office, if living.

Elections and removal of Members.

13. And We do further declare and grant, that on, or at any time and from time to time after, the said second Tuesday in February 1862, the Fellows of " the Society," or any seven or more of them, shall and may have power at the general meetings of " the Society," to be held at the usual place of meeting of the Society, or at such other place as shall have been in that behalf appointed by open voting (unless five or more Fellows then present shall in writing require a ballot, and in such case by method of ballot,) to elect such persons to be Fellows, Honorary Members, and Foreign Members of " the Society " as they shall think fit, and any of the Fellows, Honorary Members, and Foreign Members for the time being to remove from " the Society," the majority of the Fellows voting, in case of open voting, to bind the minority ; in case of equality the Chairman to have a second or casting vote, but in case of a ballot no Fellow, Honorary Member, or Foreign Member shall be declared elected or removed, unless by a majority of two-thirds of the Fellows voting at such ballot. In case of a ballot scrutineers to be appointed, and the ballot to be taken at an adjourned meeting, in the like manner as is herein-after mentioned in the 16th and 17th clauses; and further that all such persons as shall be elected Fellows or Members of " the Society " (other than Honorary and Foreign Members) shall, at the time of their election, or before they shall be entitled to enjoy the rights or privileges of members, sign a note or memorandum in writing, binding them to observe, perform, and abide by all the rules, laws, and regulations of " the Society," and that such note or memorandum shall constitute an agreement to the effect thereof with " the Society," and shall or may be enforced by " the Society ;" and provided also that if any Member should refuse or neglect to pay his first or any annual subscription for the space of six calendar months next after the same shall, according to the rules or regulations of " the Society," become due or payable, or shall neglect or fail in the observance or performance of the same rules or regulations in anywise, then such nonpayment, neglect, or failure may be treated at any general meeting of the Fellows of " the Society " as a forfeiture by the Fellow so making default as aforesaid of his rights and privileges as a Fellow or Member of " the Society," and in case of any resolution to that effect by the Fellows of " the Society " at a general meeting, every Fellow making such default shall by such default be deemed to have ceased to be a Fellow or Member, but without prejudice to the rights of " the Society " as regards the recovery of the

APPENDIX G.

arrears for the time being of the subscription of such Fellow or Member, it being hereby declared that such Fellow or Member shall continue liable to the payment of all such arrears.

14. And it is Our further will and pleasure, and We do further declare and grant, that "the Society" shall or may carry into effect the said arrangement between the said Commissioners and the first-mentioned Society, and that the Council of "the Society" shall or may do, perform, and execute such acts and things as shall or may be necessary or fit or expedient for that purpose, and generally for carrying into effect and performing on the part of "the Society" the said several Articles of Agreement, dated the 24th day of July 1860, and the 20th day of November 1860, and the 1st day of March 1861, respectively entered into between the said Commissioners and the first-mentioned Society, and in particular shall or may proceed to raise the said sum of 40,000l., which by the first-mentioned Articles of Agreement is mentioned to be intended or to be then about to be raised by debentures, or such part or parts thereof as has not now already been or for the time being shall not have been raised, and also when and as the said Council shall think fit, the said further sum of 10,000l., which by the said Articles of Agreement of the 1st day of March 1861 the said Council are to have liberty to borrow, or any part or parts thereof, and shall or may from time to time raise again or re-borrow any part or parts or sum or sums of money, in respect of any money which shall at any time or from time to time be paid off or discharged, of or in respect of the said sums of 40,000l. and 10,000l., or any part thereof respectively, and shall or may for the purposes aforesaid, or any of them, or by way of security to the lenders, issue and deliver such debentures or other securities on behalf of or upon the property of "the Society" as the Council shall think fit, and without incurring any personal responsibility on account or in respect of the moneys now already raised or so to be raised or borrowed or raised again or re-borrowed, or by virtue of or under such debentures or securities, or in anywise howsoever in respect thereof, or of the matters aforesaid, or any of them; and We do hereby declare and grant that neither the Council of "the Society" nor any persons acting for or on behalf of "the Society" in the matter of the arrangement and the several Articles of Agreement, shall be personally responsible on account or in consequence thereof, in anywise howsoever, and that they shall be respectively indemnified by or from the funds or property of "the Society" against all losses, costs, damages, and expenses, by reason or in consequence of the said arrangement, or the execution of the said Articles of Agreement or in relation thereto.

The arrangement between the Commissioners and the Society to be carried into effect.

The Council to borrow the 40,000l. and 10,000l., and to have power to re-borrow any money in respect of any part thereof paid off.

The Council indemnified from liability on account of entering into the said arrangement with the Commissioners.

15. And We do further declare and grant that the Council for the time being of "the Society," or any five or more of them (all the members thereof having been first duly summoned to attend the meetings thereof), shall and may have power, according to the best of their judgment and

The Council empowered to make byelaws.

K

discretion, to make and establish such byelaws as they shall deem useful and necessary for the regulation of "the Society," and of the estate, goods, and business thereof, and for carrying into effect, on behalf of "the Society," the said arrangement between the Commissioners and the first-mentioned Society, and the said several Articles of Agreement and the affairs in general of "the Society," and all matters or things in anywise relating thereto, and such byelaws from time to time to vary, alter, or revoke and make such new and other byelaws as they shall think fit, most useful, and expedient, so that the same be not repugnant to these presents or the laws of this Our realm. And further that the present existing byelaws of the said Society shall continue in force in their integrity, and shall be binding upon the Society hereby incorporated and the Members thereof, except and in so far as they shall be repealed or altered by any byelaw hereafter to be made by the Society.

Byelaws to be confirmed at a General Meeting of Fellows.

16. Provided that no byelaw hereafter to be made or alteration or repeal of any byelaw which shall hereafter have been established by the said Council hereby appointed, or by the Council for the time being of "the Society," shall be considered to have passed and be binding on "the Society" until such byelaw, or such alteration or repeal of any byelaw, shall have been adopted or confirmed at some general meeting of the Fellows at large of "the Society," either with or subject to any additions or amendments to or in the same which shall be resolved upon or adopted by such meeting (it being competent for any Fellow present

Amendments may be made at the meeting in byelaws proposed by the Council. Voting may be open or by ballot, if required by five Fellows present.

at such meeting to propose or move any such addition or amendment) or in its integrity. The votes upon such byelaws or any of them or the alteration or repeal in or of any such byelaws or byelaw, or upon any motion or resolution relating thereto, to be by open voting, unless any five Fellows present shall object to open voting, and shall require, by notice in writing to that effect signed by them and delivered to the Chairman, the voting to be by ballot. In the case of open voting, the majority shall bind the minority, the Chairman may vote, and in case of equality may give a second or casting vote; and provided that in the case of a ballot (but not in the case of open voting) no byelaw or alteration or repeal of any byelaw shall be deemed or taken to pass in the affirmative, unless it shall appear that two-thirds of the Fellows voting shall have voted for the same. In every case of voting by ballot two scrutineers shall be at once appointed by the Chairman, the Fellows present may proceed forthwith to vote, and the meeting shall be adjourned to some day, not being less than five days nor more than ten days from the original meeting, for taking or continuing such ballot, of which adjourned meeting, and of the object thereof, notice shall be given in some newspaper circulating in London two days at least before the day of such adjourned meeting.

Annual meeting shall be deemed a general one.

17. And, lastly, every annual meeting shall be deemed a general meeting, and the Council may call at any time and from time to time

any other general meeting of the Fellows of the Society. In case of a ballot under the 13th and 16th clauses respectively, the ballot shall be taken at an adjourned meeting on some day to be appointed at the general meeting at which the same shall be required within ten days next after such general meeting between the hours of twelve o'clock at noon and three in the afternoon.

Witness Ourself at Our Palace at Westminster this 30th day of April, in the 24th year of Our reign.

APPENDIX H.

EVIDENCE given by the SECRETARY to HER MAJESTY'S COMMISSIONERS before the SELECT COMMITTEE of the HOUSE of COMMONS, on the BRITISH MUSEUM, 1860.

3312. Sir *George Grey.*] Are you Secretary to the Royal Commissioners for the Exhibition of 1851?—Yes.

3313. Are you well acquainted with the land belonging to those Commissioners in the neighbourhood of Kensington?—Perfectly.

3314. Have you a plan of that land?—Yes; I have brought it here to hand in to the Committee (*the same being handed in*). This is the same plan as that which has already been laid before Parliament by the Commissioners in one of their Reports, and it has also been made use of in another Report of the National Gallery Site Commissioners.

3315. Of what number of acres does the whole of that land consist; how much of it has been appropriated, either permanently or temporarily; and how much of it now remains, and in what position, that is unappropriated?—The total extent of the land originally purchased by the Commissioners was about 86 acres; of that amount 12 acres have been taken by the Government for the Department of Science and Art.

3316. When you say taken by the Government for the Department of Science and Art, have those 12 acres been permanently appropriated to that object?—Yes; pursuant to clause 2 of the Act 21 & 22 Vict. c. 36. By an agreement with the Horticultural Society, $22\frac{1}{4}$ acres, in the centre of the main square of the estate, are leased to the Horticultural Society; and a space of about $16\frac{1}{2}$ acres, to the south of that land, is proposed by the Commissioners to be lent to the Society of Arts, for the purposes of an Exhibition in 1862; and they have made a proposal which, if carried into effect, will have the effect of reserving that land till the year 1872, that is, for a further period of 10 years after the Exhibition of 1862; and, therefore, for the moment, that must be considered as appropriated. I think that about 12 acres have been devoted to roads; there are eight or nine acres in outlying pieces of land, which are all shown on the plan I have handed in, and which have been let for building purposes, leaving a space, in round numbers, of between 14 and 15 acres in the main square, which are at present unappropriated.

3317. Do those 14 or 15 acres lie together, or are they separate portions of the ground; or will you point out on the plan where those unappropriated acres are situated (*the witness pointed out the same to the Committee*)?—The unappropriated land lies partly on the east side of the estate, partly on the west side, and partly on the north, fronting the Kensington-road.

3318. Are those parts co-terminous, or are they distinct and separate?—The west and northern parts may be considered co-terminous; between the north and the east parts a small property of two acres, belonging to Lord Auckland, called Eden Lodge, intervenes.

3319. What is the area of those respective lots of land?—I have laid out on this plan the exact extent of each piece of land in square feet.

3320. Will you mark upon that plan the portions of land which are now unappropriated?—They are already marked, and include all the space on the main square lying to the east, west, and north of the arcades inclosing the Horticultural Gardens.

3321. What is the acreage of those separate portions of land, take the east side to begin with?—On the east side there is, first of all, over the entrance to the Horticultural Gardens, a space which is retained by the Commissioners; only a small space, however, is available there for the purposes of building. To the north of the entrance to the gardens, on the east side, there are about 141,000 square feet in a solid block, representing about three acres and a quarter. Then there is a narrow strip higher up, to the east of Lord Auckland's, which contains about 12,000 square feet. On the west side you have 10,500 square feet, or a quarter of an acre, over the entrance to the gardens, available for public buildings; and about 250,000 square feet in round numbers, or about six acres, to the north of that again. The total acreage in round numbers, running up from the Horticultural entrance on the west side to the Kensington-road, is about six acres and a half. The remaining space, containing five or six acres, has its frontage to the Kensington-road.

3322. Has any communication been made to the Commissioners by the Trustees of the British Museum, respecting the acquisition of that land, or any part of it, for the reception of portions of the collections in the Museum?—None whatever. The only information possessed by the Commissioners on the subject is derived from the Parliamentary Paper which I hold in my hand, and which came to them in the usual way, after publication.

3323. Do you refer to the Parliamentary Paper ordered by the House of Commons to be printed on the 15th February 1860, No. 87?—Yes.

3324. Have you read the report contained in page 11 of that Paper, from a Special Committee of the Trustees of the British Museum?—Yes.

APPENDIX H.

3325. Has your attention been called to the supposed value of the land in the statement of which you have now been speaking?—I have noticed that statement, and, on seeing it, I felt it my duty to bring the Paper under the notice of the Commissioners.

3326. I need not ask you then whether that Report was made, so far as that paragraph is concerned, by any authority derived from the Commissioners?—The statement in that Paper as to the average cost of the land is unauthorized by the Commissioners.

3327. Can you state what the cost price of that land was?—The statement there much understates the cost of the land when it puts it at 5,000*l.* an acre.

3328. Would the Commissioners be disposed, if they were requested, to dispose of that land which is now unappropriated, for the purposes of the British Museum, or any part of its collections?—The position which the Commissioners hold is this; they are quite ready, when the public desire it, to receive proposals for devoting the unappropriated part of their estate to public purposes, and to entertain favourably such proposals; but they themselves have no proposals to make, and they have never originated any, for the occupation of this land, beyond indicating generally, when they first announced to the Crown their purchase of the estate, the manner in which it might be laid out.

3329. What is the marketable value of the unappropriated portion of that land?—I should be understating it when I put it at 20,000*l.* an acre.

3330. That is the price which might now be obtained in the market for it, by the Commissioners?—Certainly; it is not a merely theoretical assumption, but we have actually disposed of a piece of land exactly opposite, of about two acres and a half, on lease, for a sum which represents that amount per acre.

3331. Have the Commissioners hypothetically entertained the question of selling any part of it for any public object; and if so, have they fixed any price for that land, supposing it to be appropriated to a public object?—In consequence of having brought under their notice this Parliamentary Paper, No. 87, they thought it very probable that some questions would arise out of it; and therefore they deemed it right to take into consideration the question as to what price they would be prepared to take for this land, if applications were made to them on the subject.

3332. At what decision did they arrive?—The decision which the Commissioners arrived at as to the price they would dispose of it, for the public object in question was, that the price to be asked should be 10,000*l.* an acre, and 5,000*l.* per acre for that portion where the necessity of arching over the ground, under the agreement with the Horticultural Society, would leave no ground-floor space available.

3333. What portion of it would be sold at 10,000*l.* per acre, and what portion at 5,000*l.* per acre?—The greater part of it would be sold at

10,000*l*. per acre; and the part that would be sold at 5,000*l*. an acre seems to be about a quarter of an acre.

3334. Mr. *Ayrton.*] Those parts marked "entrance"?—It is the part on the west side, over the entrance to the Horticultural Society, and on the east side at the same rate. I should state that a part of the land on the north side, fronting the Kensington-road, is occupied by houses held under leases, which would have to be bought up, to render the whole frontage to that road immediately available for public buildings, and the Commissioners have not yet considered that question.

3335. Sir *George Grey.*] Mr. Cole stated that the 12 acres which are now appropriated, in the South Kensington Museum, to the Department of Science and Art, were bought at 5,000*l*. an acre; are you aware that that was so?—The Commissioners and the Government formerly held the estate in joint partnership; and when it was resolved to dissolve that partnership, under the powers of the Act of 1858, the Government preferred to take part of their share in money, and part in land. They wished to retain the 12 acres referred to by you, at their cost price, and to receive the balance of their advances in cash in pursuance of the provisions of the Act. Now, as respects the question of cost price of the land, I need not say that, in a case of dissolving partnership, where two partners originally advanced an equal share of capital, which has been lying unproductive during the partnership, and where it is stipulated that the retiring partner is to receive back his original capital only, the sum to be repaid him by his partner is very different from the sum which any third person would have to pay him in purchase of his interest in the capital of the concern. No question arises, for example, as to interest between partners, in the case I have put, whereas with any third party the question of interest on capital arises. In the second place, those 12 acres which the Government took, very much resembled in their general character, the whole of the estate; they consisted of a certain amount of frontage, but the greater part of the 12 acres is back ground; the same is the case with the Commissioners' estate, taken as a whole, and the cost price per acre of these 12 acres may fairly be taken as the same as that of the whole property. But on the other hand, this piece of land which the Commissioners can dispose of for the purposes of the British Museum, consists entirely of frontage, and not only that, but double frontage, to a very broad road on one side, and to the Horticultural Gardens on the other; that frontage, therefore is infinitely more valuable than the back ground. The statement of the cost price per acre of the whole, when applied to the mere frontage, is entirely deceptive; in the case of the Government 12 acres, it was frontage and back ground mixed up equally; in this case it is all frontage.

3336. Mr. *Ayrton.*] You have stated that some part of this ground has been ascertained to be worth 20,000*l*. per acre by experiment, what part of it was that?—It is the plot on the west side of Prince Albert's-road, and to the south of Gore-road; that is let on lease for 99 years to Mr. Whatman, late Member for West Kent.

3337. *Chairman.*] Is that the piece of land next to Lord Harrington's?—In front of Lord Harrington's, and next to Mr. Alexander's.

3338. Mr. *Ayrton.*] That is let at a ground rent which is equivalent in value to 20,000*l.* per acre?—Yes, as nearly as possible.

3339. Then you assume that the building frontage on the opposite side of the same road, Prince Albert's-road, would be of the same value?—To avoid any risk of overstating its value, I have only assumed it to be of the same value; I have the authority of our surveyor for the figures I have given.

3340. The building frontage along the Kensington-road would be of the same value, and along the Exhibition-road?—The building value along the Kensington road would be very much greater, and along the Exhibition-road the same value as along Prince Albert's-road.

3341. What is the estimated value of that land by the test you have given the Committee of 20,000*l.* an acre?—It depends upon the extent of acreage required; and I have no data to enable me to know what extent of land is proposed to be taken for the British Museum, except what appears from this Parliamentary Paper, where five acres are spoken of.

3342. With regard to the frontage, it is one given depth of land at the price computed?—In the case of Mr. Whatman's land it was so much per foot frontage.

3343. What was the value per foot?—3*l.* per foot, with the same depth as nearly as possible, 200 feet deep.

3344. You estimate on Prince Albert's-road, and on the Exhibition-road, that the frontage with 200 feet deep would be worth 2*l.* a foot per annum?—At least 3*l.*

3345. And in the Kensington-road it would be worth something more?—I think that cannot be put at less than 4*l.* a foot.

3346. You have stated that what is called the centre of the estate would not be of so much value, because it would not have such a frontage; but supposing roads were cut through this property from Kensington to Brompton, the same as Prince Albert's-road, and Exhibition-road, the frontage would be as good, would it not, in any of those streets, as in those which now exist?—You could not make such broad streets in the centre, without cutting up the property. The great existing roads bound the estate, and you could not sacrifice the amount of space that would be required for fresh roads intersecting the estate that we have devoted to those already made by us.

3347. If you did make a road as broad, the frontage would be as valuable would it not?—I apprehend that it could not be of the same value there.

3348. What would be the difference in a road from the Kensington-road to Brompton, between the Exhibition-road and Prince Albert's-road, and those two roads?—I think no surveyor would advise the Commissioners to intersect that ground with another great road between those two roads; it would injure the property, which is laid out upon the principle of erecting buildings only round the edges of the main square, leaving the centre unbuilt upon; the same principle, in fact, as that adopted in the case of the Louvre at Paris, and in the case of the great London squares, such as Belgrave and Eaton squares.

3349. Sir *George Grey*.] Could it be done, considering the appropriation which has actually been made for the Horticultural Society, and for the purposes of the Exhibition in 1862?—No.

3350. Mr. *Ayrton*.] You have given a certain part of this estate to the Horticultural Society for 30 years?—It is on lease for 31 years, and renewable for 31 years.

3351. And without paying any rent unless they make a profit?—Precisely.

3352. Under what conditions are they to ensure their making any profit; are they under any conditions to the Commissioners?—Yes; we have an agreement with them whereby such control is retained over the property by the Commissioners as gives them reason to think that it may be a profitable arrangement.

3353. The Commissioners then claim an absolute right to give the Government this land upon any terms they please?—Certainly.

3354. Have they completed the dissolution of partnership with the Government?—They completed it in the month of January 1859.

3355. They paid the Government half the purchase money?—Yes.

3356. Which I think was repaid without interest?—Yes, but with the addition of a moiety of the rents received during the partnership.

3357. How much did they repay?—They repaid upwards of 120,000*l.* in cash, and the remaining 60,000*l.* was taken by the Government in land.

3358. And there was left to the Commissioners the rest of the land?—Yes.

3359. Did not the Commissioners then represent to the Government, and through the Government to the House of Commons, that what Government received was equal in value to what the Commissioners retained?—Not at all; the basis of the arrangement, as shown in the Act of 1858, was, that the Commissioners were to return to the Government the exact sum in pounds, shillings, and pence, which the Government had advanced; viz., 181,379*l.* 4*s.* 2*d.*, including rents received, less the value of the 12 acres retained by them for the Department of Science and Art. The very figures are stated in the Act.

3360. Without interest?—Yes.

APPENDIX H.

3361. Was not that arrangement made on the representation that what the Commissioners retained was of no more value than that which they gave to the Government?—Certainly not; the proposal of the Commissioners was to the effect that as the partnership hampered them in their free action, it was better to dissolve the partnership.

3362. If they asked the Government to take their money, without interest, was not that asked on the representation that the land which the Commissioners retained was not of more value, after paying the amount in cash, which you have mentioned, than that which the Government received?—Certainly not; there was no such understanding. The Commissioners represented that the estate had been purchased jointly by the Government and themselves, for the development of a particular scheme, but that the absence of any decision on the part of the Government for many years, as to the national institutions for which sites were to be provided on the estate, precluded the Commissioners from taking any active steps themselves towards realizing the objects of their incorporation. They therefore proposed the dissolution of partnership on terms which, under the circumstances, were considered fair and equitable on both sides, and which, moreover, subsequently received the approval of Parliament.

3363. Sir *George Grey*.] Can you state to the Committee the inducement which influenced the Commissioners in deciding to sell this land to the Government for a public object, if requested to do so, at a lower price than the market value?—The Commissioners consider the British Museum to be an important national institution; and if Parliament wished to remove any part of the collections of the British Museum to Kensington, it would be only carrying out the spirit of their original Report to give them every facility for so doing. They felt that they should not deal with the question as if it were merely a mercantile transaction.

3364. Have you formed any opinion as to the convenience of the site, and whether it is suitable, generally speaking, for a public exhibition?—I have already been examined, on two two separate occasions, upon this subject, as to the attendance of the public at various institutions, and I have quoted in evidence certain figures which seemed to show that the supposed distance of the site from the metropolis was no interference with the accessibility of those institutions to the public.

3365. Have you formed that opinion from the fact of the large number of persons who visit the Kensington Museum?—It was founded on the statistics of the number of persons who attended the different institutions established for purposes of recreation and instruction, whether in the neighbourhood of this ground or elsewhere. I gave in to the National Gallery Committee in 1853, and to the National Gallery Site Commission in 1857, a table showing for a series of years the attendance of the public at different institutions which may be called in London, and at those which are rather farther off; and the result showed conclusively that the mere distance from the heart of London is no obstacle to their accessibility.

3366. Have you had any means of ascertaining whether the persons who visit those institutions, and the visitors who come to the South Kensington Museum, are of the same class, and come from the same districts as those who visit the British Museum?—I believe that, as respects the South Kensington Museum, the great difference is, that the proportion of the working classes who go there is larger than those who go anywhere else. I have been informed by a large employer of labour, who comes much in contact with the working classes of London, that they consider the South Kensington Museum as the greatest boon that has ever been conferred upon them by Parliament and Government.

3367. Mr. *Ayrton*.] Can you give the name of the person to whom you have alluded?—I perhaps need not mention the name; I state the fact.

3368. Where does he carry on business?—He is foreman to a very large builder in the south-west end of London.

3369. Where does he carry on business?—The business is now being wound up; it was the greatest firm in London.

3370. Was it a firm that failed?—No. I have really no objection to state my authority, if the Committee desire it; it was the foreman of the late Mr. Cubitt.

3371. Mr. Cubitt being largely concerned in building in that neighbourhood?—Not at all; he had no connexion whatever with it.

3372. Was that the Mr. Cubitt who was engaged in building houses in the neighbourhood of Belgrave-square?—It was the Mr. Cubitt who died two years before the South Kensington Museum was established and who built Belgravia, but who had no connexion whatever with the neighbourhood of South Kensington.

3373. Sir *George Grey*.] Are you aware of any increased means of access that are in contemplation to that district, by which means the working classes could come to South Kensington with greater facility than they do now?—I am not aware of there being any intention to open any fresh access, the present access being so very convenient. The public leave the London streets, and cross the London parks, and soon arrive at the site.

3374. From the east of London?—Yes.

3375. Is not that a very long distance for them to walk?—Mr. Cubitt, in his evidence before the National Gallery Committee, stated it as his opinion, from his intimate knowledge of the working classes, a large number of whom were employed under him, that when working men go to visit these public institutions, they made a half-holiday of it, and they like to take their wives and children with them, and enjoy themselves in the fresh air. It is an additional attraction to them if any institution of this kind, instead of being in the heart of London, is a little way removed from it, where not only they get fresh air, but a pleasant prospect, and have the enjoyment of the parks, and so on.

3376. Mr. *Ayrton.*] According to your view, when the public go to see the objects in the Museum, it is a matter of interest to them to have a pleasant prospect out of the window?—It certainly very much adds to the enjoyment of the working classes to have these museums in a pleasant situation.

3377. Is there any pleasant prospect out of the windows at Brompton? —I do not allude in the least to South Kensington; I am talking generally.

3378. Is there any pleasant prospect out of the windows at Brompton? —There is a pretty garden at the side, but I do not allude to that at all. I may mention a case exactly in point; only yesterday evening I was in Kensington Gardens, and I saw a large party there headed by a band of their own, enjoying themselves in the gardens.

3379. They went to enjoy nature, I presume, and the scenery of the gardens?—I may perhaps be allowed to finish the sentence. On asking the man who seemed to act as conductor, who these persons were, he stated that they were connected with some institution (I did not catch the name) at Kennington; that they had taken a half-holiday to spend at the South Kensington Museum, to which they had walked in procession a distance of four miles, and they were winding up the evening by going into Kensington Gardens, which are in the immediate neighbourhood.

3380. That observation of yours would equally apply to persons visiting the Crystal Palace, would it not?—Precisely.

3381. Then, on the same theory, it would be just as possible to put the whole collection at the Crystal Palace as at the Kensington Museum, where there is a very pleasant prospect, and a considerable distance to go, which would give all the advantages which you seem to think are sought for in making a pleasant holiday?—The figures, as to the attendance of the public at the Crystal Palace, greatly exceeding a million a year, show that its distance from London does not prevent people from going there to enjoy the exhibition, and this carries out my statement that the mere distance from the heart of London, or what has been called the non-accessibility of an institution, is not such a matter as to interfere with the attendance of the public.

3382. Are you aware that Mr. Cubitt's workmen resided at Chelsea, for the most part, and largely in the neighbourhood of Westminster, where small houses are to be found?—I do not know at all where they resided.

3383. There is a considerable population of working people, is there not, in Westminster and in Chelsea?—Yes.

3384. Are you aware whether the people come more than once in the course of 12 months to visit the South Kensington Museum?—I have no personal knowledge on the point. I have been informed, however, that the police state that they are almost all new faces.

3385. Have you taken any means to ascertain at all the classes of people who visit the South Kensington Museum?—No, the Commissioners have no connexion with that Museum.

3386. Are you aware of the number of adults, as compared with the number of children, who go there?—No.

3387. Are you aware of the class of persons who go there of an afternoon, or on the Wednesday, Thursday, and Friday?—Those are the close days, when they obtain admission only on the payment of sixpence; the attendance is comparatively small on what are called students' days.

3388. Then the open admission is on Monday?—Monday, in the morning and evening; Tuesday, morning and evening; and Saturday morning.

3389. On Saturday morning what class of people go there?—I do not know.

3390. On Monday, do you know the proportion of people who visit the South Kensington Museum as compared with other days?—I believe on Monday and Tuesday there is a larger attendance, and on Monday the greatest of all.

3391. In the evening is the attendance greater than in the morning? —It is nearly equally divided, but rather greater in the morning, on the whole. I have a table here, showing in each year, from 1850 to 1859, the number of visitors to the Science and Art Department's Museum, to the British Museum, the National Gallery, the Vernon Gallery, the Zoological Gardens, Kew Gardens, and Hampton Court Palace.

3392. Sir *George Grey*.] Will you be good enough to hand it in? (*The same was handed in.*)

3393. Mr. *Ayrton*.] Are you aware of any exhibition in London with which you can make a just comparison with regard to opening the exhibition in the evening?—I am not aware that any other national exhibition is opened in the evening.

3394. Then the comparison you have made is not one that is based upon a comparison of analogous circumstances: it is merely a comparison of numbers without reference to circumstances?—It is only in the last three or four years that the South Kensington Museum has existed; my table goes back to the year 1850, and it was prepared for a Parliamentary Committee before the Museum existed, and not to show the attendance at that Museum. In the case of the other institutions mentioned in the table there is that analogy, as none of them are open in the evening.

3395. I see that there was a very large increase from 1857 to 1858; to what do you ascribe that large increase?—Up to the middle of 1857 those collections were at Marlborough House; it was not till June that they were removed to the South Kensington Museum, and therefore the increase only relates to the second half of the year; whereas, in the last two years, 1858 to 1859, there appears to have been a normal attendance of about 500,000 a year, and I understand that the same rate is maintained during the present year.

3396. The collection of paintings was removed from Marlborough House at that time, was it not?—No, they have only lately been removed.

3397. Sir *George Grey*.] What other collections do you speak of as having been removed in the middle of 1857?—The Museum of the Science and Art Department.

3398. Mr. *Ayrton*.] The Kensington Museum is in close proximity, is it not, to a large and idle population?—I am not aware of that.

3399. I mean the population of Belgravia and that neighbourhood, which is to a very large extent an unoccupied population?—Certainly my own experience of the visitors to that Museum is, that by far the larger proportion is not of that class, and that a very small proportion indeed of the 500,000 are persons belonging to the upper classes.

3400. Refreshments are supplied, I believe, at the Museum?—I believe so.

3401. Do you know whether there is any great consumption of refreshments?—I am not prepared with any evidence upon that subject.

3402. There are no refreshments supplied at any other exhibition of a national character?—I do not remember; but in the neighbourhood there are public-houses, and so on.

3403. But not in the Exhibition, or in immediate connexion with it?—No.

3404. What is the exact distance of the South Kensington Museum from the Bank of England?—I should think it is somewhere over four miles. I hold in my hand a paper which has been delivered this Session, showing the number of visitors to the National Gallery last year, and to the Vernon Gallery; and the note states: "The expected removal of the National Gallery British School to South Kensington greatly diminished the number of visitors to Marlborough House during the whole of the year 1859." That observation certainly seems inconsistent with the correctness of the assumption that the removal to Kensington renders the pictures less accessible to the public, seeing that immediately they were removed, the attendance largely increased, and that in the very next month after the removal to South Kensington, upwards of 50,000 persons visited those collections.

3405. You have not got an account of the number of persons who visit the Museum on the Mondays and Tuesday when it is free, in the morning?—I was looking just now at one of the reports of the Science and Art Department, and it states that the morning visitors are rather in excess of the evening visitors; they are nearly equally divided. I ought to state, with regard to a question that was asked by the Honourable Member for the Tower Hamlets, as to the dissolution of the partnership between the Commissioners and the Government, and any question of the increased value of the land connected therewith, that the land which the Government had taken for 60,000*l.* was then worth 90,000*l.*, clearly showing that there was no question of increased value involved in dissolving partnership, on one side or the other.

3406. What is your impression of the basis on which the money was repaid by the Commissioners, and the number of acres taken by the Government as the half of their interest in this estimate?—The Commissioners carried out precisely what the Act of Parliament ordered them to do.

3407. What is your impression of the basis on which that Act of Parliament was passed with regard to the relative value of the interest of the Government and of the Commissioners?—I am under the impression that the Government were to be repaid the exact amount of their advances, whatever they may have been.

3408. Without any reference to the value of the property?—Yes; interest would have been charged to the Commissioners, if they had delayed payment, but they made the payment in time.

3409. What is the value of the frontage on the estate you have named, in the three roads, the Prince Albert's-road, the Exhibition-road, and the Kensington-road?—About 3*l.* a foot per annum, I have assumed.

3410. The total value?—It entirely depends upon the extent of land proposed to be taken.

3411. Can you state in gross the total value?—On Prince Albert's-road there appears to be about 1,400 feet frontage; the upper portion is certainly worth more than 3*l.* a foot; I might have assumed about 4*l.* probably,—that is per foot per annum ground-rent.

3412. Sir *George Grey.*] Is the depth of that land marked on the map?—The depth is 200 feet.

3413. Mr. *Puller.*] Prince Albert's-road is 1,400 feet: can you give the length of the other roads?—There appears to be 800 or 900 feet available in Exhibition-road.

3414. There is another, is there not, the Cromwell-road?—The north frontage is in the Kensington-road, and the frontage at present available, without pulling down any houses, is about 600 feet there. If those houses were removed, 1,000 feet frontage would be obtained.

3415. Mr. *Turner.*] I suppose there is no doubt that there will be a very large profit to somebody from this purchase of the Kensington Gore Estate, as to the value of it?—If it were disposed of as a mercantile speculation, certainly. The Commissioners, however, hold it for a very different purpose. I know, referring to the centre square alone, that its present value is estimated at 800,000*l.* and upwards, for the whole of the great square.

3416. Then the Government, who went into partnership with the Commissioners, will derive no benefit whatever from that profit?—The Government have been repaid the whole of their advances.

3417. Yes, but without interest?—Yes; but they have got for 60,000*l.* a piece of land worth at the time, at least 90,000*l*, and, I should say, now worth about 100,000*l*.

3418. Mr. *Ayrton.*] But they paid for that land more than it originally cost, for the joint undertaking?—No; they did not pay more than the original cost.

3419. Did they take it at the cost price?—Yes.

3420. Mr. *Puller.*] That was above the average, was it not?—On the contrary; I have shown that the sum of 5,000*l.* per acre, stated as the average cost of the estate, is much understated.

APPENDIX to MR. BOWRING'S EVIDENCE.

STATEMENT of the Number of Visitors admitted to visit the British Museum, the National Gallery, the Vernon Gallery, the Zoological Gardens, Kew Gardens, Hampton Court Palace, and the Museum of the Department of Science and Art in each year, from 1850 to 1859 inclusive.

Years.	British Museum.	National Gallery, Trafalgar Square.	Vernon Gallery.	Zoological Gardens.	Kew Gardens.	Hampton Court Palace.	Science and Art Department Museum.
	No.	No.	No.	No.	No.	No.	No.
1850	1,096,563	875,005	61,560	360,402	179,627	221,119	—
1851	2,527,216	1,008,708	353,152	667,243	327,900	350,848	—
1852	507,973	352,290	115,013	305,203	231,010	173,391	25,397
1853	641,113	697,740	248,998	409,076	381,210	180,753	125,453
1854	459,262	446,641	249,466	407,676	339,164	203,990	104,823
1855	384,089	891,897	298,095	315,002	313,816	141,420	78,427
1856	361,714	608,270*	227,780	344,184	344,140	161,752	111,768
1857	621,034	640,850	250,770	339,217	361,798	173,710	284,953†
1858	519,565	533,764	238,377	351,580	405,376	218,035	456,289
1859	517,895	789,401	172,727‡	364,356	384,698	208,264	475,365

* Incorrectly stated at the time by the National Gallery authorities as 208,270.
† Removed in June 1857 from Marlborough House to South Kensington.
‡ Removed in December to South Kensington; 51,404 out of the total number were visitors in that month to the collection after its removal, leaving only 121,323 as the visitors in the whole of the rest of the year at Marlborough House, where the exhibition was closed in the month of September.

N.B.—Of the above Institutions, the British Museum, the National Gallery, and the Vernon Gallery may be considered as exhibitions in town, and the remainder as exhibitions out of town, to which the supposed objection of non-accessibility would apply.

APPENDIX I.

CORRESPONDENCE between HER MAJESTY'S COMMISSIONERS and the SOCIETY of ARTS respecting the PROPOSED EXHIBITION of 1861.

I.—The SOCIETY of ARTS to HER MAJESTY'S COMMISSIONERS.

Society of Arts, Manufactures, and Commerce,
SIR,   Adelphi, London, December 16th, 1858.

I AM instructed by the Council of the Society of Arts to request you to call the attention of Her Majesty's Commissioners for the Exhibition of 1851 to the fact, that in February last the subject of holding a second Great International Exhibition of Industry was brought before the Council of the Society of Arts, and that after five meetings, each specially summoned to consider the subject, and each fully attended, the following resolutions, based on such information as the Council could obtain, were passed :—

" The Council of the Society of Arts, bearing in mind the part which the Society took in originating the Great Exhibition of 1851, have considered it to be their duty carefully to examine various suggestions for holding an Exhibition in 1861 which have been submitted to them, and have resolved—

" 1. That the institution of Decennial Exhibitions in London, for the purpose of showing the progress made in Industry and Art during each period of 10 years, would tend greatly to the encouragement of Arts, Manufactures, and Commerce.

" 2. That the first of these exhibitions ought not to be a repetition of the Exhibition of 1851, which must be considered an exceptional event, but should be an exhibition of works selected for excellence, illustrating the progress of Industry and Art, and arranged according to classes and not countries, and that it should comprehend music, and also painting, which was excluded in 1851.

" 3. That foreigners should be invited to exhibit on the same conditions as British exhibitors.

" 4. That the Council will proceed to consider how the foregoing resolutions can be best carried into effect."

The Council, after arriving at these conclusions, considered that, as more than three years had to elapse before the date of the contemplated exhibition, it would be well to put forth the resolutions at once, in order that the opinions of the commercial public at large might be the better ascertained. They were accordingly published in April last.

APPENDIX I.

The newly-elected Council of the Society, at their third meeting in November, having in the interim learnt the feeling of increased numbers of the commercial world, have confirmed the views of their predecessors in office, and further resolved that it would be proper to address themselves to Her Majesty's Commissioners who conducted the Exhibition of 1851.

In accordance with this resolution, I am instructed to ask you to bring the subject before Her Majesty's Commissioners, and to inform me whether they will be willing to entertain the question of undertaking the management of the Exhibition of 1861. The Council feel it unnecessary to give any detailed reasons for submitting this application, for it will be obvious that the great success which attended the labours of Her Majesty's Commissioners in 1851, and their announcements when soliciting public subscriptions on behalf of the Exhibition, make this application one of the greatest propriety.

In the event of Her Majesty's Commissioners being prepared to act, I am directed by the Council of the Society of Arts to say that they are prepared, as in 1851, to render every assistance in their power to them.

I am, &c.

P. LE NEVE FOSTER,
Secretary.

Edgar A. Bowring, Esq.

II.—HER MAJESTY'S COMMISSIONERS to the SOCIETY OF ARTS.

SIR, Palace of Westminster, 19th February 1859.

I AM directed by Her Majesty's Commissioners for the Exhibition of 1851 to acknowledge the receipt of your letter, transmitting a copy of certain resolutions passed by the Council of the Society of Arts on the subject of a proposed International Exhibition to be held in London in the year 1861, and inquiring on behalf of the Council whether the Commissioners will be willing to entertain the question of themselves undertaking the management of such an Exhibition.

In reply, I am directed to state, for the information of the Council of the Society of Arts, that Her Majesty's Commissioners consider that they could only be justified in complying with this application upon its being made to appear to them, not only that the scheme of the proposed Exhibition meets with the general sympathy and support of the public to an extent sufficient to warrant a reasonable confidence of success, but also that the necessary funds would be at once forthcoming for the purpose of defraying the expenses of the Exhibition until those expenses are met by the receipts derivable from it.

The Society of Arts are aware that the Commissioners have themselves no funds at their disposal applicable to the purposes of the proposed Exhibition; nor have the Commissioners at the present moment any

L

APPENDIX I.

information before them on which to found an opinion as to the amount of public support that may be anticipated for the undertaking. In the absence of this information they do not consider themselves in a position to return a positive answer to the inquiry contained in your letter.

Upon being made acquainted with the result of any inquiries on this subject which may be instituted by the Society of Arts, it will give Her Majesty's Commissioners much pleasure to proceed to consider (should that result prove to be satisfactory) how far it may be in their power to contribute to the success of the Exhibition, and also to determine the position to be taken by them with respect to its management.

I have, &c.

P. Le Neve Foster, Esq.   EDGAR A. BOWRING.

III.—The SOCIETY of ARTS to HER MAJESTY'S COMMISSIONERS.

Society of Arts, Manufactures, and Commerce,
SIR,   Adelphi, London, W.C., 11th March 1859.

THE Council of the Society for the Encouragement of Arts, Manufactures, and Commerce has carefully considered your letter of the 19th February last.

With much satisfaction the Council perceives that Her Majesty's Commissioners raise no question as to the beneficial effects of the intended international Exhibition in 1861 ; but lay down the important condition that, before they can decide how far it may be in their power to contribute to the success of the Exhibition, and what position they can take in respect to its management, they must be satisfied that it will receive sufficient support, and that means to meet the expenditure will be at once forthcoming.

On both of these points the Council will have much pleasure in doing all in its power to satisfy and aid the Commissioners.

Looking upon the intended Exhibition as a stimulus to the development of the industrial resources of the country, and to the advancement of science and the arts, the Council is aware that, while Her Majesty's Commissioners cannot take a mere financial view of the undertaking (as if the expectation of pecuniary profits could alone induce them to embark in it), they must not be exposed to a large pecuniary risk, or to any serious failure.

To provide means for meeting the expenditure, the Council proposes that a guarantee fund of 250,000*l.* should at once be subscribed for ;. and it is presumed the Commissioners will regard such a subscription as a sufficient test of the probability of success. To enable the Council, however, to obtain this guarantee, the previous co-operation of the Royal Commissioners appears at present to be indispensable. To make this

APPENDIX I.

clear, it is necessary to explain in some detail the position and views of the Society of Arts.

Her Majesty's Commissioners are aware that His Royal Highness the President of the Society of Arts, and the other members of the Society who were the originators of the Great Exhibition of 1851, never contemplated that it should be the last as well as the first International Exhibition of Industry. The beneficial effects of periodical exhibitions in painting, agriculture, and horticulture having been proved, it could not have been intended to do no more for general industry than to hold one industrial exhibition without successors; and accordingly, in the letter addressed in 1849, on behalf of the Society of Arts, to Her Majesty's Principal Secretary of State, by His Royal Highness the President, applying for the appointment of Royal Commissioners to manage the Exhibition of 1851, it was expressly stated that the Society's object was that quinquennial exhibitions of industry should be established. The Society was well aware that any beneficial results which the Exhibition of 1851 might accomplish could only be fully known when the condition of general industry should be again tested, after a proper interval, by a similar exhibition; and that if none such should be held, the good effects of the Exhibition of 1851 would subside and evil would ensue, the stamp of authority having been so fixed by the jurors of 1851 on past improvements as even to create an obstacle to further improvements.

Early in 1858 the Council received suggestions that it was the duty of the Society of Arts to renew the action by which the Society originated the Exhibition of 1851, and to originate a new Exhibition in 1861. The subject was carefully considered by the Council, and the results of its repeated deliberations were expressed in the resolutions which have been submitted to the Royal Commissioners.

Having re-affirmed the conclusion arrived at and published in 1849, that the interests of arts, manufactures, and commerce require international exhibitions of industry to be held periodically; and considering, with the experience obtained in 1851, that decennial periods would be more expedient, the Council announced the Exhibition of 1861, in the full conviction that when it should be satisfactorily settled where and under what management the Exhibition was to be held, a guarantee for the expenditure would be easily obtained, as in 1849, and the requisite support would certainly ensue.

The Council, however, has been constantly met by inquiries on the part of the public whether the Exhibition will be held at South Kensington, on the land purchased by Her Majesty's Commissioners; whether the Commissioners will manage the Exhibition, and what part they will take in guaranteeing the requisite funds. The public refer to the Royal Commission as appointed and continued in existence by Her Majesty for

L 2

purposes strictly analogous to those of the Exhibition now intended, and as having exclusive control for those purposes over the large property which has been created with the proceeds of the previous Exhibition ; and it will be very difficult indeed to obtain a satisfactory list of guarantees until replies have been given to those inquiries. If Her Majesty's Commissioners will place the name of the Royal Commission at the head of the list of guarantees, the Council will immediately proceed to complete it.

The Council, though not hitherto in a position to determine absolutely the success of the Exhibition, has done enough by inquiries to satisfy itself that the Exhibition of 1861, managed with the same spirit and intelligence as its great predecessor in 1851, will elicit still more definite and valuable results.

The Council submits to Her Majesty's Commissioners the following general considerations :—

Since 1851 commerce has been so extensively developed, not only at home and with the colonies, but with foreign countries, that a knowledge of the productions of other nations has become everywhere a necessary part of mercantile education. In manufactures there have been numberless inventions and improvements. Population and wealth have greatly increased. In the metropolis alone, in 1861, 500,000 persons will have been added to the population, and 700,000 young persons of 1851 will have become adults. The means and popular habits of locomotion have been immensely extended at home and abroad. In England, the railways have already increased from 6,000 miles in 1851, to 9,000 in 1858 ; and the railway travellers from 85,000,000 in 1851, to 139,000,000 in 1858. On the Continent the increase has been far greater. The desire to see, and, by seeing, to attain knowledge, coupled with the love of art, has received an extraordinary stimulus in all civilized countries. The same influences will be at work in 1861 as in 1851 to induce manufacturers and inventors to exhibit their productions. Those who are insufficiently known, young, and enterprising will be foremost to meet the competition. Those who are better known and established will not be left behind.

Much will depend on the selection of the site, and on the authority in which the management of the Exhibition is vested. To give proper confidence to guarantees and exhibitors, the undertaking should have a national character, and be carried on under the countenance, if not under the immediate direction of a constituted authority.

The Council expresses its conviction that if Her Majesty's Commissioners join in the guarantee, and allow it to be announced that, provided it be completed by a given day, they will hold the Exhibition of 1861 on their own ground at South Kensington, the elements of success will be such that failure will be almost impossible ; and the Council feels sure that Her Majesty's Commissioners may have at least as much confidence in the public spirit and intelligence of all classes of the community in 1859 as they had in 1849.

I am, &c.

Edgar A. Bowring, Esq.,
Secretary to the Commissioners
for the Exhibition of 1851.

P. LE NEVE FOSTER,
Secretary.

IV.—The SOCIETY of ARTS to HER MAJESTY'S COMMISSIONERS.

Society of Arts, Manufactures, and Commerce,
Adelphi, London, W.C., 2nd June 1859.

SIR,

I HAVE the honour to enclose a copy of resolutions passed by the Council of the Society of Arts in reference to the proposed Exhibition of 1861, and I am directed to request that you will be good enough to lay them before the Royal Commissioners for the Great Exhibition of 1851.

I am, &c.

Edgar A. Bowring, Esq.,
Secretary to the Royal Commissioners
for the Exhibition of 1851.

P. LE NEVE FOSTER,
Secretary.

Resolved—

That with reference to the present and prospective condition of the Continent, the Council is of opinion that the International Exhibition proposed to be held in 1861 should be postponed to a more favourable opportunity.

That this resolution be communicated to His Royal Highness the President of the Society, and to Her Majesty's Commissioners for the Great Exhibition of 1851.

V.—HER MAJESTY'S COMMISSIONERS to the SOCIETY of ARTS.

SIR, Whitehall, 6th July 1859.

I AM directed by Her Majesty's Commissioners, &c. to acknowledge the receipt of your further letters of the 11th March and 2nd June last, on the subject of the proposed International Exhibition of 1861, and in reply I am to acquaint you, for the information of the Council of the Society of Arts, that the Commissioners entirely agree with the opinion of the Council, as indicated in the resolutions transmitted in the last-named letter, to the effect that, in the present and prospective condition of the Continent, it is expedient that the proposed Exhibition should be postponed to a more favourable opportunity.

I have, &c.

EDGAR A. BOWRING.

P. Le Neve Foster, Esq.

APPENDIX K.

CORRESPONDENCE on the SUBJECT of the INTERNATIONAL EXHIBITION of 1862.

I.—The SOCIETY of ARTS to HER MAJESTY'S COMMISSIONERS.

Society of Arts, Manufactures, and Commerce,
John Street, Adelphi, London, W.C., 8th March 1860.

SIR,

I AM directed by the Council of the Society of Arts to transmit, for the information of Her Majesty's Commissioners for the Exhibition of 1851, a copy of the guarantee agreement by which the Society seeks to secure the means of holding an International Exhibition of Art and Industry in 1862, and to express a hope that the Council may receive the co-operation of Her Majesty's Commissioners collectively and individually in the undertaking.

I am also directed by the Council to inquire whether, considering the interest of the Society of Arts in the permanent buildings to be erected, the Commissioners will now grant a portion of the ground at South Kensington, purchased out of the surplus funds of the Exhibition of 1851, for the purpose of holding exhibitions of Art and Industry, and for other purposes tending to the encouragement of Arts, Manufactures, and Commerce, and if so, on what terms.

I am, &c.
P. LE NEVE FOSTER,
Secretary.

Edgar A. Bowring, Esq.,
Secretary to the Royal Commissioners
for the Exhibition of 1851.

Enclosure in I.

An AGREEMENT for HOLDING an INTERNATIONAL EXHIBITION in 1862.

WHEREAS the Society for the Encouragement of Arts, Manufactures, and Commerce is of opinion that decennial Exhibitions of works of Industry and Art, showing the progress made during each period of ten years, would tend greatly to the encouragement of Arts, Manufactures, and Commerce; and it is intended that the first of such exhibitions shall be held in London in the year 1862; that foreigners shall be invited to contribute; and that a guarantee fund shall be formed, in order to obtain adequate means for originating and holding the same:

In furtherance, therefore, of the said intention, we, the undersigned, severally agree with the Trustees and Managers of the intended Exhibition in manner following:—

1st. The sum of 250,000l. sterling at least shall be and is hereby subscribed as the guarantee fund, in the sums set opposite to our respective signatures; and no liability shall be incurred by any person subscribing this agreement, unless the sum of 250,000l. be subscribed within six

APPENDIX K.

calendar months from this date, nor shall any subscriber be liable beyond the amount of his subscription. And every subscriber shall contribute in rateable proportion to his subscription to liquidate any loss, should such attend the undertaking.

2nd. The undertaking shall be under the management of five persons, herein-after called Trustees, in whom all monies received on account of the undertaking shall be vested, and they shall have full and absolute powers to expend the same, and to enter into contracts, as well for works as for loans of money, and to do all things which may in their judgment be necessary for the undertaking.

3rd. The Earl Granville, K G., the Marquis of Chandos, Thomas Baring, Esq., M.P., Charles Wentworth Dilke, Esq., and Thomas Fairbairn, Esq., shall be invited to become, and if they shall accept the office, shall be the first Trustees of the undertaking.

4th. On the death, resignation, incapacity, or refusal to act of any person invited to become a Trustee, or of any Trustee, another Trustee shall be appointed to supply the vacancy, by the majority in value of the subscribers present at a meeting specially called for the purpose, and every Trustee shall sign a memorandum, on these presents, testifying his acceptance of the appointment; but, notwithstanding any vacancy, the actual Trustees shall have full power to act in the management of the undertaking.

5th. The Trustees shall apply to Her Majesty's Commissioners for the Exhibition of 1851 to grant a portion of the ground purchased at South Kensington out of the surplus funds of that Exhibition as a site for the intended Exhibition; and should they not obtain such ground on terms satisfactory to themselves, they shall have power to acquire, by purchase or otherwise, any suitable site.

6th. The Trustees shall erect on the site they acquire all such buildings and conveniences, as well permanent as temporary, as shall in their judgment be necessary, and one-third part at least of the sum thus expended shall be employed in erections of a permanent character, suitable for such decennial or other periodical exhibitions, and, when not so used, suitable for other purposes tending to the encouragement of Arts, Manufactures, and Commerce.

7th. Subject to the provisions herein contained, arrangements shall be made for vesting the site and buildings of a permanent character in the Society for the Encouragement of Arts, Manufactures, and Commerce, for holding exhibitions of Art and Industry, and for other purposes tending to the encouragement of Arts, Manufactures, and Commerce, on such terms as may be arranged with the Council of the said Society.

8th. After the close of the Exhibition, or the previous termination of the undertaking, its affairs shall be wound up, and the temporary buildings sold. And should there be a deficit which the Society of Arts shall decline to liquidate, a sale shall be made of the interest of the Trustees in the permanent buildings. And if, after such sale, there shall remain a deficit, the ultimate loss shall be paid by the subscribers rateably. But in case there shall be a surplus, it shall be applied to the encouragement of Arts, Manufactures, and Commerce, in such manner as shall be determined by a majority in value of the subscribers present at a meeting specially called for that purpose.

9th. In case the undertaking be attended with loss, the Trustees shall assess such loss rateably upon the subscribers, and make a call or calls upon each of them for payment of his proportion of such loss; and if such calls shall not be paid on demand, the Trustees may recover the same from the defaulting subscriber as a common debt, in an action to be brought in the names of the Trustees. And a notice from the Trustees, requiring payment from any subscriber, sent by the post addressed to his usual or last known residence, shall be sufficient evidence of the calls having been made, and the production of this agreement shall be conclusive evidence of the liability of every subscriber to pay the money demanded.

10th. Every meeting of the subscribers shall be held at the rooms of the Society of Arts, or some other convenient place in London, and be called by the Trustees, or any two of them, or by not less than 10 subscribers, representing a total subscription of at least 50,000l., by notice sent to each subscriber through the post addressed to his usual or last known residence, 14 days at least prior to the day fixed for such meeting. At each meeting a chairman shall be elected, and all resolutions shall be determined by a majority in value of the subscribers present. If subscribers, 10 at least in number, representing a total subscription of 50,000l., do not attend within 30 minutes of the time appointed for holding any meeting, no business shall be transacted.

Witness our hands, this   day of   1860.

Signatures.	Addresses.	Amounts.

II.—The SOCIETY of ARTS to HER MAJESTY'S COMMISSIONERS.

Society of Arts, Manufactures, and Commerce,
John Street, Adelphi, London, W.C., 8th June 1860.

SIR,

ADVERTING to my letter of the 8th March, on the subject of the International Exhibition of 1862, which appears to be still under the

APPENDIX K.

consideration of Her Majesty's Commissioners of the Exhibition of 1851, I am directed by the Council of the Society of Arts to urge on Her Majesty's Commissioners the propriety of permanently appropriating a portion of the land at South Kensington for the purpose of holding exhibitions of Art and Industry. This land was in great part purchased by means of surplus funds arising from the Exhibition of 1851, and being admirably situated for exhibitions, whether of a national or international character, has been naturally looked to as the site for future exhibitions.

The Council desire to impress on the Commissioners their conviction of the importance of periodical exhibitions, and the value attached to them by the public as a means whereby the growth of Art and Industry may be stimulated, and their progress ascertained and recorded at suitable intervals. The views of the Council have received remarkable confirmation in the fact that, without any public appeal, and in a very short period of time, 455 persons have intimated their intention to subscribe to a Guarantee Fund sums which in the aggregate amount to 308,350*l.*

The minimum of a quarter of a million originally proposed for the Guarantee Fund has thus been already much exceeded, and, in the opinion of the Council, the amount subscribed will be largely and rapidly increased when they can announce that arrangements for the site at Kensington are definitively settled with Her Majesty's Commissioners.

The object of the Guarantee Fund is not limited to holding an Exhibition in 1862, but is intended to secure, by the investment of a sum of 50,000*l.* at least, in permanent buildings, the repetition of exhibitions whenever the public desire them; and the Council look with confidence to the assistance of the Commissioners in promoting that object, which, in their opinion, can in no way be more effectively afforded than by appropriating a portion of the land acquired by them.

In considering the application of the Council the Commissioners will doubtless bear in mind the liberality with which the Society, in order to promote the accomplishment of the great object of international exhibitions, unconditionally surrendered its right to a share of the surplus profits of the Exhibition of 1851, the maintenance of which right would have enabled it now, without assistance, to undertake the Exhibition of 1862.

In conclusion, I am directed to express the earnest desire of the Council that they may be favoured with an early answer to their application, inasmuch as the preparations for the Exhibition of 1862 ought to be no longer delayed.

I have, &c.

Edgar A. Bowring, Esq.,   P. LE NEVE FOSTER,
Secretary to the Royal Commissioners   Secretary.
for the Exhibition of 1851.

III.—HER MAJESTY'S COMMISSIONERS to the SOCIETY of ARTS.

Palace of Westminster,
SIR,   June 28, 1860.

I AM directed by Her Majesty's Commissioners for the Exhibition of 1851 to acknowledge the receipt of your letters of the 8th March and 8th instant, on the subject of the proposed Exhibition of 1862, and applying on behalf of the Council of the Society of Arts, for the grant of a site upon the Commissioners' Estate at Kensington Gore for the purposes of that and future exhibitions of Art and Industry.

Her Majesty's Commissioners direct me, in the first place, to request that you will acquaint the Council of the Society that, until the receipt of your second letter, they were not in possession of the information as to the ability of the Society to carry out their proposal to hold an Exhibition in 1862, which was necessary to enable them to return an answer to it.

From the tenor of your two letters, and from the terms of the Draft Guarantee Agreement, enclosed in that of the 8th March, the Commissioners gather that the objects sought to be attained by the Society of Arts, so far as the Commissioners are concerned, are three in number:— first, the acquisition of a site on the Commissioners' Estate for the purposes of the proposed Exhibition; secondly, the erection of permanent buildings on that site to the value of 50,000*l.*, in addition to the temporary buildings erected for the Exhibition in question, such permanent buildings to be vested, after the close of the Exhibition, in the Society of Arts, and to be available for future exhibitions, and "other purposes tending to the encouragement of Arts, Manufactures, and Commerce;" and thirdly, the permanent appropriation by the Commissioners of a portion of their Estate for the purpose of future exhibitions corresponding to the proposed International Exhibition of 1862.

With reference to the first of these objects, viz., the grant of a site for the Exhibition of 1862, I am directed to acquaint you that it will afford Her Majesty's Commissioners much pleasure to grant, rent free, until the 31st December 1862, for the purposes of that Exhibition, the use of the whole of the land on the main square of their Estate, lying on the

APPENDIX K.

south side of the arcades and entrances to the gardens of the Horticultural Society, estimated at 16 acres, on the understanding that all the buildings to be erected for the Exhibition shall be subject to their approval, and, further, subject to the conditions referred to in the Appendix to this letter.

As respects the erection of permanent buildings on the site in question as part of the buildings to be erected for the Exhibition, such permanent buildings being afterwards vested in the Society of Arts, I am to acquaint you that the Commissioners fully appreciate the motives which have induced the Council of the Society to propose that the whole of the buildings required for the Exhibition of 1862 should not be entirely temporary in their character, but that a certain portion of them should be suffered to remain after the close of the Exhibition, as permanent erections, available for the promotion of the general objects for which the Society of Arts is incorporated. The Commissioners are at the same time glad to take advantage of the present opportunity of again recognizing the services of the Society in advancing the interests of the Arts and Manufactures during the long period of its existence, and especially in preparing the way for the Great Exhibition of 1851.

Under these circumstances, and adverting to the provisions of the Guarantee Agreement, so far as they relate to this part of the question, Her Majesty's Commissioners direct me to state that they will be happy to grant to the Society a lease for 99 years of the permanent buildings referred to, on condition of the sum of not less than 50,000*l*. being expended by the Trustees on their erection, and of their not covering more than one acre of ground; it being understood that they shall be used by the Society during the continuance of the lease solely for holding exhibitions, and for purposes connected with the promotion of Arts and Manufactures. For further details I am again to refer you to the Appendix.

With regard to the third question raised in your letters, viz., the appropriation by the Commissioners of a portion of their Estate for the purpose of future exhibitions analogous to the proposed Exhibition of 1862, Her Majesty's Commissioners direct me to state that, with the view of meeting the wishes of the Council as far as is consistent with their public duty, and at the same time bearing in mind their obligations to their mortgagees, they will undertake, in the event of the payment to them of the sum of 10,000*l*. out of the profits (if any) of the Exhibition of 1862, to reserve for the purposes of another International Exhibition in 1872, to be conducted by such body as may be approved by the Commissioners, the remainder of the land now proposed to be lent by them for the Exhibition of 1862, that is not covered by the permanent buildings already referred to; such reservation not interfering in any

172   APPENDIX K.

way with the free use by the Commissioners of that land in the intervening period, and being, as well as all other arrangements of the Commissioners with the Society, subject to the rights and powers which may be exercised by the mortgagees.

I am directed, in conclusion, to append, for the information of the Council of the Society, a copy of the terms to which Her Majesty's Commissioners are prepared to accede, with the view of giving effect to the various arrangements above indicated.

I have, &c.

The Secretary to the Society of Arts.   EDGAR A. BOWRING.

Enclosure in III.

TERMS referred to in the FOREGOING LETTER.

I.

The Royal Commissioners shall grant rent free, until the 31st December 1862, for the purposes of the Exhibition of 1862, the use of the whole of the land on the main square of their estate, which is on the south side of the arcades and entrances to the gardens of the Horticultural Society, estimated at 16 acres.

II.

Any buildings, whether permanent or temporary in their character, to be erected for the purposes of the Exhibition of 1862, shall be subject to the approval of the Commissioners.

III.

The Trustees of the Exhibition of 1862 shall be bound to remove all the buildings, except the permanent buildings herein-after referred to, and reinstate the site, within six months after the close of the Exhibition, if required by the Commissioners. The Trustees shall, on the other hand, be at liberty to remove the permanent buildings in question, if the Exhibition should be attended with pecuniary loss.

IV.

Any buildings that may be intended to be permanent, which the Trustees of the Exhibition shall erect, shall cost not less than 50,000*l*., and shall not cover more than one acre of ground.

V.

If the Trustees give notice to the Commissioners on behalf of the Society of Arts, on or before the 31st December 1862, of the desire of that Society to retain the permanent buildings in question, the Commissioners shall grant to the Society a lease of those buildings for 99 years from the 1st January 1863, at a ground rent calculated at the rate of

240*l.* per acre per annum, payable half-yearly, the first payment becoming due on the 1st July 1863. The buildings to be used for holding exhibitions, and for purposes connected with the promotion of Arts and Manufactures, and no other. The lease to be subject to forfeiture if the buildings are used otherwise than for the purposes described. The Society shall not be at liberty to require the concurrence of the mortgagees in such lease, and shall not assign, underlet, or otherwise part with the lease except with the consent in writing of the Commissioners. The Society shall be subject to no personal or corporate liability under the lease, but the Commissioners shall have a right of re-entry if the full amount of ground rent is not paid for three consecutive years.

VI.

In the event of the payment to the Commissioners by the Trustees of the Exhibition of 1862, on or before the 31st March 1863, out of the surplus profits of that Exhibition, of the sum of 10,000*l.*, the Commissioners shall undertake to reserve for the purposes of another Exhibition in 1872, to be conducted by such body as may be approved by the Commissioners, the remainder of the land originally lent by them for the Exhibition of 1862, that is not covered by the permanent buildings referred to in the previous clauses. Should the land be so reserved, the Society of Arts, on their part, shall hold those permanent buildings also available for the purposes of the Exhibition of 1872, failing which the Commissioners may enter into possession of the buildings, and hold the same for such time as may be necessary for those purposes, the ground rent payable on them under Clause V. being suspended for the time when the buildings are so resumed by the Commissioners.

VII.

The above contingent reservation by the Commissioners for the purposes of an International Exhibition in 1872 of the land not occupied by permanent buildings shall not interfere in any way with the free use by them of that land in the intervening period.

VIII.

The Society of Arts are to understand that all arrangements between the Commissioners and the Society, or the Trustees of the Exhibition of 1862, must be subject in all respects to the rights and powers of the mortgagees, and that the Commissioners are to be under no liability to protect or indemnify the Society, or the Trustees, against any exercise of those rights and powers.

IV.—The SOCIETY of ARTS to HER MAJESTY'S COMMISSIONERS.

Society of Arts, Manufactures, and Commerce,
SIR, Adelphi, London, W.C., July 5, 1860.

I AM directed by the Council of the Society of Arts to acknowledge the receipt of your letter of the 28th ultimo, notifying the willingness of Her Majesty's Commissioners for the Exhibition of 1851 to grant a portion of the Commissioners' Estate at South Kensington for the International Exhibition of 1862, rent free; to vest in the Society at a moderate rent the site of the permanent buildings proposed to be erected on a portion of such ground; and to reserve the remainder of the ground for an International Exhibition in 1872.

I am directed by the Council to request that you will express to Her Majesty's Commissioners the thanks of the Council for this communication, and their sense of the important influence which the approval by the Commissioners of the object in which the Society is engaged cannot fail to exert.

The terms on which Her Majesty's Commissioners propose to accede to the request of the Council are in their general scope and character entirely satisfactory to the Council, but there are a few matters of detail to which it is necessary they should request the attention of the Commissioners.

1st. It is proposed by the Commissioners to limit the site of the permanent buildings to an acre of ground; but it appears to the Council that the actual area required cannot be properly ascertained until the plans of the buildings are approved by the Commissioners.

2ndly. The Council would desire that the uses to which the permanent buildings shall be applicable by the Society of Arts should be described in the terms of the Charter by which the Society is incorporated.

3rdly. The Council assume it to be the intention of Her Majesty's Commissioners that the body by whom the contemplated Exhibition of 1872 shall be conducted shall be nominated by the Society of Arts, subject to the approval of the Commissioners.

I have, &c.

Edgar A. Bowring, Esq. P. LE NEVE FOSTER,
Secretary.

V.— HER MAJESTY'S COMMISSIONERS to the SOCIETY of ARTS.

SIR, Whitehall, July 10, 1860.

I AM directed by Her Majesty's Commissioners for the Exhibition of 1851 to acknowledge the receipt of your letter of the 5th instant, calling attention, on behalf of the Council of the Society of Arts, to certain matters of detail connected with the terms transmitted in the Commissioners' letter to the Society of the 28th ultimo, respecting the proposed Exhibition of 1862, &c.

As regards the first point mentioned in your letter, viz., the area to be covered by the permanent buildings proposed to be leased to the Society of Arts, I am to acquaint you that the proposal contained in the Commissioners' letter is intended to define the extent to which they are prepared to bind themselves to grant a lease of 99 years to the Society, and may accordingly serve as a guide in the preparation of the plans of the proposed erections for the approval of the Commissioners.

Upon the second point raised by the Council of the Society respecting the uses to which the permanent buildings in question may be applied, I am to observe that Her Majesty's Commissioners propose to limit those uses to objects connected with the promotion of Arts and Manufactures, in order that no question might hereafter arise as to the possibility of applying the buildings in a manner not contemplated by them to purposes of commerce, the encouragement of which appears, from the title of the Society, to be one of its chartered objects. Her Majesty's Commissioners, however, do not apprehend that there will be any difficulty in defining, to the mutual satisfaction of the Society and themselves, the exact uses to which the buildings may be devoted, should the time arrive for giving formal effect to the proposed lease to the Society.

With respect to the third question referred to by you, the Council are in error in assuming it to be the intention of Her Majesty's Commissioners to intrust the conduct of the contemplated Exhibition of 1872 to a body nominated by the Society of Arts. They feel it to be inconsistent with the duty they owe to the public to fetter their power of free action, with regard to future Exhibitions, by entering into any engagement, either expressed or implied, as to the body by which such Exhibitions shall be conducted. They must hold themselves entirely free to act on this, as on all other points connected with such undertakings, in the manner that shall appear to them, at the time, to be most conducive to the success of the object they have in view.

I have, &c.

EDGAR A. BOWRING.

The Secretary
to the Society of Arts.

second International Exhibition, which it has been proposed to hold in 1862. Since the date of my last communication the Guarantee Fund has not only been raised to the full amount which had been considered indispensable, of 250,000*l.*, but has been carried beyond that sum till it has reached no less an amount than 365,200*l.*

The Council have latterly been engaged in a correspondence with the gentlemen named in the Guarantee Deed as the proposed Trustees for the management of the Exhibition, with a view to obtaining their definite acceptance of the trust thus offered to them.

The proposed Guarantee Agreement, as you are aware, invests the Trustees with the most ample powers for giving effect to the intention of holding a second International Exhibition; but they have felt, in accordance with the opinion which has always been entertained by the Council, that to enable them to exercise the powers intrusted to them with effect, it was indispensable that in some mode or other the sanction and approval of the Sovereign and of the Government to the undertaking should be made apparent.

Various modes of effecting this object, whether by the grant of a Royal Charter or otherwise, have been suggested, and three of the proposed Trustees (viz., Lord Chandos, Mr. Dilke, and Mr. Fairbairn), assuming that the required evidence of that sanction, in one shape or another, will not be withheld, have accepted the offered trust without reserve. Two of them, Lord Granville and Mr. Baring, both members of the Royal Commission for the Exhibition of 1851, have written a letter, a copy of which is enclosed.

The Council do not infer that the adoption of the first course of action suggested in this letter would interfere with the maintenance of the Guarantee Agreement, and they came at once to the conclusion that at the earliest possible period they ought to lay the letter before the Commissioners, to learn whether they would be prepared, whilst preserving the conditions of the Guarantee Agreement, to afford their valuable support in either of the modes suggested by Lord Granville and Mr. Baring; and from the interest which the Royal Commissioners have already displayed in the success of the intended Exhibition, by the liberal terms on which they have announced their readiness to allow the use of their property at Kensington for the purpose, the Council are induced to hope with confidence that their present communication will be favourably received, and that early arrangements may be made for giving effect to the wishes of the public manifested by their liberal support of the necessary guarantee.

I have, &c.
P. LE NEVE FOSTER,
Secretary.

Edgar A. Bowring, Esq.,
Secretary to the Royal Commissioners
for the Exhibition of 1851.

APPENDIX K.

Enclosure in VI.

SIR, 16, Bruton-street, August 29, 1860.

We have to acknowledge the receipt of your letter of the 20th. Lord Chandos is in America, Mr. Dilke in France, and Mr. Fairbairn is not at present in London. We shall not be able to meet together till the end of October, and it is not likely that the Government, to whom application would have to be made for a Charter, will be regularly assembled before that time. There are other circumstances at the present moment which add to the difficulty of our becoming responsible for the success of an International Exhibition in 1862. It is therefore impossible, if the Society of Arts require an immediate answer, for us to give one in the affirmative.

It may, however, be useful to the Society of Arts to be made acquainted with some of our opinions, in order that they may be better able to judge of the probable issue of any further communications. The fact of our being members of the Commission for the Exhibition of 1851 prevented our doing more than *indicate*, by our letter of the 21st of June, that in our opinion it was desirable for the Society to apply to that body who had conducted with success the last Exhibition, to give the benefit of their authority to the repetition of the undertaking. We believe that that Commission, with certain modifications of its working arrangements, would furnish the best mode of directing the next Exhibition, and that an application from the Society of Arts to that effect to the Commission, agreed to by them, would be the best solution of the present question. It is, on the other hand, possible that His Royal Highness the President of the Commission, and other distinguished members of the Commission, might feel that they would not be justified in again undertaking the labour and responsibility which they willingly underwent for the first experiment, when the work to be done was new, and not understood by the public. In that case it would strengthen the hands of any persons charged with the direction of the work, if that Commission expressed an opinion favourable to the holding of another Exhibition, and of the mode of management proposed by the Society of Arts, and sanctioned by those who have already promised to sign the guarantee. If, further, the Commission would consent to advise the Trustees as to certain important principles, such as whether jurors should be appointed, and prizes should be given, and if some of the members of the Finance Committee would give the Trustees the advantage of their experience in occasionally advising them on other matters, and if Her Majesty's Government consented to grant such a Charter as the Trustees might think it expedient to apply for, we should think it our duty to comply with the flattering offer which has been made to us.

We beg, in conclusion, to thank the Society of Arts for the courtesy of their communications, and to state that we consider them (if they dissent

M

APPENDIX K.

from our views or require immediate action) as perfectly free to take any course which they may think proper, without reference to us.

We have, &c.

(Signed) GRANVILLE.
THOMAS BARING.

The Secretary to the Society of Arts.

VII.—HER MAJESTY'S COMMISSIONERS to the SOCIETY of ARTS.

SIR,   Palace of Westminster, November 20, 1860.

I AM directed by Her Majesty's Commissioners for the Exhibition of 1851 to acknowledge the receipt of your letter of the 24th October, enclosing copy of a letter from Lord Granville and Mr. Baring, two of the proposed Trustees for the contemplated Exhibition of 1862, on the subject of the management of that Exhibition, and requesting to be informed, on behalf of the Council of the Society of Arts, whether the Commissioners would be prepared, whilst preserving the conditions of the guarantee agreement, to afford their support to the undertaking in question in either of the modes indicated in the above-mentioned letter.

It appears from the communication of Lord Granville and Mr. Baring, that they are of opinion that the Commission for the Exhibition of 1851, with certain modifications of its working arrangements, would furnish the best mode of directing the next Exhibition; but they intimate their readiness, in the event of the Commissioners not being willing to undertake the labour and responsibility of managing it, to accept the office of Trustees of the Exhibition (their proposed three colleagues having already, as stated in your letter, accepted that office without reserve), upon condition of the Commission expressing an opinion favourable to the holding of another Exhibition, and the proposed mode of management, and of their consenting to advise the Trustees as to certain important principles, and of some of the members of the Finance Committee being willing to give them their advice occasionally on other matters.

The question, therefore, submitted for the consideration of the Commissioners is, whether, on the one hand, they will be willing themselves to undertake the management of the Exhibition, not with entire liberty of action, and in such manner as they may deem best adapted to insure its success, but subject to the provisions of the Guarantee Agreement, a copy of which was enclosed in your letter of the 8th March last; or whether, on the other hand, leaving the Exhibition to be managed by Trustees, as originally proposed, they will be prepared to give that more limited amount of assistance to the undertaking which Lord Granville and Mr. Baring make the condition of their accepting the proffered trusteeship.

In reply, I am to acquaint you, for the information of the Council of the Society of Arts, that, having given their careful consideration to the

APPENDIX K.

subject, Her Majesty's Commissioners have come to the conclusion that they could not with propriety accede to any proposal for undertaking themselves the management of the Exhibition of 1862 that is submitted to them, accompanied by any restriction such as that of the maintenance of all the conditions of the Guarantee Agreement required by the Council; and the Commissioners direct me to express their regret that this consideration, irrespective of any other, renders them unable to entertain the question of managing the Exhibition.

There remains the more limited question raised by the alternative alluded to by Lord Granville and Mr. Baring: and it affords Her Majesty's Commissioners much pleasure to state that, to this extent, they will be happy to meet the wishes of the Council, and to render such support and assistance to the undertaking as may be consistent with their position as a chartered body, and with the powers conferred upon them by their Charter of Incorporation.

The Commissioners have therefore no difficulty in expressing their general approval of the object which the Society of Arts have in view in organizing the scheme of the proposed Exhibition; and they have already sufficiently indicated, by the terms upon which (as set forth in their letter of the 28th June last) they are prepared to lend a portion of their estate for the purposes of the Exhibition, their readiness to co-operate with the Society in the matter, and their confidence in the mode of management by means of Trustees, proposed by the Society and sanctioned by the parties to the Guarantee Agreement.

Her Majesty's Commissioners will also be happy to communicate with the Trustees from time to time upon any points, whether of principle or of detail, connected with the undertaking, upon which the latter may think proper to seek their advice; and with the view of facilitating those communications as far as possible, it will afford them much pleasure, when the trust is definitely constituted by the acceptance of the whole of the five gentlemen who have been requested to act as Trustees, to elect as members of the Commission, under the powers conferred upon them by their Charter of Incorporation, those two of the five Trustees who are not already members of the Commission, viz., Lord Chandos and Mr. Thomas Fairbairn.

I have, &c.
EDGAR A. BOWRING.

The Secretary to the Society of Arts.

APPENDIX K.

together with a copy of the plan therein referred to; and I am directed to request that you will bring before the Commissioners for the Exhibition of 1851 the proposition therein contained for a modification of the terms contained in your letter to me of the 28th of June 1860, and to request, on the part of the Society of Arts, that the Commissioners for the Exhibition of 1851 will assent to such a modification being made.

I am, &c.

Edgar A. Bowring, Esq.,
&c. &c.

P. LE NEVE FOSTER,
Secretary.

Enclosure in VIII.

SIR, London, January 8, 1861.

I AM directed by the Trustees for the Exhibition of 1862 to request that you will have the goodness to inform the Council of the Society of Arts that in settling the arrangements of the buildings which will be required for that Exhibition, the Trustees find it impossible, without serious injury to the general interests of the undertaking, to carry out literally the condition laid down in the 4th clause of the Appendix to the Royal Commissioners' letter of the 28th June 1860, wherein it is stipulated that "any buildings that may be intended to be permanent which the Trustees shall erect" (and which, by the 5th clause, are under certain conditions to be leased to the Society of Arts) "shall cost not less than 50,000*l.*, and shall not cover more than one acre of ground."

While it does not appear, from the general tenor of the correspondence that passed between the Society of Arts and the Royal Commissioners, that any question of principle was intended on either side to be involved in the specification of the sum of 50,000*l.*, the Trustees have reason to believe that the general objects had in view in stipulating for the expenditure of a certain sum on a certain area, may be realized in a manner that will be satisfactory both to the Society and to the Commissioners, although the amount to be spent on the permanent buildings, to be leased to the Society at the close of the Exhibition, be reduced.

The object of the Society of Arts on the one hand, is to secure the erection of a building which will not only be available for the annual Exhibitions of the Society, and for otherwise promoting the general purposes for which it is incorporated, but which will also facilitate the "repetition of International Exhibitions whenever the public desire them."

The Royal Commissioners, on the other hand, who are no less interested than the Society in promoting such periodical Exhibitions, naturally look to the security against loss which a permanent building of considerable value will give them in the event of any failure on the part of the Society to pay their stipulated yearly rent.

APPENDIX K.

The Trustees believe that plans which they at present have under consideration will enable them to satisfy the requirements both of the Society and of the Commissioners.

They have not yet definitely adopted any plan for the whole of the buildings that will be required for the Exhibition, but sufficient progress has been made in the matter to justify them in proposing that the building which shall be the first to be chosen as permanent, with the view of being leased to the Society of Arts, in the event of the Exhibition succeeding, shall be the centre portion of the picture galleries facing Cromwell-road, as shown on the accompanying plan.

This portion, which occupies a little less than an acre of ground, will be the handsomest part of the façade of the proposed buildings, and will form perfectly lighted galleries, suitable for the exhibition of pictures or of any other objects.

The Trustees consider that, with due regard to the interests of the Exhibition, they would not be justified in expending more than 20,000*l*. on this part of the site, especially as the average cost per acre of the whole Exhibition is estimated not to reach 12,000*l*.

Under these circumstances, the Trustees direct me to request that the Council of the Society of Arts will ask the Royal Commissioners for the Exhibition of 1851 so far to modify the terms of their letter of the 28th of June 1860, as to be satisfied with an expenditure of 20,000*l*. upon the portion of the building above referred to, in case it should remain permanent, and should be leased to the Society in trust for future Exhibitions.

I am to beg that you will favour the Trustees with as early a reply as possible to this communication.

           I have, &c.

P. Le Neve Foster, Esq., (Signed) F. R. SANDFORD.
 &c. &c.
  Society of Arts.

IX.—HER MAJESTY'S COMMISSIONERS to the SOCIETY of ARTS.

SIR,   Whitehall, January 21, 1861.

I AM directed by Her Majesty's Commissioners for the Exhibition of 1851 to acknowledge the receipt of your letter of the 15th inst., enclosing a copy of a letter from the Trustees of the Exhibition of 1862 and of the plan therein referred to, and requesting, on the part of the Council of the Society of Arts, that the Commissioners will assent to the modification of the terms contained in my letter of the 28th June last that the Trustees desire, viz., a reduction of the amount required to be expended, by Clause 4 of those terms, on the acre of permanent buildings proposed by Clause 5 to be leased to the Society, from 50,000*l*. to 20,000*l*.

APPENDIX K.

In reply, I am directed by Her Majesty's Commissioners to acquaint you, for the information of the Council of the Society, that, under the circumstances set forth in this communication from the Trustees, they are prepared to assent to the modification in question, the *maximum* extent of the buildings to be leased by the Society remaining fixed at one acre, as previously agreed upon.

This assent on the part of the Commissioners is subject to the provision by the Trustees hereafter of such access as the Commissioners shall find requisite through the buildings proposed to be leased to the Society to the Commissioners' land in the rear of those buildings.

The Commissioners' consent to this large reduction in the value of the permanent buildings intended to be left on their land is given upon condition that there shall be expended upon those buildings, at the close of the Exhibition, should a surplus remain in the hands of the Trustees, such portion of the difference between the original sum of 50,000*l.* agreed to be spent thereon, and the reduced amount of 20,000*l.* as may, in the judgment of the Commissioners and the Trustees of the Exhibition, be deemed requisite for the completion of the buildings in a suitable architectural manner.

The Commissioners take this opportunity of observing that it is of course to be understood that the Society of Arts are not to be allowed at any time during the continuance of their lease to alter or change in any way the buildings intended to be leased to them without the consent and approval of the Commissioners being previously obtained.

I am to state, in conclusion, that the Commissioners agree to accept the line A A A marked in the plan enclosed in your letter, as defining the northern boundary of the ground to be reserved for the purposes of an Exhibition in 1872, in accordance with Clause 6 of the terms already spoken of.

I have, &c.

The Secretary to the Society of Arts.   EDGAR A. BOWRING.

X.—The TRUSTEES of the EXHIBITION of 1862 to HER MAJESTY'S COMMISSIONERS.

SIR,   London, January 17, 1861.

ADVERTING to the arrangements made between the Royal Commissioners for the Exhibition of 1851 and the Society of Arts, with reference to the grant of a site on the Commissioners' estate at Kensington Gore, for the purposes of an Exhibition to be held in the year 1862, I am directed by the Trustees of the proposed Exhibition to forward to you for the approval of the Commissioners, pursuant to Clause 2 of the terms laid down in the Appendix to the Commissioners' letter of 28th June last, the accompanying ground plan and elevation of the buildings which (subject to modifications in the minor details of internal arrangements) the Trustees propose to erect on the site in question, in the event of the requisite funds being forthcoming.

I am to state at the same time, for the information of the Commissioners, that the Trustees have found it impossible, without serious detriment to the general interests of the Exhibition, to comprise in the plan any structure which will fulfil, in their integrity, the conditions laid down in Clause 4 of the terms above mentioned, viz., that any buildings intended to be permanent, which the Trustees shall erect (and which by Clause 5 are, under certain conditions, to be leased to the Society of Arts) shall cost not less than 50,000*l.*, and shall not cover more than one acre of ground. On the one hand, the portion of the buildings which it is proposed to erect in accordance with the accompanying plan, and which possess every necessary quality of permanence, should it hereafter be deemed desirable to retain them, will considerably exceed an acre in extent; and on the other, no single acre admits of the outlay upon it of so large a sum as 50,000*l.*, except at the cost of greatly injuring the character of the remaining buildings.

The Trustees have addressed a separate letter to the Council of the Society of Arts on the same subject, with especial reference to the acre of building that may eventually be leased to the Society, and the Council will doubtless communicate direct with the Commissioners respecting it.

It is the earnest hope of the Trustees that Her Majesty's Commissioners may find it consistent with their duty to assent to such modifications in the terms arranged by them with the Society of Arts as may admit of the adoption of the plans now submitted for their approval, as it is highly desirable that no time should be lost in taking the necessary steps for proceeding with the erection of the buildings.

I have, &c.
F. R. SANDFORD.

Edgar A. Bowring, Esq.,
Secretary to the Royal Commissioners
for the Exhibition of 1851.

XI.—HER MAJESTY'S COMMISSIONERS to the TRUSTEES of the EXHIBITION of 1862.

SIR,
Whitehall, January 21, 1861.

I AM directed by Her Majesty's Commissioners for the Exhibition of 1851 to acknowledge the receipt of your letter of the 17th instant, transmitting on behalf of the Trustees of the Exhibition of 1862, for the approval of the Commissioners, in accordance with the terms contained in my letter of the 28th June last to the Secretary of the Society of Arts, on the subject of the proposed Exhibition, a ground plan and elevation of the buildings which the Trustees propose to erect for the purposes of the Exhibition on the Commissioners' estate at Kensington Gore.

In reply, I am to acquaint you, for the information of the Trustees, that Her Majesty's Commissioners are pleased to approve of the plans in question, so far as relates to the buildings proposed to be erected on the Commissioners' land lying to the south of the arcades and entrances of the Horticultural Society, to which alone the original agreement made with the Society of Arts refers.

With regard to the temporary structures shown in the ground plan, which the Trustees desire to erect on the western side of the Commissioners' estate, and on land not included in that above alluded to, to which subject reference is made in your other letter of the 17th instant, I am to acquaint you that Her Majesty's Commissioners also approve of the plan submitted to them, subject to their subsequent approval of the buildings to be erected thereon, and also subject to the acceptance by the Trustees of the terms proposed by the Commissioners in their reply to your last-mentioned letter as the condition of the loan to the Trustees of the land in question, and of the Commissioners' south arcades.

I am to add that the Society of Arts have already addressed Her Majesty's Commissioners upon the question which forms the subject of the latter portion of your letter, viz., the suggested reduction to some smaller amount of the sum of 50,000*l.* required to be expended, by the terms of the existing agreement with the Society of Arts, upon the acre of permanent buildings proposed to be leased to the Society; and I am directed to enclose herewith, for the information of the Trustees, a copy of the reply which they have made to the Society of Arts, assenting to a reduction to a *minimum* sum of 20,000*l.* of the above-mentioned sum of 50,000*l.* I am to call the special attention of the Trustees to this reply, as embodying the conditions upon which the Commissioners are willing to agree to the reduction in question.

Her Majesty's Commissioners direct me to observe, in conclusion, that they notice from your letter that the portion of the buildings which it is proposed to erect in accordance with the plans submitted by you, and which possess every necessary quality of permanence, should it be hereafter deemed desirable to retain them, will considerably exceed an acre in extent. Upon this point I am to acquaint you that the Commissioners are not at present prepared to enter into any engagement for permanently retaining on the ground any of the buildings erected for the purposes of the Exhibition, beyond those intended to be leased to the Society of Arts (and which are not to exceed a *maximum* of one acre in extent). Should any proposal be made at some future time to the Commissioners by the Trustees, with a view to the retention, after the close of the Exhibition, of any of the buildings other than those last specified, the question will then have to be dealt with on its own merits, and the Commissioners

APPENDIX K.

will take such course as they may consider proper under the circumstances. But in the meantime it is necessary for them to retain to its full extent and unimpaired the power possessed by them under Clause 3 of the agreement made by them with the Society of Arts in June last, of requiring the removal of the whole of the buildings erected for the Exhibition within six months after its close, except the portion agreed to be leased to that Society.

F. R. Sandford, Esq.

I have, &c.
EDGAR A. BOWRING.

XII.—The TRUSTEES of the EXHIBITION of 1862 to HER MAJESTY'S COMMISSIONERS.

SIR, London, January 17, 1861.

I AM directed by the Trustees for the Exhibition of 1862 to request that, in submitting to the Royal Commissioners the enclosures transmitted in my other letter of this day's date, you will have the goodness to invite their special attention to the plan of the site which the Trustees are anxious to be allowed to occupy for the purposes of the proposed Exhibition.

The Trustees find that it will be impossible to provide sufficient exhibiting space in a building confined to the sixteen acres which the Commissioners have already granted on the application of the Society of Arts.

They would, therefore, be glad to know whether, in addition to those 16 acres, the Royal Commissioners would be willing to grant them the use of that portion of their land, at present unoccupied, lying between the Western Arcades of the Horticultural Society and Prince Albert's-road, which is marked off on the plan above referred to. Even with this additional land, if it can be granted to them, the Trustees, after deducting the amount of space that will be required for the erection of the contemplated picture galleries, will have a smaller site available for the general purposes of the Exhibition of 1862 than was occupied in 1851.

As it will, therefore, be necessary to carry the walls of the Exhibition building to the extreme verge of whatever site may be assigned them, it has occurred to the Trustees that an arrangement might possibly be made, through the intervention of the Royal Commissioners, by which they could obtain temporary possession of the Southern Arcades, erected by the Commissioners, in which they understand that the Horticultural Society have a right of promenade, and could also be allowed to make use of the ground which has at present been reserved for the western entrance to the Society's gardens. The Arcades would provide suitable space for refreshments, and, by strengthening their roofs, similar accom-

APPENDIX K.

modation might probably be obtained on a level with the galleries of the Exhibition; while, as regards the entrance to the gardens, the Trustees feel that there would be considerable difficulty in providing satisfactory means of direct communication between their main building and the annexe that would be erected to the north of it, between Prince Albert's-road and the Western Arcades, if these two parts of the structure were separated by a thoroughfare open to the public.

Under these circumstances the Trustees are desirous of learning whether, and, if so, upon what terms, the Royal Commissioners will be disposed to meet their wishes by granting them the additional land now applied for, and by making such arrangements with the Horticultural Society as may be required to carry out the present proposal, so far as it affects the interests of the Society.

The Trustees, in respect to this additional accommodation, will be prepared to accept the second and third conditions laid down in the Appendix to the Commissioners' letter to the Society of Arts, of 28th June 1860 (with respect to the approval of the plans, and the removal of the buildings); but, so far as the entrance to the gardens is concerned, it would probably be in their power to restore it to the Horticultural Society at a much earlier date than is specified in the third of those conditions.

As every day is of importance to the Trustees at the present stage of their proceedings, I am to beg that you will have the goodness to lay this letter before the Commissioners, and to inform me of their decision at the earliest opportunity in your power.

I have, &c.

F. R. SANDFORD.

Edgar A. Bowring, Esq.,
Secretary to the Royal Commissioners
for the Exhibition of 1851.

XIII.—HER MAJESTY'S COMMISSIONERS to the TRUSTEES of the EXHIBITION of 1862.

SIR, Whitehall, January 29, 1861.

I AM directed by Her Majesty's Commissioners for the Exhibition of 1851 to acknowledge the receipt of your letter of the 17th inst., inquiring, on behalf of the Trustees of the Exhibition of 1862, whether the Commissioners will be willing to grant to them, for the purposes of the Exhibition, in addition to the 16 acres already agreed to be lent, the use of that portion of their land, at present unoccupied, lying between the Western Arcades of the Horticultural Gardens and Prince Albert's-road; and further inquiring upon what terms the Commissioners will be prepared to grant to the Trustees the use of their South Arcades, and also

APPENDIX K.

of the ground at present reserved for the western entrance of the Gardens, which last ground is included in the lease granted by the Commissioners to the Horticultural Society.

Being desirous of affording every facility in their power to the Trustees of the Exhibition of 1862, in the discharge of the duties undertaken by them, Her Majesty's Commissioners are anxious, if possible, to make arrangements for meeting the wishes of the Trustees as set forth in your letter. It is necessary, however, to observe, that while, on the one hand, the consent of the Horticultural Society is required to any terms for the loan to the Trustees of the South Arcades and western entrance, on the other, the Commissioners, by assenting to the loan of those Arcades, will deprive themselves, for such period at the loan continues, of the large rental expected to be derived by them from letting stalls as hitherto proposed in those Arcades, such rental being estimated to amount to 3,200*l.* a year. By lending to the Trustees the land, at present unoccupied, lying between the Western Arcades and Prince Albert's-road, as proposed by them, Her Majesty's Commissioners will, moreover, be precluded for a considerable period from entertaining any proposals for devoting it to any of the public purposes contemplated in their Charter, should such proposals be made to them.

The Commissioners gather from your communication that the buildings proposed to be erected by the Trustees will come into actual contact with the wall of the South Arcades and also with that of the West Arcades, both of which are at present intended to be only temporary in their nature. It also appears that in the event of the South Arcades being lent to the Trustees, they desire to provide suitable space for refreshments, not only inside them, but also on their roof, which roof also, as at present designed, is only of a temporary character.

It is obvious that Her Majesty's Commissioners could not, in justice to themselves or the Horticultural Society (which last body has a considerable interest in the questions now under consideration), assent to any arrangement whereby the stability of either of those Arcades could be endangered.

Under all the circumstances of the case, and after communicating with the Council of the Horticultural Society, Her Majesty's Commissioners have to acquaint the Trustees, on behalf of themselves and the Society respectively, that they will be prepared to make over to the Trustees for the purposes of the Exhibition of 1862, the entire use of the South Arcades, the use of the western entrance to the gardens, and the use of the vacant land to the north of that entrance applied for by the Trustees, on condition of their providing, to the satisfaction of the Commissioners, a permanent wall and roof to the South Arcades, and a permanent wall to the West Arcades, in place of the temporary ones at present intended to be constructed. With regard to the use by the Trustees of the western entrance to the gardens now leased to the Horticultural Society, that Society further stipulate, in agreeing to defer using it as a public entrance till after the close of the Exhibition, that they shall possess in the meantime a right of entrance for carts, &c., through that entrance until nine o'clock in the morning, and after six o'clock in the evening.

I have, &c.

F. R. Sandford, Esq.
Edgar A. Bowring.

XIV.—The Commissioners for the Exhibition of 1862 to Her Majesty's Commissioners.

International Exhibition, 1862.
Offices, 454, West Strand, London, W.C.
Sir, April 13th, 1861.

Adverting to your letters of the 21st and 29th of January last, I am directed to inform you that the plans which have been adopted by Her Majesty's Commissioners for the occupation of the several portions of the premises of the Royal Commissioners for the Exhibition of 1851, to which those letters refer, fulfil the various conditions laid down on the part of the Royal Commissioners, and that by the terms of the arrangement which has been made with the contractors, the permanent walls of the two Arcades, and the roof of the south Arcades, will remain the property of Her Majesty's Commissioners at the close of the Exhibition, whatever may be the decision then arrived at with respect to the removal or retention of the other parts of the building. The stipulation of the Horticultural Society, with respect to the western entrance to the Gardens, will also be observed.

There is one point, however, in your letter of the 29th January, to which I am directed to request you will invite the attention of the Royal Commissioners.

As it is necessary to contemplate the possibility of the proposed Exhibition being, from unforeseen circumstances, attended with a pecuniary loss, Her Majesty's Commissioners would be glad to know whether, in the event of such a contingency occurring and of a call having in consequence to be made upon the guarantors, the Royal Commissioners would be willing to credit Her Majesty's Commissioners with the sum of 1,300*l*. (say one thousand three hundred pounds), being the amount of saving which is estimated to accrue to the Royal Commissioners by their being relieved from the expense of erecting the temporary wall and roof of the south Arcades, and the temporary wall of the west

Arcades, previously intended to be erected by them, under their agreement with the Horticultural Society.

I am, &c.

Edgar A. Bowring, Esq.   F. R. SANDFORD, Secretary.

XV.—HER MAJESTY'S COMMISSIONERS to the COMMISSIONERS for the EXHIBITION of 1862.

SIR,   Whitehall, April 18th, 1861.

I AM directed by Her Majesty's Commissioners for the Exhibition of 1851 to acknowledge the receipt of your letter of the 13th inst. intimating, with reference to the Commissioners' letters of the 21st and 29th of January last, that the Commissioners for the Exhibition of 1862 assent to the conditions laid down in those letters for the loan to them for the purposes of that Exhibition of the south Arcades and the unoccupied ground lying between Prince Albert's Road, and the west central Arcades.

With reference to the request of the Commissioners of 1862 to be informed whether, in the event of the Exhibition being attended with such a pecuniary loss as may involve the necessity of their making calls upon the guarantors, the Royal Commissioners will be willing to credit them with the sum of 1,300*l.*, that amount representing the saving estimated to accrue to the Royal Commissioners by their being relieved under the arrangement now made from the expense of erecting the temporary wall and roof of the south Arcades, and the temporary wall of the west Arcades, previously intended to be erected by them under their agreement with the Horticultural Society,—I am to acquaint you that, although Her Majesty's Commissioners consider that such an addition to the conditions originally laid down by them is not strictly called for, and that those conditions were fair and reasonable in themselves, they will nevertheless, under the special circumstances of the case, be prepared to make the concession sought for by the Commissioners for the Exhibition of 1862, and credit them with the above mentioned sum of 1,300*l.* in the event of the contingency referred to by you.

I have, &c.
EDGAR A. BOWRING.

F. R. Sandford, Esq.

APPENDIX L.

CHARTER of INCORPORATION of the COMMISSIONERS for the EXHIBITION of 1862.

VICTORIA, by the Grace of God of the United Kingdom of Great Britain and Ireland Queen, Defender of the Faith, To all to whom these Presents shall come greeting: Whereas the Society for the Encouragement of Arts, Manufactures, and Commerce, incorporated by Charter under Our Great Seal, bearing date at Westminster the 10th day of June, in the 10th year of Our reign, and whereof Our most dearly beloved Consort is President (and which Society is herein-after referred to as the Society of Arts), did previously to the year 1851, establish and cause to be held from time to time, exhibitions of the products of Industry and Art, which exhibitions resulted in, or conduced to, the holding of the Exhibition of the Works of Industry of all Nations in the year 1851, and which last-named Exhibition was attended with great success and public advantage: And whereas the said Society, in order to promote the objects for which it was incorporated, is desirous that facilities should be afforded for holding from time to time International Exhibitions of the Products of Industry and Art, and it hath been represented to Us by the said Society, that many of its members and others of Our loving subjects, are desirous that such an International Exhibition should be holden in the metropolis in the year 1862, or so soon after as conveniently may be, and the said Society is desirous that the entire control and management of such Exhibition shall be confided to the Right Honourable Granville George Earl Granville, Lord President of Our Council, and Knight of Our most noble Order of the Garter; the Right Honourable Richard Plantagenet Campbell Temple Nugent Brydges Chandos Grenville, commonly called Marquis of Chandos; Thomas Baring, Esq., M.P.; Charles Wentworth Dilke the younger, Esq.; and Thomas Fairbairn, Esq.; who are willing to undertake the duty of conducting such Exhibition, provided that the holding thereof be approved by Us, and that We should be willing to grant to them Our Charter of Incorporation, to enable them to conduct and manage the same: And whereas it hath also been represented to Us that it is essential to the success of such undertaking that We give Our Sanction thereto, in order that it may have the confidence not only of all classes of Our subjects, but of the subjects of foreign countries, and for such objects, as well as for other the purposes herein appearing, the said Society hath besought Us to authorize the said Earl Granville, the Marquis of Chandos, Thomas Baring, Charles Wentworth Dilke, and Thomas Fair-

APPENDIX L.

bairn, to carry into effect such undertaking, and to grant to them Our Charter of Incorporation: And whereas it hath been further represented to Us that, with a view to the arrangements for the said Exhibition, it will be necessary for the Corporation to be hereby created forthwith to borrow sums not exceeding in the whole 250,000*l.*, and that the Governor and Company of the Bank of England, or other persons, will be willing to advance that sum, on having the repayment thereof secured by the covenant of the Corporation, to be hereby created, and by the covenant of a sufficient number of other persons: And whereas it hath been further represented to Us, that, with a view of forwarding the undertaking, many of Our loving subjects are willing to enter into proper covenants to effect such purpose, the covenants to be so framed as in the event of any payment being made thereunder, as far as practicable to subject the covenantors to bear such payment rateably, according to the amounts by them subscribed, but not exceeding in each case the amount of the subscription: And it hath also been represented to Us that it is essential to the well-conducting of the affairs connected with the undertaking, and with the view of preventing disputes and litigation hereafter in reference thereto, that the general nature of the undertaking, as sanctioned and approved by Us, and of the duties, rights, and powers of the persons conducting the same, shall, so far as conveniently may be, be defined, and shall be notified to all whom it may concern, by means of such Charter: And whereas it is further represented to Us, that under arrangements made between the said Society and the Commissioners for the Exhibition of 1851, incorporated by Our Royal Charter bearing date the 15th day of August, in the 14th year of Our reign, and continued and endowed with further powers by Our Royal Charter bearing date the 2nd day of December, in the 15th year of Our reign, those Commissioners have agreed to grant, rent free, the use of a certain site for the said Exhibition of 1862, subject to certain regulations relating to the approval by them of the buildings to be erected thereon, and with a provision that, in case the persons having the conduct of that Exhibition should, before the 31st day of December 1862, give notice of the desire of the said Society to retain certain permanent buildings intended to be erected for the Exhibition of 1862, the Commissioners for the Exhibition of 1851 would grant to the said Society a lease of the site to an extent not exceeding one acre, whereon those permanent buildings should be erected, with a view, amongst other things, to assist the holding of future exhibitions; and, in case the same persons shall, out of the profits of the undertaking, pay to the same Commissioners a sum of 10,000*l.*, those Commissioners have agreed to reserve (subject to certain conditions) a certain site for an Exhibition to be held in the year 1872. Now know ye, that We, being earnestly desirous to promote the holding of an International Exhibition of

APPENDIX L.

Industry and Art, in the year 1862, do, by these Presents, for Us, Our heirs and successors, give, grant, and ordain that the said Earl Granville, the Marquis of Chandos, Thomas Baring, Charles Wentworth Dilke, and Thomas Fairbairn, and the survivors and survivor of them, and such other persons, if any, as shall be appointed, in manner herein-after provided, to be Commissioners, in lieu of them or any of them, shall be one body politic and corporate, by the name of "The Commissioners for the Exhibition of 1862," and by that name shall and may sue and be sued, implead and be impleaded, and shall have perpetual succession and a common seal, with full power to alter, vary, break, or renew the same at their discretion: And We will and ordain that the Corporation hereby incorporated, herein-after referred to as "Our Commissioners," is incorporated for the purpose of conducting and managing an International Exhibition of the Products of Industry and Art of all Nations, such Exhibition to be held in or near the metropolis in the year 1862, or within such further time as is herein-after provided in that behalf; and We will and ordain that Our Commissioners shall have the entire conduct, control, and management of the said Exhibition, and of the funds that may arise from that undertaking, and that such Exhibition may be carried on either in accordance with the precedent afforded by the Exhibition of 1851, or in such other mode or manner as Our Commissioners shall in their discretion think fit, but subject to such special directions as are herein-after contained. And We will and ordain that Our Commissioners shall have power to borrow and take up at interest for the purposes of the said undertaking, such sum or sums of money as they may think fit, and may from time to time for such purpose mortgage or pledge the funds or other property of the said Corporation, and may under their common seal execute any deed or deeds of covenant or other deed or deeds for securing repayment of any sum or sums so to be borrowed, with interest, and may also procure any persons willing to guarantee the repayment of any such sum or sums or any part thereof, to execute a deed of covenant for payment of such sums as the covenantors may be willing to become liable for, so as to guarantee the due repayment of any sum or sums which may be so borrowed with interest, and all costs, charges, and expenses caused by the non-payment thereof, and that the said deed or deeds of covenant shall contain all necessary and proper provisions, and in particular provisions to insure, as far as practicable, that none of the covenantors shall ultimately bear more than his fair and proper proportion of the sums which they may respectively covenant to pay, and the several persons who shall make and enter into such covenants are herein-after referred to as the guarantors, and the sum or sums of money which shall be so borrowed and secured to be paid are herein-after referred to as "The Guaranteed Debt of the Corporation." And We will and ordain that each of the several persons hereby incorporated, and any person who may, as herein-after provided, be appointed in the place of any of them, may execute the said deed of guarantee in his own individual capacity for such sum as he may think fit. And We do hereby direct and authorize our Commissioners to make and enter into such arrangements as they and the Commissioners for the Exhibition of 1851 may mutually agree upon, for holding the Exhibition on a portion of the estate of those Commissioners at Kensington Gore, in accordance with the arrangements already made with them by the Society of Arts, or which may hereafter be made by Our Commissioners with the Commissioners for the Exhibition of 1851, so as such other or further arrangements shall not, without the approval of the Society, be inconsistent with the arrangements already made between the Society and those Commissioners; or they may choose and contract for the occupation of any other site for holding the intended Exhibition, provided such site be situate within ten miles from St. Paul's Cathedral, in the city of London, measured in a direct line. And We will and direct that in case the Exhibition shall be held on any part of the lands of the Commissioners for the Exhibition of 1851, then that Our Commissioners shall cause a sum not exceeding 50,000l. to be expended on buildings of a permanent character, and such as may be adapted for the purposes for which the Society of Arts may require to have a lease of the site of such buildings, under the arrangements now made or contemplated between them and the Commissioners for the Exhibition of 1851, and which buildings are herein-after referred to as "The Permanent Buildings." And We will and ordain that Our Commissioners may contract for, erect, and, subject to such special directions as are herein contained, may remove, or may leave standing at the close of such Exhibition, any building or buildings erected for the same in accordance with such arrangements as have been or shall be lawfully made in that behalf; and may, if they think fit, distribute prizes to exhibitors, and may do all matters and things connected with such distribution; and shall have full power to receive and take such sums of money as they may direct, for entrance to the Exhibition, or for the rent of any part of the buildings to be erected or otherwise relating to the premises, and to dispose of all monies which shall come to their hands as they shall think fit, for and towards the purposes of the said Exhibition or otherwise, in the execution of the powers hereby given to them, including the payment of all expenses, charges, and liabilities which they may incur or become subject to; and that they shall have full power to give effectual discharges to any persons paying any monies to them, and to settle and adjust any accounts relating thereto; and generally, to do all matters and things that may be necessary, or may appear to them to be expedient for promoting the ends and designs of the said Exhibition. And We do hereby ordain, that it shall be lawful for Our Commissioners, and they shall have full power and authority,

APPENDIX L.

from time to time, to depute or choose any persons, and to give to them all or any of the powers and authorities hereby given to our Commissioners as they shall think fit, for managing and conducting all or any of the matters and things hereby authorized to be done by Our Commissioners, and which may be necessary for conducting, or in any manner relate to or concern the said Exhibition. And We do hereby ordain that it shall be lawful for Our Commissioners from time to time to appoint one or more Secretaries and such other officers as they may think fit, and to remove all persons appointed by them, and to appoint others or not, as they see fit. And We do hereby ordain that our Commissioners may elect one member of their Corporation to be the Chairman thereof, and from time to time may vary such Chairman as they think fit; and also that Our Commissioners may elect such other person or persons as they may think fit to be Commissioners in lieu of any one or more of them who may die or desire to be discharged from or become incapable to act in the execution of the office of Commissioner before the duties of such office shall be fully performed. And We will and ordain that such appointment of a Commissioner or Commissioners shall be made by a resolution to be passed at a meeting specially to be called for that purpose, but no appointment shall be effectual and valid unless and until the person or persons appointed shall be approved by Us, such approval to be testified by a minute in writing, to be signed by one of Our Principal Secretaries of State, and published in the "London Gazette." And We order and direct that Our Commissioners shall meet when and at such place or places as, from time to time, they shall direct or determine, and that all and every the powers hereby given to Our Commissioners may be exercised at any meeting of any two or more of the Commissioners, and that the decision of the majority attending at any meeting shall be binding, and determine any question proposed; and that when the votes shall be equal the Chairman of the Corporation for the time being, if present, shall, in addition to his vote as a member, have the casting vote, and that Our Commissioners shall and may from time to time make and repeal or alter such rules, orders, regulations, and bye-laws for the management of the business of the undertaking as they may think fit, so as the same be not contrary to the laws of this Our realm, and such rules, orders, regulations, and bye-laws, shall, when made, and till the same shall be repealed or altered, be as effectual as if they were contained in this Our Royal Charter: Provided always, and We will and ordain that in case it shall appear to Our Commissioners, from any cause not now foreseen, expedient to postpone the holding of such Exhibition until some time in the year 1863, it shall be lawful for them, with the consent in writing of any one of Our Principal Secretaries of State, to do so, by inserting in the "London Gazette," on or before the 1st day of March 1862, notice that the said

APPENDIX L. 195

Exhibition is to be so postponed, and in that case they shall and may hold such Exhibition accordingly in the year 1863, and in case after making any contracts or engagements for the holding of such Exhibition, they shall from like cause see fit to abandon it altogether, they may, with the like consent so do, giving like notice thereof, upon and subject to their making compensation to persons with whom they may have entered into any contracts in relation to the holding thereof, or incident thereto, which in such case We require and authorize them to make. And We do will and ordain, that so soon as conveniently may be after the closing or abandonment of the Exhibition, Our Commissioners shall sell, dispose of, and convert into money, all property and effects belonging to them which can be so sold and converted, particularly all the buildings erected by them for the purposes of the undertaking, save and except "The Permanent Buildings." And We will and ordain that immediately after such sale and conversion into money, Our Commissioners shall, out of the monies to arise by such sale and conversion, or of which they shall be otherwise possessed, proceed, after payment of all costs, charges, and expenses incident to the undertaking to pay and discharge, so far as such monies will extend, in such order and priority as the law may require or our Commissioners see fit, all their debts and liabilities, save and except the guaranteed debt of the Corporation; and after payment of all such debts and liabilities, except as aforesaid, and providing and setting apart a reasonable sum for the payment of future expenses incident to the completion of their duties, our Commissioners shall apply the surplus of such monies, if any, in or towards the payment and satisfaction of the guaranteed debt of the Corporation, or in case the guarantors, or any of them, shall have been called upon to pay, and have paid, any monies in respect of the guaranteed debt of the Corporation, then in repaying to them, so far as the monies applicable for such purposes will extend, the amount which the guarantors shall have so paid, in such manner, as far as practicable, as to secure that none of the guarantors shall pay more than his just and fair proportion of the sum which he shall have bound himself to contribute. And We will and ordain that as soon as may be after such sale and conversion as aforesaid, Our Commissioners shall cause a statement of the accounts relating to the undertaking to be made up, and shall submit for examination the vouchers for the receipt and expenditure to the Governor of the Bank of England, the Deputy Governor of the Bank of England, and the Comptroller-General of the National Debt, or such person or persons as such Governor, Deputy Governor, and Comptroller-General, or any two of them, shall appoint to make such examination, and shall submit a duplicate of such statement to the Society of Arts for their information; and Our Commissioners shall then proceed to ascertain whether or not (having reference, if necessary, to the value of the permanent buildings, and calculating such value according to the amount such buildings are likely to realize if taken down and the materials sold,) there has been a gain or loss attendant upon the undertaking, and shall forthwith certify, under their common seal, whether there shall have been a gain or loss, and, as near as may be, the estimated amount of such gain or loss, having reference to the value of the permanent buildings, and shall cause their certificate to be forthwith published in "The London Gazette." And in case, irrespective of the value of the permanent buildings, there shall have been a loss attending the said undertaking, then if the Society of Arts shall, with a view to obtain a lease of the permanent buildings in accordance with such arrangement as hereinbefore in that behalf mentioned, be willing out of their corporate funds to bear and sustain that loss, it shall be incumbent upon Our Commissioners, if so required by the Society of Arts, by notice in writing under the hand of their Secretary, to be delivered within one calendar month from the publication of such certificate, to make and enter into such arrangement with the Society as may secure to them the benefits of such lease subject to the Society bearing such loss and undertaking to provide sufficient funds to enable Our Commissioners to pay and satisfy all the remaining debts and liabilities of the said Corporation, including the guaranteed debt of the Corporation, or so much thereof as shall remain unpaid, and the Society undertaking to indemnify the guarantors from all loss and liability in respect thereof, but in default of the said Society serving such notice in due time, or of their duly and effectually performing all acts to carry out such arrangement as provided for by the clause last herein-before contained, then our Commissioners shall forthwith or so soon as conveniently may be, sell the permanent buildings, and out of the proceeds thereof, after payment of all cost incident to such sale, or otherwise incident to the undertaking and remaining unpaid, shall discharge all debts and liabilities, if any, attending the undertaking, remaining unpaid, except the guaranteed debt of the Corporation, and shall apply the surplus, if any, in or towards satisfaction of the guaranteed debt of the Corporation, or in case the guarantors, or any of them, shall have been called upon to pay, and have paid, any monies in respect of the guaranteed debt of the Corporation, then in repaying to them, so far as the monies applicable for such purposes will extend, the amount which the guarantors shall have so paid, in such manner, as far as practicable, as to secure that none of the guarantors shall pay more than his just and fair proportion of the sum which he shall have bound himself to contribute; and if any surplus shall remain after all such payments, then such surplus shall be disposed of in manner herein-after directed as to and concerning the ultimate disposable profit of the undertaking in case of there being a gain attending the undertaking. And we will and ordain that in case, after payment of all the debts and liabilities attending the undertaking, it shall be found that, irrespective of the permanent buildings, there shall have been a gain attending the undertaking, then the permanent buildings shall be left standing for the Society of Arts, in accordance with the aforesaid arrangements, and out of such gain Our Commissioners shall firstly pay to the Commissioners for the Exhibition of 1851, if desired by the Society of Arts, as herein-before recited, a sum not exceeding 10,000$l.$ as a consideration for their reserving a site containing 16 acres or thereabouts for an Exhibition of the Products of Industry and Art, to be held in the year 1872, on the lands belonging to such Commissioners, and shall, secondly, apply in completing the permanent buildings in an architectural manner, and in a manner suitable for the objects for which they are to be employed by the Society of Arts, so much of the unexpended portion of the sum herein-before mentioned to be intended to be expended on the permanent buildings not exceeding 50,000$l.$, as in the judgment of Our Commissioners jointly with that of the Commissioners for the Exhibition of 1851 may be requisite for that purpose. And We will and ordain that if there shall remain any surplus of such gain arising from the said undertaking after all the payments herein-before provided for, such gain shall be considered as the ultimate disposable profit of the undertaking, and shall be disposed of as herein-after in that behalf provided, viz., We will and ordain that Our Commissioners shall apply the ultimate disposable profit of the undertaking for such purposes connected with the encouragement of Arts, Manufactures, and Commerce, as shall be determined by the guarantors at a meeting to be called for the purpose, at such time and place, and in such manner, by advertisement or otherwise, as Our Commissioners shall think fit, and whereof 28 days' notice, at the least, shall be given, at which meeting the question to be determined shall be decided and settled by the votes of guarantors representing the majority in value of the subscriptions of the persons actually present and voting: Provided further, that before proceeding to ascertain the amount of each subscription, for the purpose of such decision, it shall be lawful for the Chairman of the meeting to take a show of hands on any question to be submitted to the meeting, and his decision, if not objected to as to such show of hands, shall be considered conclusive and binding without the actual necessity of ascertaining the exact amount for which each guarantor shall have signed the agreement. And We will and ordain that the services of Our said Commissioners shall be rendered gratuitously: but We direct that Our Commissioners may, out of the corporate funds, allow and pay to their Secretaries and Officers, and other persons who may aid them in the conduct of such Exhibition, such salaries and gratuities or other remuneration as they may think fit; and they may thereout also pay the costs, charges, and expenses incurred, or to be incurred, by the Society of Arts, in pro-

APPENDIX M.

moting the said undertaking, and in getting the requisite instruments made and executed by the guarantors: Provided always, that when and as soon as any sum or sums of money which may have been borrowed by Our said Commissioners under the powers aforesaid, and all interest thereon shall be fully paid, and all other the matters and things entrusted to be done by this Our Charter by the said Commissioners hereby incorporated shall be fully performed, or become incapable of being executed, and when the same shall have been certified under the Corporate Seal to one of Our Principal Secretaries of State, then these Presents, and every matter and thing herein contained, shall be absolutely void.

In witness whereof We have caused these Our Letters to be made Patent. Witness Ourself at Our Palace, at Westminster, this 14th day of February, in the 24th year of Our Reign.

APPENDIX M.

DEED of GUARANTEE given to secure an ADVANCE to be made by the BANK of ENGLAND to the COMMISSIONERS for the EXHIBITION of 1862.

THIS INDENTURE made the fifteenth day of February in the year of our Lord one thousand eight hundred and sixty-one, between the several persons who have subscribed their names in the first column of the second schedule hereto, and who have affixed their Seals hereto, of the first part; and Sir Alexander Spearman, of the National Debt Office, London, Baronet, Matthew Marshall of the Bank of England, Esquire, and George Earle Gray, of the Bank of England, Esquire, herein-after called the said Trustees, of the second part. Whereas the Commissioners for the Exhibition of one thousand eight hundred and sixty-two, incorporated by Her Majesty's Letters Patent, dated the fourteenth day of February one thousand eight hundred and sixty-one, have applied to the Governor and Company of the Bank of England, and have requested them to advance the sum of two hundred and fifty thousand pounds, to be repaid with interest on the first day of January one thousand eight hundred and sixty-three, or if the Exhibition should be postponed until the year one thousand eight hundred and sixty-three, then on the 1st day of January one thousand eight hundred and sixty-four, which the said Governor and Company have consented and agreed to do, on the security of a covenant by the Corporation (to be embodied in a separate deed) and of the covenants herein-after contained. And whereas for

APPENDIX M.

the convenience of execution of this Indenture, by the parties hereto of the first part, the same has been prepared in ten parts. Now this Indenture witnesseth, that each party hereto, of the first part, for himself, his heirs, executors, and administrators, hereby covenants with the said Trustees, their executors and administrators, that the covenantor, his or her heirs, executors, or administrators, shall at any time, or from time to time when required so to do by the Trustees or Trustee, for the time being of these presents, or any two of the Trustees for the time being (if more than two), at any time after the period when the repayment of the said loan shall become due, pay to the said Trustees, or the survivors or survivor of them, or the executors or administrators of the survivor of them, any sum or sums of money, not exceeding in the whole the sum set after his or her seal in the third column of the Second Schedule hereto: Provided nevertheless, and it is hereby agreed as follows :—

1. That when and so soon as the aggregate of the sums expressing the limits of the liability of the persons who shall become Covenantors (by affixing their Seals to any part of these presents), shall amount to two hundred and fifty thousand pounds at least, the Commissioners, or any two of them, shall sign and publish in the "London Gazette" an advertisement in the form contained in the First Schedule hereto, and unless and until an advertisement in such form or to the like effect shall be published, none of the parties hereto of the first part, shall be liable under the covenant herein-before contained.

2. That whenever any sum of money shall be required to be paid under the preceding covenant, a notice, signed by one at least of the Trustees for the time being, of the sum required to be paid, and of the day (not being less than twenty-eight clear days after the date of the notice) at which the same is to be payable, shall be delivered or sent by post to the usual or last known place of abode of the Covenantor, or the executors or administrators of any Covenantor, from whom such payment is required, or to the address mentioned in the fifth column of the Second Schedule for that purpose; and such notice shall also name a bank or banks into which, or one of which, the required payment may be made.

3. That the calls to be made by the Trustees or Trustee for the time being shall, subject to the provisions of the fourth stipulation, be made rateably on each person who shall become a Covenantor hereunder by executing any part of these presents, according to the amounts set opposite to his or her seal in the Second Schedule to the part hereof which he or she shall so execute, the intention of the parties being, that as far as is practicable, and subject to the fourth stipulation, each Covenantor and his estate shall ultimately bear his rateable proportion, and no more than his rateable proportion, of the entire sum to be raised.

4. That the Trustees or Trustee for the time being may abstain or desist from enforcing any requisition for payment against any Covenantor or the estate of any Covenantor, if they or he shall be satisfied that an attempt to enforce it will be useless or unproductive, and may compromise any such requisition against any Covenantor or his estate, on such terms as to reduction of amount, postponement of payment (with or without security), or otherwise as they or he shall think proper, and in determining the amount to be called for may take into consideration the probability that some of the Covenantors may be unable or cannot be compelled to pay their proportion of the sums to be paid.

5. That the monies recovered under these presents shall be applied first in paying all costs and expenses incurred in the execution of the trusts, next in payment to the Governor and Company of the Bank of England of whatever sum may be due to them from the Commissioners, and any costs and expenses incurred by them by reason of the non-payment thereof, and the balance shall be returned by the Trustees or Trustee for the time being, to the persons who have contributed it, in such manner as they or he may think just, and calculated to give effect, as far as practicable, to the principle of rateable contribution between the Covenantors, and that the Trustees or Trustee for the time being may, after full satisfaction of the Commissioners' debt to the said Governor and Company, enforce the preceding covenant against any Covenantor or his estate, for the purpose of setting right any discrepancy between what has been, and what ought according to that principle to have been, contributed by any contributor or contributors, and may apply for that purpose the money raised by so enforcing the covenant.

6. That no person sued under the preceding covenant shall be entitled to resist the claim on the ground that the requisition for payment is improperly made, or unnecessary, or excessive in amount, or that no such notice as is required by the second stipulation has been given.

7. That if the said Commissioners shall keep a banking account with the Bank of England, and while the said sum of two hundred and fifty thousand pounds, or any part thereof, shall be due and owing by the said Commissioners to the Governor and Company of the Bank of England, any sum shall be standing or paid to the credit of such banking account, the said Governor and Company shall not be bound or required to retain or apply any such sum as last aforesaid, in or towards payment of what may be due in respect of the said sum of two hundred and fifty thousand pounds. In witness whereof the said parties hereto have hereunto set their hands and seals, the day and year first above written.

The FIRST SCHEDULE above referred to.

We hereby certify that the aggregate of the sums, expressing the limits of the liability of the persons who have executed the Deed of

APPENDIX M.

Guarantee for enabling the Commissioners for the Exhibition of one thousand eight hundred and sixty-two to obtain advances from the Bank of England, amounts to the sum of two hundred and fifty thousand pounds. *Signatures of the Commissioners, or any two of them.*

The SECOND SCHEDULE above referred to.

1st Column.	2nd Column.	3rd Column.	4th Column.	5th Column.	6th Column.
The signature of the Guarantor.	The Seal of the Guarantor.	Sum for which the Guarantor renders himself liable.	Christian and Surname (or the usual Name) of the Guarantor to be written in full length by the Witness who attests the Signature at, or immediately after, the time at which the Signature of the Guarantor is affixed.	Address of the Guarantor, to which Address all Notices may be sent, Notices so sent being hereby declared sufficient for all purposes connected with these presents or the intended Exhibition.	Name and Address of the Witness attesting the Signature and sealing of the Agreement by the Guarantor, whose Name is set opposite to that of the Witness in the fourth Column of this Schedule.

APPENDIX N.

APPEN

DR.   ACCOUNT of the RECEIPTS and EXPENDITURE of HER
From 1st January 1856

1856.	RECEIPTS.	£	s.	d.
Jan. 1	Balance as per last Account (see Appendix C. to the Third Report of the Commissioners. Page 84) - - -	101,742	16	10
May 15	Parliamentary Grant, being the Balance due upon the Vote of 1854–5 - - -	20,000	0	0
1859.				
Jan. 12	Loan from the Commissioners of Greenwich Hospital, for the purpose of returning the Parliamentary Grants (see page 12) -	120,000	0	0
1860.				
April 27	Loan from the Commissioners of Greenwich Hospital, for purposes connected with the Agreement with the Horticultural Society (see page 22) - - - -	50,000	0	0
Dec. 31	Rents received to this day - - -	6,542	13	4
		298,285	10	2

We hereby certify, that we have examined the above Accounts of the Receipts and Payments of the Royal Commissioners for the Exhibition of 1851, for the period commencing 1st January 1856, and ending 31st December 1860, and that we have found the same to be correct.

BONAMY DOBREE, Governor of the Bank of England.
ALFRED LATHAM, Deputy Governor of the Bank of England.

DIX N.

MAJESTY'S COMMISSIONERS for the EXHIBITION of 1851, to 31st December 1860.   CR.

1859.		PAYMENTS.			£	s.	d.
Jan. 12		To the Lords Commissioners of Her Majesty's Treasury for repayment of Parliamentary Grants pursuant to the Act 21 & 22 Vict. cap. 36, less 60,000*l.*, fixed by their Lordships as the value of the land retained by the Department of Science and Art (see page 12)			121,379	4	2
1860.			£	s. d.			
Dec. 31		For Purchase of Land, Leases, &c.	77,954	13 9			
	„	Making Roads and improving Estate	5,895	11 8			
	„	Parliamentary and Law Expenses	2,910	7 4			
	„	Surveyor's Charges	2,529	8 10			
					89,290	1	7
	„	Interest on Mortgage Loan	6,213	0 2			
	„	Loss on Sale of Exchequer Bills	757	15 5			
					6,970	15	7
	„	Museum Building and Collection of Animal Produce presented to the Government			7,476	12	0
	„	Printing	170	2 8			
	„	Office Expenses, Postage, Stamps, and Incidentals	418	17 2			
	„	Salaries and Wages for Labour	4,088	3 3			
					4,677	3	1
	„	Repairs to Houses on the Estate	323	16 8			
	„	Taxes on do. do.	1,417	16 3			
					1,741	12	11
	„	Outlay on Arcades on account of Contracts			24,300	0	0
					255,835	9	4
	By	Balance, Cash, and Securities, viz.—					
		Cash at Bank of England	318	1 6			
		Petty Cash	5	16 0			
		Cost of 3 per cent. Reduced Annuities	31,496	12 1			
		Cost of 5 per cent. New South Wales Bonds and East India Railway Company's Stock	10,629	11 3			
					42,450	0	10
				£	298,285	10	2

13th March 1861.   H. R. WILLIAMS, Financial Officer.

We certify, that the above Balance of 42,450*l.* 0s. 10*d.*, stated to be in the hands of the Commissioners on 31st December 1860, is correct, viz., 318*l.* 1s. 6*d.* deposited at the Western Branch of the Bank of England, 5*l.* 16s. in the hands of the Financial Officer, 31,496*l.* 12s. 1*d.* invested in 3 per cent. Reduced Annuities, and 10,629*l.* 11s. 3*d.* invested in New South Wales Bonds and East India Railway Company's Stock.

                   GRANVILLE, Chairman of Finance Committee.
                   THOMAS FIELD GIBSON, } Commissioners.
                   C. WENTWORTH DILKE, }
                         EDGAR A. BOWRING, Secretary.

LONDON
Printed by GEORGE E. EYRE and WILLIAM SPOTTISWOODE,
Printers to the Queen's most Excellent Majesty.
For Her Majesty's Stationery Office.

www.ingramcontent.com/pod-product-compliance
Lightning Source LLC
Chambersburg PA
CBHW020914230426
43666CB00008B/1450